INTERNATIONAL DEVELOPMENT

Edited by **Seth Appiah-Opoku**

International Development
http://dx.doi.org/10.5772/63034
Edited by Seth Appiah-Opoku

Contributors

Makoto Kimura, Yoshinori Fukubayashi, Ricardo Stratta Fernández, Miriam López González, ignacio de los Rios-Carmenado, Colin Pritchard, Luke Strongman, Nehal Mohammed Elmashad, Azza Hassan, Sherif Shehata, Razvan Barbulescu, Gabriel Staicu, Nicolette Hall, Beulah Pretorius, Hettie Schonfeldt, Julius Juma Okello

Published by InTech
Janeza Trdine 9, 51000 Rijeka, Croatia

Publishing Process Manager Iva Simcic
Technical Editor SPi Global
Cover InTech Design team

First published April, 2017
Printed in Croatia
Legal deposit, Croatia: National and University Library in Zagreb

Additional hard copies can be obtained from orders@intechopen.com

International Development, Edited by Seth Appiah-Opoku
p. cm.
Print ISBN 978-953-51-3103-8
Online ISBN 978-953-51-3104-5

For EU product safety concerns:
IN TECH d.o.o., Prolaz Marije Krucifikse Kozulić 3, 51000 Rijeka, Croatia,
info@intechopen.com or visit our website at intechopen.com.

Meet the editor

Dr. Seth Appiah-Opoku is an associate professor of Geography at the University of Alabama, Tuscaloosa, AL, USA. He teaches world regional geography, regional geography of Africa, environmental management, land use regulation, principles of planning, regional planning and analysis, and Ghana summer abroad course. He is also a member of the American Institute of Certified Planners and the author of *The Need for Indigenous Knowledge in Environmental Impact Assessment: The Case of Ghana* (Edwin Mellen Press, NY, June 2005). His research focuses on development and planning issues in the Third World. He serves on the international editorial board of the journal of *Environmental Impact Assessment Review* and has published scholarly articles in several renowned journals including *Environmental Management, Society and Natural Resources, Environmental Impact Assessment Review, Journal of Cultural Geography*, and *Plan Canada*. He is a member of the Technical Advisory Team advising the government of Ghana on the preparation of a 40-year development plan for the country.

Contents

Preface

Development is a multidimensional process involving positive changes in social structures, popular attitudes, and the acceleration of economic growth. The end result is a reduction in equality and eradication of absolute poverty. According to the United Nations Development Program, the components of development are improved life sustenance, equity, empowerment, and sustainability. In the realm of international development, nations are expected to strive for the ability to provide the basic necessities of life without which life will be meaningless. No matter how fast a nation grows, if only a small segment of the population benefits from it, then development hasn't addressed inequities. Empowerment implies giving leverage to the poor and marginalized people to participate in decisions affecting their lives. Finally, sustainability implies that the development of a nation must be in harmony with the environment in both the short and the long run. The finiteness of a nation's natural resources requires it to consider the prospects of a sustainable future. In other words, development must be conducted in ways that meet the needs of the present generation without compromising the ability of future generations to meet their own needs. The converging effects should indicate in time a rise in the standard of living or favorable changes in the way of life of the citizenry.

It is in the light of this that this book brings together leading researchers in the field of international development to examine issues relating to food security, health, rural development, human development, and institutional strengthening in developing countries. Using empirical research, the book discusses a variety of topics including nutrition-sensitive agricultural development in South Africa, household food security in Tanzania, medical research in Egypt, child mortality in Christian and Islamic countries, spot improvement of rural roads in Asia and Africa, resilience in natural disaster, the relationship between foreign aid and human development in Africa, and developing competencies for rural development project management through the creation of local action groups in Argentina.

This book must be seen as a wide brush stroke pointing the way to matters to be addressed in the latter volumes because it does not cover every important issue in international development. It is concise, insightful, and easy to understand and could serve as an important reference material on international development.

Seth Appiah-Opoku, PhD, AICP
Geography Department
University of Alabama
Tuscaloosa, AL, USA

Section 1

Food Security

Chapter 1

Nutrition-Sensitive Agricultural Development for Food Security in Africa: A Case Study of South Africa

Hester Carina Schönfeldt, Nicolette Hall and
Beulah Pretorius

Additional information is available at the end of the chapter

http://dx.doi.org/10.5772/67110

Abstract

The paradox of persistent under-nutrition and food insecurity; as well as the increasing the incidence of over nutrition is particularly observed in middle –income countries experiencing rapid westernisation such as South Africa (SA). Values of household Food insecurity remains high, whereas overweight and obesity are increasing at a rapid rate. Agriculture and the food system play a key role in nutrition, health and food security. It provides for the primary sources of energy along with essential nutrients, while simultaneously being a source of income, creating jobs and earning foreign exchange. This case study presents the current nutrition sensitivity of the South-African agriculture and food systems (including governmental prioritization) and highlights the importance of this for future development towards improved food and nutrition Security and nutritional status. Since 2013, discussions on a single, comprehensive, food security and nutrition policy and implementation plan for South Africa have been in process with the aim to coordinate the improvement of both food security and all forms of malnutrition. Yet, the case study findings indicate an unfortunate lack of understanding about nutrient density and dietary diversity and the role which this could play in combating non-communicable diseases in addition to food insecurity and hunger.

Keywords: South Africa, food security, policies, programmes, Africa, nutrition sensitivity

1. Introduction

The relationship between the causes and consequences of malnutrition is complex [1]. Poverty and high food prices reduce consumer purchasing power and can leave the nutritionally vulnerable even more powerless when it comes to acquiring healthy foods. On the other hand, nutrition plays a fundamental role in the sustainable development of human capital [2]. Malnutrition adversely affects both mental and physical development and significantly reduces the productivity and economic potential of an individual [3].

Agriculture and the food systems play a key role in linking nutrition, healthand food security. It provides for the primary sources of energy and essential nutrients, while simultaneously being a source of income, creating jobs and earning foreign exchange. Agricultural development is fundamental for sustaining the lives of the world's population, yet agricultural activities often face many challenges due to population growth, urbanization and climate change, which threaten the availability of water, land and other natural resources.

The importance of agriculture to health has been increasingly recognised, but the link between agriculture, nutrition and health policies and programmes is still weak in most countries, with serious implications for the effectiveness and efficiency of the efforts to improve overall health and nutrition outcomes. Although the agriculture and health sectors are all aiming at alignment and improved well-being, agricultural interventions and actions frequently undermine health and nutrition [4]. For instance, the failure of agriculture to provide access to nutritious foods and support high-quality food choices contributes to micronutrient deficiencies and 'hidden hunger', which are a persistent health concern in many countries. Monotonous diets which mainly include inexpensive, energy-dense, nutrient-poor (staple) foods could further aggravate the emerging epidemic of obesity and chronic diseases.

South Africa (SA) has an abundant supply of natural resources, well-developed financial and service sectors and modern infrastructure. The country is considered nationally food secure as agricultural production is high and at the national level, there is enough food available for the whole population [5]. SA is in a nutrition transition in which under-nutrition (including stunting and micro-nutrient deficiencies) continue to co-exist with a rising incidence of overweight and obesity and the associated consequences such as hypertension, cardiovascular disease and diabetes. Within the context of the HIV and AIDS pandemic and food insecurity, the high prevalence of under-nutrition, micro-nutrient deficiencies and over-nutrition presents a complex series of challenges.

Using findings from a South African case study, as commissioned by the United Nations Standing Committee on Nutrition (UNSCN), this chapter provides an overview of the nutrition sensitivity of agricultural development.

2. The concept of food and nutrition security

Food security is said to exist when all people in a society at all times have enough food for an active, healthy life. Food security as an umbrella term includes the availability of food that is nutritious and safe and an assured ability to procure and acquire food of good quality in a socially acceptable way. Measuring food security continues to exist as a challenge due to the multidimensional nature thereof. As a result, there is no standardised methodology to measure or monitor food security [6].

Main measures for food security are related to income versus food basket expenditure, agriculture production, consumption and household expenditure. Often, investigating the adequacy of daily energy intake or access is considered the best direct measure of food security. However, it has been globally recognised that the provision of energy, without the adequate intake of critical macro- and micro-nutrients such as protein or vitamins and minerals, may increase weight but not length, promoting adipose tissue gain resulting in overweight and obesity [7]. The combined term *"food and nutrition security"* has been used more frequently to emphasise the need for considering complete dietary requirements (nutrients) in addition to dietary energy, when food security strategies are discussed.

3. The status of food and nutrition security in South Africa (case study)

South Africa (SA) is considered food secure at the national level, producing or importing enough dietary energy for the whole population (more than 3000 kcal/capita/day) [5]. The same cannot be said about households, especially those in rural areas. The majority of households live in poverty with a limited variety of foods (mainly staples) available at home [8]. Although no national survey has been conducted to assess all the dimensions of food insecurity in South Africa, some surveys have included components of food insecurity.

A review of published studies indicates that food insecurity threatens 50–80% of South-African households, whereas the incidence of obesity is increasing to levels affecting more than half of South-African adults. These statistics indicate the co-existence between obesity and food insecurity, possibly even for the same individual.

In addition, SA is one of only 12 countries in the world in which mortality rates for children younger than 5 years have increased since 1990 [6]. Despite the relatively high per capita income, rates of childhood stunting in South Africa (although a middle- income country) are similar to low-income countries in the region [7]. While some indicators show improvement, several conditions seem to have worsened over the past decade [6]. High incidence of stunting observed in children indicate a chronic deficiency in essential nutrients during the growing years, yet 25% of adolescents and 56% of the adult population were recorded as overweight or obese in 2013, indicating excessive intakes of energy with nearly 30% of all deaths attributed to non-communicable diseases [6].

When populations modernize as a result of socio-economic development, urbanization and acculturation as is observed in SA, it is characterized by changes in dietary patterns and nutrient intakes that increase the risk of the diet-related non-communicable diseases [9]. Non-communicable diseases have emerged in Sub-Saharan Africa at a faster rate and at a lower economic level than in industrialized countries before the battle against under-nutrition could be won. Adverse changes in dietary patterns include increased consumption of foods from animal origin rich in total and saturated fat, decreased intakes of legumes and vegetables and increased intakes of energy-dense, micro-nutrient-poor snack foods, convenience foods (often high in sodium), vegetable oils and sweetened carbonated beverages as well as added sugar, fats and oils during the preparation of food [10]. Although increases in fruit and meat consumption have been observed, the increased intake has not been sufficient to meet all micro-nutrient needs [9].

The average household income of the poor in South Africa equips many households to procure mainly low-cost staple foods like maize-meal porridge, with limited added variety. The five most commonly consumed foods include maize-meal porridge, bread, sugar and tea supplemented with small amounts of milk [8]. Although this ability to procure enough food to maintain satiety of all family members might categorise them as being food secure, the nutritional limitations of such monotonous diets might have severe implications in terms of health, long-term development and quality of life.

3.1. Understanding the South African agriculture and food system

3.1.1. *Food availability*

South Africa has an area coverage of nearly 122 million hectares. The area utilised for agriculture amounts to nearly 80%, distributed between permanent pastures for extensive grazing of animals (69%), arable land (10%) and permanent crops (0.34%). Of the arable land available, only 22% is high-potential arable land, with the availability of water presenting the greatest constraint to the farming sector. The agricultural sector is also characterised by inequalities among different types of farmers, in particular between large commercial farmers and small subsistence farmers in the communal areas.

The food balance sheet for South Africa [5], indicates that the country produces enough food for local consumption for a wide selection of commodities, including maize, sorghum, other cereals, millet, potatoes, sweet potatoes, sugar, pulses (excluding peas and beans), soya beans, sunflower oil, groundnuts, vegetables, fruits, bovine meat, animal fats, eggs, milk and fish. The sectors with the highest contributions to the gross value of agricultural production are (from highest) poultry, maize, cattle, deciduous and other fruit, milk, vegetables, eggs, citrus fruit, sugar cane and potatoes. The major agricultural export products (based on 2011/2012 export values) are citrus fruit, wine, maize and grapes [11].

The commodities in short supply to support recommended consumption (thus relying on imports) are reported by the FAO food balance sheets to include wheat, barley, oats, rice, rye, sweeteners, honey, beans, peas, tree nuts, vegetable oils, rape and mustard seed, soya bean oil, cottonseed, groundnut oil, poultry meat, pig meat, mutton and goat meat, butter, ghee, crustaceans, freshwater fish, molluscs, tea, coffee, cocoa beans, pimento, pepper and spices [5]. The major agricultural import products according to the national statistics include rice, wheat, poultry, palm oil and undenatured ethyl alcohol [11].

3.1.2. *Food affordability*

Despite significant development in the past 15 years, SA remains a country with a complex combination of developed and developing regions, in terms of its people, economy and infrastructure. The country has a consistently unequal economy where two-thirds of the populations live under third world conditions, with the rest living under first world conditions [12]. According to the Development Indicators Mid-term Review issued by the Presidency in 2006, 43.2% of the country's population lived in poverty. In 2004, 7.6% of the population was recorded to be living below the US$1 per day, indicating extreme poverty [13].

With high-unemployment rates, the reality is that one salary often carries an entire household. The poorest South Africans (30%) spend 31% of their total expenditure on food according to the latest Statistics South African Income and Expenditure Survey [14] and this population group is also the most vulnerable to food price increases.

With food price inflation being a global phenomenon, the price of staple foods has continued to increase over the past 2 years at a relatively high rate. Yet, although the Food and Agricultural Organisation (FAO) indicates that world food prices declined by 18.5% in 2015, Statistics South Africa (StatsSA) measured a 5% increase in the cost of its benchmark food basket during 2015. The South African Reserve Bank (SARB) announced that food price inflation is expected to rise to 11% by the end of 2016. The rural poor is also more severely affected. In 2013, rural consumers payed $0.37 more than their urban counterparts for the same food basket consisting of rice (2 kg), maize meal (5 kg), full cream-long life milk (1000 ml), sunflower oil (750 ml) and a loaf of white bread (700 g) [15].

3.1.3. *Food access*

Food retailing in South Africa is characterised by two distinct sectors: the formal food retail sector and the informal sector. The shop formats within the formal food retail sector include hypermarkets, supermarkets, superettes, convenience stores, urban counter stores, urban self-serve stores, rural counter stores and rural self-serve stores. It is estimated that the formal food retail sector accounts for at least 60% of food retailing in South Africa.

The informal food retail sector includes informal markets, small retail stands, hawkers (street vendors), food vendors and spaza shops (informal stores found in rural areas and informal settlements in SA). These informal retailers play a significant role in the food security of the most vulnerable population groups in South Africa [16].

In terms of own production, a recent study on food security among poor households in the Limpopo province of South Africa found that in terms of food production, 57and 50% of households were involved in crop production and livestock production, respectively. The most popular crops were maize, mangoes, papaya, spinach, tomatoes, oranges, bananas and guavas. The most prominent livestock production activities focused on poultry, cattle and goats [17].

Although South Africa has the ability to meet national food requirements, large-scale inequality and poverty means that many households do not enjoy food security or adequate access to nutritious and safe food. Apart from poverty increasing vulnerability to hunger and food insecurity, many households do not have sufficient access to diverse or nutrient-dense foods that will allow adequate nutrition. At the national level, South Africa is considered to be a food-secure nation, yet stunting and micro-nutrient deficiencies continue to co-exist with a rising incidence of overweight and obesity and the associated consequences such as hypertension, cardiovascular disease and diabetes [18]. This high prevalence of under-nutrition, micro-nutrient deficiencies and over-nutrition within a complex agriculture and food system presents a series of challenges which has significant implications for policies and programmes.

4. Methodology

To conduct the case study, a South-African country team was formed representing academics and professionals working in nutrition, food security and the agricultural policy environment. Members of the country team were selected based on their level of involvement in nutrition and agricultural activities and frameworks within South Africa.

As a point of departure, a literature review was conducted on the nutrition situation in South Africa to serve as the background to contextualize the case study. A review of previous nutrition surveys and data was conducted simultaneously with the collection of primary data in the field. Nutrition information was sourced from the previous nutrition-related national surveys that have been conducted in South Africa since 1994 namely, the review of the South African Vitamin A Survey (SAVACG) and the National Food Consumption Survey (1999 and 2005). The main nutrition policies at the time were also reviewed and summarised in comparison with the findings of the Landscape Analyses Report performed for the World Health Organization (WHO) in 2010 [19]. The information was discussed and insights were obtained through stakeholder interviews with members from the Directorate of Nutrition of the National Department of Health.

Secondly, to get a thorough understanding of the South African policy environment, 29 key stakeholders were interviewed. Interviews at the national level involved mainly senior staff (Directors and managers) at key government ministries and agencies, departmental heads of academic and training institutions and national programme officers.

In addition, a questionnaire was distributed extensively throughout the country to stakeholders as well as through professional associations, e.g. the South African Association for Food Science and Technology (SAAFOST) and Nutrition Society of South Africa (NSSA)). The questionnaire was developed and adapted based on a scientific article from Haddad [20] and a report from the Leverhulme Centre for Integrative Research on Agriculture and Health [21]. The questionnaire was adopted to be applicable to the South African situation.

Once the policy environment within which programmes are rolled out was well understood, key programmes and policies were identified which do/could impact on the nutrition sensitivity of agriculture and food systems. A desktop review was done to isolate relevant programmes. This was done by means of reviewing the current strategic plans of all the national departments in South Africa, identifying any frameworks and programmes containing the words 'nutrition', 'food security' or 'health' or 'agriculture'. The programmes excluded medical based interventions and programmes such as supplementation programmes by the Department of Health and medicinal programmes such as the Farmer-to-Pharma programme by the Department of Science and Technology.

Once the list of programmes was compiled, confirmation that the list was complete was obtained from stakeholders in South Africa through the distribution of the list to them for comments and approval, as well as presentation of the report to the National Department of Agriculture, Forestry and Fisheries (DAFF).

To review the nutrition sensitivity of the programmes included in the list, a template was developed to evaluate the nutrition sensitivity of each of the interventions, adopted from the UNSCN guideline provided [22] (**Table 2**).

5. Findings

The national government of South Africa functions through three spheres, i.e. national, provincial and local governmental departments. At the national level, the Bill of Rights in the Constitution of the Republic of South Africa (Act 108 of 1996) states that: *Everyone has the right to have access to sufficient food and water and the state must take reasonable legislative and other measures, within its available resources, to achieve the progressive realisation of each right* (Section 27); and *Every child has the right to basic nutrition, shelter, basic health care services and social services* (Section 28) [13]. This Constitution is considered the supreme law of the land and cannot be superseded by any other governmental action.

The Medium-Term Strategic Framework (MTSF) of South Africa is an electoral mandate and a statement of intent identifying the development challenges facing South Africa. It guides planning and resource allocation during a 5-year cycle. National and provincial departments need to develop their own strategic plans and budgets taking the medium-term imperatives reported in this document into account. In the 2014–2019 MTSF of the current ruling party, their objectives are:

- Radical economic transformation, rapid economic growth and job creation.
- Rural development, land and agrarian reform and food security.
- Ensuring access to adequate human settlements and quality basic services.
- Improving the quality of and expanding access to education and training.
- Ensuring quality health care and social security for all citizens.
- Fighting corruption and crime.
- Contributing to a better Africa and a better world.
- Social cohesion and nation building.

Based on the MTSF, a set of 14 national outcomes were developed (**Table 1**). These outcomes reflect the desired development impacts the Government seeks to achieve. Each outcome is articulated in terms of measurable outputs and key activities to achieve the outputs. The President of South Africa then proceeds to sign Negotiated Service Delivery Agreements with all Cabinet Ministers, in which they are requested to establish and participate in

Outcome	Department responsible for coordination
1. Improved quality of basic education	Department of basic education
2. A long and healthy life for all South Africans	Department of health
3. All people in South Africa are and feel safe	Department of defence
4. Decent employment through inclusive economic growth, coordinated by the	Department of trade and industry
5. A skilled and capable workforce to support an inclusive growth path	Department of higher education
6. An efficient, competitive and responsive economic infrastructure network	Department of rural development and land reform
7. Vibrant, equitable and sustainable rural communities with food security for all	Department of rural development and land reform
8. Sustainable human settlements and improved quality of household life	Department of human settlements
9. A responsive, accountable, effective and efficient local government system	Department of cooperative governance
10. Environmental assets and natural resources that are well protected and continually enhanced	Department of environmental affairs
11. Create a better South Africa and contribute to a better and safer Africa and World	Department of telecommunications and postal services
12. An efficient, effective and development oriented public service and an empowered, fair and inclusive citizenship	Department of public service and administration
13. A comprehensive, responsive and sustainable social protection system	Department of social development
14. A diverse, socially cohesive society with a common national identity	Department of arts and culture

Table 1. The 14 key outcomes of the 2014–2019 Medium-Term Strategic Framework.

Implementation Forums for each of the outcomes, prioritise funds and develop the related policies and programmes accordingly.

An organogram summarizing relevant food and agricultural policies, programmes and frameworks and the responsible national levels of power are presented in **Figure 1**.

In 2011, the National Planning Commission (NPC) released a diagnostics report setting out the achievements and shortcoming of SA since 1994. It identified a failure to implement policies and an absence of broad partnerships as the main reasons for slow progress and set out nine primary challenges: (1) too few people work, (2) the quality of school education of black people is poor, (3) infrastructure is poorly located, inadequate and under-maintained, (4) spatial divides hobble inclusive development,(5) the economy is unsustainably resource-intensive,(6) the public health system cannot meet demand or sustain quality, (7) public services are uneven and often of poor quality,(8) corruption levels are high and(9) South Africa remains a divided society.

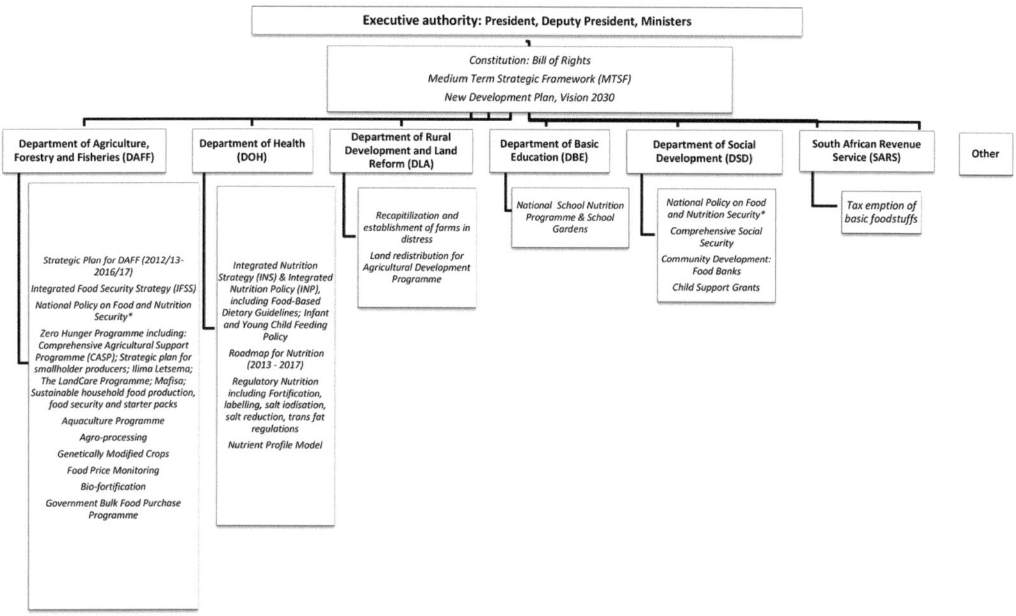

Figure 1. Organogram of the national levels of power responsible for the relevant food and agricultural policies, programmes and frameworks included in this case study.

The National Development Plan (Vision 2030) was released later in 2011 as a broad strategic framework that was set out by the NPC to guide the development of the new cycles of the presidential MTSF. It identified the key challenges South Africa as a country has to face but argues that the country can eliminate poverty and reduce inequality by 2030. It emphasises the importance of hard work, leadership and unity. It furthermore identifies infrastructure development, job creation, health, education, governance, inclusive planning and the fight against corruption as key focus areas and spells out specific projects for each.

In summary, the principal indicators of the NDP are to eliminate income poverty by 2030 (reduce the proportion of households with a monthly income below R419 per person in 2009 prices from 39% to zero) and reduce inequality (the Gini coefficient should fall from 0.69 to 0.06 by 2030). Apart from increased employment from 13 million in 2010 to 24 million in 2030, affordable access to quality health care and household food and nutrition security are listed as specific milestones required for enabling the achievement of these indicators.

The results of the findings related to the nutrition sensitivity of the various programmes and policies according to the Food and Agriculture Organization of the United Nations (FAO) guiding principles for linking agriculture and nutrition [22] are presented in **Table 2**.

Already in the early 2000s, lack of coordination was recognised and in 2002, Cabinet approved the Integrated Food Security Strategy (IFSS) to streamline, harmonize and integrate the diverse food security programmes. The strategy was implemented through among others the Zero Hunger Programme and there have been achievements in many of the

Nutrition sensitivity of agriculture policies and programmes	Integrated food Security Strategy	Zero Hunger	Food Security and Nutrition Programme	Aquaculture	Agro-processing	Food Price Monitoring	TAX	Fortification	Integrated Nutrition Strategy & Programme	Roadmap to nutrition	Regulatory nutrition	Recapitilization & establishment of farms in distress	Land Redistribution for Agricultural Development Programme	National School Nutrition Programme	Comprehensive social security	Food banks	Grants
1. Have explicit nutrition objectives	Yes	Yes	Yes	Partial	Partial	No	Yes	Partial	Yes	Yes	Yes	Partial	Partial	Yes	Partial	Yes	Partial
2. Have explicit nutrition indicators/link with nutrition M&E system	Yes	Yes	Yes	No	No	No	No	No	Yes	Yes	No	No	No	Yes	No	Yes	No
3. Have goals/ activities based in the local nutrition context	Yes	Yes	Yes	No	No	Yes	Yes	No	Yes	Yes	Yes	No	No	Yes	No	Yes	No
4. Target the most vulnerable	Yes	Yes	Yes	Yes	Yes	Yes	Yes	Yes	Yes	Yes	Partial	Yes	Yes	Yes	Yes	Yes	Yes
5. Empower women	No	No	Yes	No	No	No	No	No	No	Yes	No	No	No	No	No	No	No
6. Increase food production	Yes	Yes	Yes	Yes	No	No	No	Partial	Yes	Yes	No	Yes	Partial	Yes	No	No	No
6. One of nutrient-rich foods	No	No	Partial	Yes	No	No	No	Yes	Yes	Yes	No	No	No	Yes	No	No	No
7. Reduce post-harvest losses	No	No	Yes	No	Yes	No	No	No	Yes	Yes	No	No	No	No	No	Partial	No
8. Promote diversification of agricultural products	Partial	Yes	No	Partial	No	No	Partial	Yes	Yes	Yes	No	No	No	Partial	No	No	No

http://dx.doi.org/10.5772/67110

Nutrition sensitivity of agriculture policies and programmes	Integrated food Security Strategy	Zero Hunger	Food Security and Nutrition Programme	Aquaculture	Agro-processing	Food Price Monitoring	TAX	Fortification	Integrated Nutrition Strategy & Programme	Roadmap to nutrition	Regulatory nutrition	Recapitilization & establishment of farms in distress	Land Redistribution for Agricultural Development Programme	National School Nutrition Programme	Comprehensive social security	Food banks	Grants
9. Presence of nutrition promotion/ education components	Yes	Yes	Yes	No	No	No	No	No	Yes	Yes	Yes	No	No	Yes	No	No	No
10. Improve processing of foods	No	No	Yes	No	Yes	No	No	No	No	No	Partial	No	No	No	No	No	No
10. One to retain nutritional value	No	No	No	No	Partial	No	No	No	No	No	Yes	No	No	No	No	No	No
11. Improve storage	No	No	Yes	No	No	No	No	No	No	No	No	No	No	No	No	Partial	No
11. One storage of nutrient-rich foods	No	No	No	No	No	No	No	No	No	No	No	No	No	No	No	No	No
12. Expand markets and market access of the most vulnerable	Yes	Yes	Yes	No	No	No	Partial	No	No	No	No	Partial	Partial	Yes	Partial	No	Partial
12. One of nutrient-rich foods	No	No	Yes	No	No	No	Partial	Partial	No	No	No	No	No	Yes	No	No	No
13. Collaborate with other sectors	Yes	Yes	Yes	Partial	Partial	Partial	Partial	Partial	Partial	No	Partial	Partial	Partial	Yes	Yes	Yes	Yes
14. Maintain/ improve the natural resource base (sustainability approach)	Partial	Yes	Yes	Partial	No	No	No	No	No	No	No	No	No	Partial	No	No	No

Table 2. Summary of the nutrition sensitivity of relevant South African policies and programmes.

strategic priority areas [i.e. NSNP, INP, EPWP, Working for Water, CASP, Ilema/Letsema, Land Care etc.]. Today SA is able to attain national food sufficiency through a combination of own production and importation, but access to nutritious foods by all households is not yet guaranteed.

Within the context of food security and nutrition, South Africa still faces serious challenges, including inadequate safety nets and food emergency management systems, lack of knowledge and resources to make optimal food choices by citizens, in cases where land is available, it is not always optimally utilised for food production, limited access to processing facilities or markets for small-scale primary producers, climate change, undermining of ecosystems, lack of sustainability and no adequate, timely and relevant information on food security and food security programmes.

Although nutrition is frequently included within governments' policies, frameworks and programmes, it is mostly reported upon in terms of 'under-nourishment', focusing on vulnerable people rather than adopting a more integrated approach. Although reference is made to nutrition in many programmes, it is not always clear how they will contribute to better nutrition as expressed in these goals. There is, in particular, a lack of inclusion of(1) the promotion of diversifying agricultural production, (2) improved processing of foods to retain nutrient value and (3) improved storage of nutrient-rich foods (**Table 2**).

Apart from the health sector, there seems to be a knowledge gap on the role which essential nutrients (in addition to kilojoules/calories) play on the health status of the population. Furthermore, there is still a general lack of understanding of the economic and social burden which malnutrition plays in the country. There is consequently very little coordination across technical areas in relation to nutrition. A deeper understanding of the relevance of the interlinkage between agriculture and nutrition for improved food and nutrition security is still an area that needs more attention.

6. Policy implications

A collective vision or 'game plan' to implement nutrition outcomes in agriculture is required and the NDP can be seen as creating the correct architecture. It provides a plan for the reduction of poverty and inequality, with increased employment, affordable access to quality health care and household food and nutrition security as milestones. It fed the development of the current MTSF and evidence of deeper political commitment towards nutrition within food security programing has become evident in the new Food Security and Nutrition Policy for South Africa which was gazetted in 2014.

The policy has an over-arching mandate, with the Presidency at the apex of the policy. Implementation will entrench public, private and civil society partnerships. An Inter-Ministerial Committee on Food Security is advised by a National Food Security Advisory Committee, comprised of recognised experts from organized agriculture, food security and consumer bodies, as well as climate change and environmental practitioners. Although ambitious, this has the potential to allow for more effective coordination among sectors for nutrition outcomes. However, specific areas where this policy is still lacking include(1) promoting diversification of agricultural production,(2) improving processing to retain nutritional value of foods and (3) improvement of storage of nutrient-rich foods. These gaps along with stakeholder comments still indicate misunderstanding of the importance of nutrient density and dietary diversity.

In the past 24 months, the ministerial partners involved have engaged in order to plan and streamline the policy prior to gazetting the implementation plan. The associated stakeholder communication has resulted in a more informed group of policy influencers with the hope that the long-awaited implementation plan will include nutrition-sensitive considerations.

It is not yet clear what community level roll-out will include, but it is anticipated that individual departmental programmes will be developed to build clear evidence of the link between agriculture and nutrition. These programmes and projects need to sufficiently articulate how the evidence base and lessons learned from the projects will contribute to other interventions. Projects like these could be designed and studied as potential models for greater nutritional impact, i.e. how to make it work, the extent of impact etc., including those linked to:

a. Improved agricultural growth and development (such as vitamin A-rich vegetable gardens), including rural and community household food production such as home gardens, agricultural commodity development, including animal husbandry/livestock, aquaculture/fisheries, dairy and cultivation and sustainable resource management.

b. Increasing the production of nutritious foods, e.g. through agro-biodiversity contributing to dietary diversification or a mix of different crops (e.g. fruits and vegetables and livestock), focussing on traditional/indigenous/local foods, bio-fortification (crop breeding, e.g. orange-fleshed sweet potatoes, brown sorghum, yellow maize, cassava, rice, pearl millet, legumes and beans) and aquaculture technology development.

c. Focus on value chains to make nutritious foods more available and specifically to vulnerable groups such as children and women, e.g. school-based nutrition programmes such as SEED, school feeding programmes such as the National School Nutrition Programme (NSNP), alternative marketing and retail channels such as Harvest for Hope providing more fruits and vegetables through an alternative food supply chain, food price monitoring such as the pre-determined food basket of the NAMC which serves as a database to demonstrate food price trends (could be more aligned with the FBDG), tax incentives and scaling up food fortification.

d. Other entry points could include linking small-scale food production and nutrition education, strengthening initiatives that combine low external input farming and nutritional education, strengthening alternative marketing channels and local food economies and including different commodity chains in food price monitoring.

Advocacy is a critical element of any effort to raise the policy profile and social consensus for nutrition. Placing nutrition outcomes high on the agenda of agriculture and the food system requires strong leadership (champions for nutrition and food security) with a multi-dimensional understanding. The government needs to also invest in scientific evidence such as conducting baseline surveys and, undertake formative research; develop community awareness; achieve behaviour change and conduct regular monitoring and evaluation, as well as document findings and lessons learned. Organisational arrangements allowing for shared resources, responsibility, accountability and decision-making with incentives for collaboration will have to be put in place.

With increased economic growth the South-African agricultural sector is becoming less of a provider of food for direct consumption, to more a supplier of raw ingredients to the food industry. The post-harvest value chain of the food system is thus also becoming more important. Policy action to incentivize, regulate and educate the food industry and to encourage consumers to make more nutritious choices is currently limited and needs to be further explored.

7. Conclusions

Although South Africa produces and imports enough energy per person per day, energy alone does not ensure nourished communities. High intakes of low cost, low nutrient, higher energy staple foods have inevitably contributed to the prevailing scenario of malnutrition. Malnutrition, in turn, negatively impacts on productivity and livelihoods.

While many poor South African households produce own fresh produce, the majority of food accessed and consumed is procured through the formal or informal food systems. The importance of the agriculture and food sectors should thus not be ignored when nutrition considerations for political commitment are made.

Although there has been a general lack in the nutrition sensitivity within policies and programmes and coordination within the government spheres, it seems as if an era of increased awareness is on the horizon with the prioritization of an overarching policy, governed by The Presidency that not only includes nutrition outcomes but lists nutrition within the policy title. The National Food Security and Nutrition Policy for South Africa was gazetted in 2014 and although it has its shortcomings in terms of nutrition sensitivity, it is a step in the right direction. Moving away from policies exclusively promoting a food system which primarily generates profit to one which generates adequate, affordable and nutritious foods, should be the future focus.

Author details

Hester Carina Schönfeldt*, Nicolette Hall and Beulah Pretorius

*Address all correspondence to: profhettie@gmail.com

Department of Animal and Wildlife Sciences, Institute of Food, Nutrition and Well-being, University of Pretoria, Pretoria, South Africa

References

[1] Kimani-Murage, E. W. et al. The prevalence of stunting, overweight and obesity and metabolic disease risk in rural South African children. BMC Public Health, v. 10, pp. 158, 2010.

[2] Vorster, H. H. The link between poverty and malnutrition: a South African perspective. Health SA Gesondheid, v. 15, n. 1, pp. 1–6, 2010.

[3] Lanigan, J. Singhal, A. Early nutrition and long-term health: a practical approach. Proceeding of the Nutrition Society, v. 61, pp. 422– 429, 2009.

[4] Pinstrup-Andersen, P. Improving human nutrition through agricultural research: Overview and objectives. Improving Human Nutrition Through Agriculture: The Role of International Agricultural. United Nations University: Nutrition Bulletin. pp. 352–355, 2000.

[5] FAOSTAT (2013). South Africa Country Overview. Available at: http://faostat.fao.org/ Last accessed 25 June 2013.

[6] Koch, J. The food security policy context in South Africa: Country study number 21. International Policy Centre for Inclusive Growth. Brazil. 2011.

[7] UAUY, R., KAIN, J. The epidemiological transition: need to incorporate obesity prevention into nutrition programmes. Public Health Nutrition, v. 5, n. 1A, pp. 223–229, 2002.

[8] NFCS, 1999. *The National Food Consumption Survey: children aged 1-9 years*, Pretoria: Department of Health.

[9] Vorster, H. H., Kruger, A., Margetts, B. M. The nutrition transition in Africa: can it be steered into a more positive direction? Nutrients, v. 3, n. 4, pp. 429–441, 2011.

[10] Mchiza, Z. J. et al. A Review of Dietary Survey's in the Adult South African Population from 2000 to 2005. *Nutrients*, v. 7, pp. 8227–8250, 2015.

[11] Department of Agriculture, Forestry and Fisheries. Abstract of Agricultural Statistics. [S.l.]. 2012.

[12] Nkonki, L. L., Chopra, M., Doherty, T. M. Explaining household socio-economic related child health inequalities using multiple methods in three diverse settings in South Africa. International Journal of Equity in Health, v. 10, pp. 13, 2011.

[13] Steyn, N. P., Temple, N. Community based nutrition textbook for South Africa: a rights based approach. Cape Town: Medical Research Council & Food and Agriculture Organization of the United Nations, 2008.

[14] STATSSA. Income and Expenditure Survey (IES) 2010/2011. Statistics South Africa. Pretoria. 2012.

[15] National Agricultural Marketing Council. Food Price Monitro - Media Release. NAMC. Pretoria. 2013.

[16] Battersby, J. Urban food insecurity in Cape Town, South Africa: an alternative approach to food access. Development Southern Africa, v. 28, n. 4, pp. 545–561, 2011.

[17] D'haese, L. Food security in the Limpopo Province. International Research Report. [S.l.]. 2011.

[18] Shisana, O. et al. South African National Health and Nutrition Examination Survey (SANHANES-1). Cape Town. 2013.

[19] World Health Organization. Country Assessment in South Africa. [S.l.]. 2010.

[20] Haddad, L. From nutrition plus to nutrition driven: how to realize the elusive potential of agriculture for nutrition? Food and Nutrition Bulletin, v. 34, n. 1, pp. 39–44, 2013.

[21] Hawkes, C., Turner, R., Waage, J. Current and Planned Research on Agriculture for Improved Nutrition: A Mapping and a Gap Analysis. Report for the Department of International Development (DFID). Leverhulme Centre for Integrative Research on Agriculture and Health/University of Aberdeen/Center for Sustainable International Development. London. 2012.

[22] Food and Agriculture Organization of the United Nations. Synthesis of guiding principles on agricultural programming for nutrition. FAO of the UN. Italy, Rome. 2013 (E-ISBN 978-92-5-107560-9).

Chapter 2

A Study of Household Food security and Adoption of Biofortified Crop Varieties in Tanzania: The Case of Orange-Fleshed Sweetpotato

Julius J. Okello, Kirimi Sindi, Kelvin Shikuku,
Margaret McEwan and Jan Low

Additional information is available at the end of the chapter

http://dx.doi.org/10.5772/67677

Abstract

Food insecurity has become a key issue in the field of development in recent years with major inadequate intake of vitamin A-rich foods. Specifically, vitamin A deficiency (VAD) remains a major health problem among poor developing-country households, especially in Africa. Efforts to combat VAD currently focuses on food-based approach that entails breeding for crops that are rich in beta carotene, a precursor for Vitamin A. Success has been registered in sweetpotato, cassava and maize. Among these crops, the greatest effort has gone into promoting the production and consumption of orange-fleshed sweetpotato (OFSP). These efforts include sensitization of farmers on the nutritional benefits of OFSP and the provision of clean sweetpotato planting materials. This study used a rich dataset collected from 732 farm households in Tanzania to assess of effect of household food insecurity and benefit awareness on the adoption of OFSP varieties. The study found that the household food security and awareness of the benefit of OFSP affect the decision to adopt OFSP varieties. It also found evidence that agroecology and farmer endowment with financial and physical assets affect the decision to grow OFSP varieties. It discusses lessons and policy implications of the findings for other countries.

Keywords: food insecurity, benefit awareness, biofortified sweetpotato, farmer adoption, Tanzania

1. Introduction

Hidden hunger has become a major development issue, especially in developing countries. The concept refers to a situation where households and individuals may have access to food in sufficient amounts but fail to attain the required quantities of micronutrients. These micronutrients include zinc, iron, and vitamin A. Hidden hunger is especially a major problem among poor rural households who cannot afford purchased supplements. The problem of hidden hunger, first coined in the 1990s, led to greater emphasis on defining food security to include the nutritional content of the food.

The inability of households to afford purchased food supplements required to meet micronutrient needs has led to the rethinking of the strategies to improve access to essential micronutrients. One approach that has gained importance is the biofortification of crops most frequently used by poor/rural households [1]. Hence, the last one decade has witnessed concerted efforts to breed for crops that have enhanced quantities of essential micronutrients. Some of the essential nutrients targeted by these efforts are zinc, iron, and vitamin A. The crops targeted by these efforts include sweetpotato, maize, sorghum, beans, and cassava. These staple crops are consumed by a large number of rural households in developing countries and are often labeled as the food security crops [2].

Sub-Saharan Africa (SSA) has one of the largest number of food insecure households. Global hunger index (For details, see http://www.ifpri.org/pressrelease/global-hunger-index-calls-greater-resilience-building-efforts-boost-food-and-nutrition-) developed by the International Food Policy Research Institute ranked this region among those with highest levels of hunger. The high incidence of hunger results from inadequate intakes of both micro and macronutrients needed by the body to function adequately. Foremost among the micronutrients that are contributing to micronutrient-based food insecurity in SSA is vitamin A [3–5]. Prevalence of vitamin A deficiency (VAD) is high among the East African countries, including Ethiopia, Uganda, Rwanda, Kenya, and Tanzania [6]. High incidence of VAD is also reported in Southern African countries such as Zambia, Malawi, and Mozambique. For instance, vitamin D deficiency in Uganda is estimated to be about one-third of the population. In Kenya, about 70% of pre-school children suffer from VAD [7, 8].

To combat VAD among these countries, the consultative group for International Agricultural Research (CGIAR) has focused biofortification efforts on maize, sweetpotato, and cassava. Among these, the greatest investment, and success, has been in the development of vitamin A rich orange-fleshed sweetpotato (OFSP). These efforts have been recognized by the award of the 2016 World Food Price to biofortification of sweetpotato. At the same time, past studies have found increased intakes among rural women and children [4, 5] and evidence of reduced incidence of VAD among these vulnerable groups [9]. These studies further suggest regular consumption of OFSP can reduce VAD among vulnerable groups by 13–15%.

Theoretically, the increased intake of OFSP should, in turn, result in higher adoption of OFSP varieties. To date, however, evidence regarding early adoption of OFSP varieties in SSA remains mixed, with experts (i.e., scientists) predicting much higher adoption than what empirical studies suggest [10]. At the same time, there is still rather limited presence of OFSP in the local markets even where extensive campaigns have occurred. This chapter draws from a rich dataset collected from 732 households and the multivariate regression technique to assess the factors that influence a farmer's decision to grow/adopt OFSP varieties. To date, evidence on the factors that drive adoption of OFSP remains very limited. At the same time, no study has systematically examined the effect of awareness of the nutritional benefits of OFSP and household food security status on early adoption OFSP varieties in the presence of the more popular white-fleshed varieties. This chapter uses the multivariate probit regression technique to control for the effects of competing interests in the planting of different varieties of sweetpotato by including the more popular local (white-fleshed) varieties. The chapter then tests two hypotheses. The null hypothesis tested in the two cases state that participation in the project (a proxy for awareness of benefits of OFSP) and food insecurity (a proxy for poor households) have no effect on the decision to plant the sweetpotato varieties examined in this study.

That is, it first tests the hypothesis that the likelihood of adopting OFSP is affected by food insecurity status of the households. Second, the chapter tests the hypothesis that awareness of the nutritional benefits of the OFSP increases the likelihood of planting OFSP.

The chapter focuses on smallholder farm households in the four regions of Tanzania, namely, Mara, Mwanza, Shinyanga, and Kagera. The households are stratified by participation in a project known as Marando Bora, which, among other things, sensitized farmers on nutritional benefits of consuming OFSP varieties. The Tanzania project provides an interesting case study because of the high incidence of poverty in the study regions and activities of the project that created awareness about the importance of growing OFSP and of consuming diets rich in vitamin A to combat vitamin A deficiency.

The rest of this chapter is organized as follows: Section 2 provides the study background and describes the Marando project. Section 3 outlines the study methods while Section 4 presents and discusses the results. Lastly, Section 5 concludes and highlights key policy implications.

2. Study background

2.1. The concept of food insecurity and food-based approach to fighting micronutrient deficiency

Food security has been defined variously in the literature. However, the most widely used definition of food security is that of [11]. It states that food security is "a situation that exists when all people, at all times, have physical, social, and economic access to sufficient, safe, and nutritious food that meets their dietary needs and food preferences for an active and healthy life." Among the pillars emphasized by this definition is the fact that food needs to meet nutritional requirements of the people. The failure to access food that meets the nutritional needs of the household, also known as hidden hunger, is, therefore, one of the subtle yet equally dangerous forms of food insecurity. It specifically arises when households do not have access to a diverse diet that supplies their micronutrient needs.

A new strategy being used to combat hidden hunger among poor rural households is the promotion of production and consumption of biofortified crops that are bred to supply the essential micronutrients. This strategy, often referred to as the food-based approach to enhancing household nutrition, particularly aims at tapping into the local food production system to tackle the problem of poor or inadequate consumption of foods that supply essential nutrients. The strategy uses the locally produced staple foods to introduce essential micronutrients into the locally available and preferred foods.

One of the micronutrients targeted by this strategy is vitamin A. Vitamin A deficiency (VAD) is widespread in many rural communities of Africa. It is especially prevalent among pregnant or lactating women and children who are less than five years of age. Young children need vitamin A to fight common childhood diseases (e.g., diarrhea) and for healthy growth. Pregnant women, on the other hand, are in greatest need for vitamin A during the third trimester when they and the unborn child have the highest demand for vitamin A. Thus inadequate consumption of vitamin A–rich foods by these vulnerable household members can significantly compromise the development of the child and health of the mother. Thus growing and consuming vitamin A–rich crops can act as a vehicle for tackling VAD. Indeed, proof-concept studies and efficacy trials have demonstrated that consumption of modest amounts (125g a day) of orange-fleshed sweetpotato (OFSP), a biofortified crop, can supply the daily needs of vitamin A [1, 12, 13].

Following the findings of past studies, several countries have intensified efforts to promote the growing and consumption of biofortified sweetpotato varieties (i.e., orange-fleshed varieties that are rich in vitamin A). The countries include Ethiopia, Kenya, Uganda, Tanzania, Zambia, and Mozambique. Promotion of the varieties usually includes provision of clean planting material to farmers at subsidized rates along with information about the nutritional benefits of growing and consuming orange-fleshed sweetpotato (OFSP). These efforts usually target the farming households and enable them to grow vitamin A–rich foods.

2.2. The case for sweetpotato production in Tanzania and benefit awareness

Sweetpotato is an important food security crop in many districts of Tanzania, including the Lake Victoria region. Throughout these districts, it helps bridge the hunger gap often characterized by acute shortage of staple foods. There are several reasons why sweetpotato plays a significant role in bridging the hunger gap among sweetpotato producing communities. First, sweetpotato can stay in the soil for an extended period making it easy for farmers to "store" it in the field and harvest piecemeal or as needed. Second, it can withstand moisture stress caused by lack or insufficient rains hence it fills in the food gap during inclement weather. Third, sweet potato does not require much use of external inputs and is often grown without fertilizers and pesticides.

Until recently, farmers planted mainly the white and yellow-fleshed varieties of sweetpotato. These varieties contribute to household food security by providing starch (sugars) needed to supply body energy. They, however, lack (for the case of white-fleshed varieties) or contain inadequate amounts of the beta-carotene, the precursor for vitamin A. Nonetheless, the majority of households grow these non-OFSP varieties to meet household food/subsistence needs. Varieties that are richer in vitamin A, popularly known as the orange-fleshed sweetpotato, due to the deep orange color of the flesh, have been bred for the dual purpose of supplying household energy (starch) and micronutrient needs.

The study targeted Tanzania because of the high incidence of poverty among the rural farm households [14] leading to poor nutritional intake hence inability to access purchased food supplements needed to remedy the vitamin A deficiency. Tanzania also has one of the world's highest rates of undernutrition [1]. It is estimated that around 2.4 million children in Tanzania are malnourished and that 42% of children suffer from stunting. The authors [1] further indicate that about one-third of children in Tanzania are deficient vitamin A. The Tanzania Food and Nutrition Center (2012) estimated that vitamin A deficiency would contribute to one out of 10 child deaths between 2006 and 2015.

The intervention in Tanzania through a project known as Marando Bora, a Swahili phrase for better quality vines, was launched in 2009. The Marando Bora project specifically focused on promoting the use of clean/quality sweetpotato planting materials. It was aimed at resolving the clean seed bottleneck by developing and testing effective strategies for multiplication, dissemination, and exchange of disease-free (i.e., clean/quality) vines from which new plants can be propagated. The project was implemented in several districts of the Lake Victoria region of Tanzania. The project used two strategies to reach out to farmers namely decentralized vine multipliers (DVM) and mass distribution (MD). Under the DVM model, 88 trained vine multipliers were provided with quality planting materials to bulk. Farmers were then informed about these multipliers and given information about where to find them. The MD model used open-air meetings, conducted by partner nongovernmental organizations and government extension personnel, to create awareness among farmers about quality vines.

The Marando Bora project expanded to cover four regions of Tanzania. An estimated 110,000 households were reached through the project between 1999 and 2012. The regions the project has covered are Mara, Mwanza, Shinyanga, and Kagera (**Figure 1**). These regions fall the drier

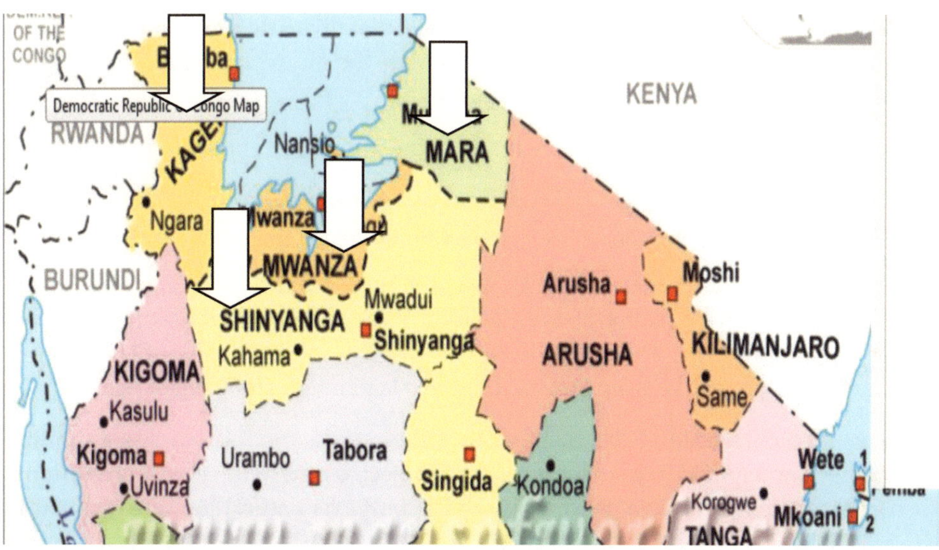

Figure 1. A map of the southern region of Tanzania showing the study areas. *Source*: http://www.mapsofworld.com/tanzania/tanzania-political-map.htm.

agroecological zones namely zone P4, zone P5, zone P8, zone W3, and zone N10. The sensitization on the use of quality planting materials focused on the sweetpotato agronomy, pest and disease diagnosis, and protection and methods for conserving vines for future planting.

3. Methodology

3.1. Empirical analysis of adoption

Adoption of a different technology (i.e., improved variety of sweetpotato) from the existing one usually entails both costs and benefits. In the case of OFSP, these costs could include conventional (such as having to purchase new planting materials from neighbors) and transaction costs related to search and transportation of planting materials to the firm.

The decision to adopt of improved technology is often modeled using a logit or probit regression model. In the case where OFSP varieties coexist with other improved local varieties, it is also expected that farmers make the decision to adopt OFSP fully knowing of the existence of the other varieties. Thus the adoption decisions relating to OFSP and improved local varieties are interdependent [15, 16]. More formally, this means that the decision to adopt variety j by farmer i is correlated to the decision to adopt variety k. The correlation in decision to adopt multiple varieties of sweetpotato, in turn, suggests the likelihood of correlation of the error terms across the different equations. This correlation renders the use of probit or logit regressions models inappropriate because the estimates coefficients will be biased [16].

To overcome the above problem, a multivariate probit regression was used to model the choice of sweetpotato varieties to plant. The multivariate probit regression technique has been used in several past studies [17–19]. It is an extension of bivariate probit model [20] and uses Monte Carlo simulation techniques to jointly estimate the multivariate probit regression equation system [21].

The implicit form along with the variables included in the estimation of the model is given by

$$\begin{aligned}\text{variety} &= \text{f}(\mathit{intervened}, \mathit{foodsec}, \mathit{gender}, \mathit{lneduc}, \mathit{lnage}, \mathit{credit}, \mathit{lnusedfarm},\\ &\quad \mathit{valley\_bottom}\ \mathit{lndistmkt}, \mathit{lncrpinc}1, \mathit{grpmember}, \mathit{assetindex}, \mathit{moreyield},\\ &\quad \mathit{sugary},\ \mathit{aezP4N10}, \mathit{aezP8}) + \text{error term}\end{aligned}$$

The dependent variable in the equation above is a dummy variable equal 1 if a farmer *i* decided to plant variety *j* and 0 otherwise. That is, the dependent variable takes the value of 1 if *variety* = *j*, for *j* = Kabode, Ejumala, Jewel, or New Polista, Ukerewe is planted, and 0 otherwise.

The explanatory variables used in the estimation of the model are: *intervened* is a dummy equal 1 if a farmer participated in the Marando Bora project, 0 otherwise; *gender* is a dummy equal 1 if the respondent is a male, zero if otherwise; *lneduc* is natural log of education in years; *foodsec* is an index of food security computed as discussed above; *valley* is a dummy equal 1 if farmer has access to valley bottom, 0 if otherwise; *lndistmkt* is natural log of distance to market in walking minutes; *lnfamsize* is natural log of size of farm in acres ; *grpmember* is a dummy equal 1 if the farmer belongs to a farmer organization, 0 if otherwise; *credit* is a dummy equal 1 if a farmer received credit in 2012; *lncropinc* is natural log crop income in Tanzania Shillings; *assetindex* is wealth index computed from physical (household and farm) assets. The index was computed following [22]; *moreyield* is a dummy equal 1 if a higher root yield is important in decision to conserve vines, 0 if otherwise; *sugary* is a dummy equal to 1 if the sweetness (high sugar content) is important to the farmer, 0 if otherwise; *aezP5N10* is a dummy equal to 1 if a farmer is in the more wet area, 0 if otherwise; *aezP8* is a dummy equal to 1 if a farmer is in moderately wet area, 0 if otherwise; *eazP4W3* is a dummy equal 1 if a farmer is in drier area, 0 if otherwise.

In this study, other variables that should be included in the model, based on a priori expectations, but are highly correlated with participation in the Marando Bora project were dropped. This is because their inclusion along with intervention (i.e., participation in Marando Bora) could result in "double counting" (For example, see [23] for similar treatment but in an unrelated study). The variables dropped are voucher, dummy equal to 1 if a farmer received a voucher that allowed him/her to get sweetpotato vines at discounted rate, 0 otherwise and know_DVM is a dummy equal 1 if a farmer knew where to find a DVM, and 0 otherwise. In addition, the Wald joint-exclusion restriction test is used to assess and drop variables that do not explain much of the variability in the decision to adopt OFSP.

3.2. Computation of household food insecurity index

Food insecure households engage in several activities/actions in efforts to obtain food. Food insecurity status of the household can thus be deduced from a set of actions that it engages in to get food in situations of food shortage. Typically, the more the number of such actions undertaken by a household, the more food-insecure that household is likely to be. In this study, we use these "set of actions" undertaken by the households in the sample, and the Rasch model, to measure the food insecurity status of the household. Under the Rasch model, a farmer's behavior can be expressed as a matrix X containing the response xij of i=1,...,n farmer to j=1,...,m food insecurity statements. The actions typically correspond to a set of binary statements that capture what the farmer did in response to food insecurity situation in his/her household. An index of food insecurity was therefore computed for each of the 732 households by subjecting the collected statements to the Rasch analysis in RUMM2030. The more the actions a household undertook in response to food scarcity, the higher the food insecurity index. Households with a higher index are more food-insecure than the rest of the households in the sample. Moreover, it means that most of the statements they engaged in were extreme/severe.

3.3. Data

This study uses the data collected from 732 households in January and February 2013 as part of the Marando Bora endline household survey. The map of the study areas covered is presented in **Figure 1**. A multi-stage sampling technique was used. First, four regions (Mara, Mwanza, Shinyanga, and Kagera) were purposively selected. Within each region, farmers were categorized into those that participated in the decentralized vine multiplier scheme, the mass distribution scheme and those who did not participate in any of the two schemes. For the purposes of this study, the first two groups of farmers comprise the "intervened" group (i.e., participants) and the last group constitutes the nonintervention group (i.e., nonparticipants). The list of farmers in each category (i.e., intervened and nonintervention) was then compiled at the village levels in each of the project wards and districts. A random sample of farmers was selected from each category of farmers for personal interviews. In total 481 project participants and 251 nonparticipants were interviewed. The sample contained 221 and 511 male and female farmers, respectively. The high number of female farmers reflects the fact that women mostly grow sweetpotato and that the project also targeted female household members. Data collected included farmer and farm characteristics, asset endowments, institutional characteristics, and varietal traits.

4. Findings

Table 1 summarizes the data used in estimating the regression models. The results are presented for farmers that participated in the project (and hence were sensitized about the benefits

Variable	Participant (*N*=481)		Nonparticipant (*N*=251)		Test of diff. in means	
	Mean	Std Dev	Mean	Std Dev	t-stat	*p*-value
Farmer/household specific variables						
gender	0.31	0.03	0.02	0.47	−0.81	0.4182
lneduc	0.58	3.13	0.27	3.41	−1.23	0.2175
lnage	3.79	0.27	3.84	0.28	1.97	0.0246
Farm specific variables						
valley	0.68	0.47	0.64	0.48	−1.32	0.0939
lndistmkt	1.26	1.61	1.24	1.58	−0.14	0.8878
lnfmsize	1.08	0.81	1.02	0.98	−0.89	0.1966
Capital endowment factors						
lncropinc	6.84	8.59	5.63	8.6	−1.79	0.0363
group	0.64	0.48	0.39	0.49	−6.59	0
assetindex	3.56	2.15	3.4	2.02	−1.01	0.1549
Varietal trait variables						
moreyield	0.93	0.25	0.9	0.29	−1.41	0.0808
sugary	0.75	0.43	0.78	0.41	0.91	0.819
Agroecological factors						
aezP8	0.34	0.47	0.5	0.5	4.09	0
aezP5N10	0.17	0.38	0.02	0.15	−5.97	0
aezP4W3	0.48	0.5	0.47	0.5	0.15	0.4373

Table 1. Summary statistics and t-test of differences in means by project participation.

of OFSP) and those that did not. Growers of orange-fleshed sweetpotato were participants of the project. As results indicate, project participants differed from the nonparticipating ones in terms of age, many of the asset endowment variables, agroecology, and varietal traits, as shown by the very low *p*-values of tests of differences in means. Specifically, participating farmers differed in terms of income and membership to farmer groups. There is also weak evidence that farmers significantly differed with regard to access to land on valley bottoms.

Figure 2 presents the proportion of farmers growing different varieties of orange-fleshed sweetpotato as well as the cleaned-up local white-fleshed variety, New Polista. New Polista and Kabode were planted by nearly one-half of the farmers interviewed while only about one-quarter of the farmers planted Ejumula and Jewel. The high percentage of farmers planting New Polista is due to its popular traits such as high dry matter content and relatively high sugar content making it tastier than orange-fleshed varieties. New Polista is also more tolerant to the sweetpotato pests, especially the sweetpotato weevil, and to sweetpotato virus disease (SPVD). Among the orange fleshed varieties, Kabode is most widely grown by the farmers owing to its resistance to SPVD, good taste, and the fact that it is rich in vitamin A. However, compared to New Polista, Kabode has a lower dry matter content and is less tolerant to moisture stress caused by droughts.

The low adoption of Ejumula and Jewel is mainly attributed to their susceptibility to SPVD, hence requiring higher disease management, and low dry matter content (for the case of Jewel), despite the latter being more tolerant to moisture stress than Kabode.

This study estimated a multivariate regression model to understand the factors that drive the choice of variety of sweetpotato to grow, and to test the null hypothesis that choice of sweetpotato variety planted is not affected by awareness of nutritional benefits of OSFP. The sweetpotato varieties included in the estimated regression model were Jewel, Ejumula, Kabode (for orange-fleshed varieties), and New Polista (for improved local varieties, also promoted by the project but quite popular among the consumers).

Table 2 presents the tests of interdependence/correlation in the decision to plant different varieties promoted by the Marando Bora project, i.e., the atrho and rho. As expected, the

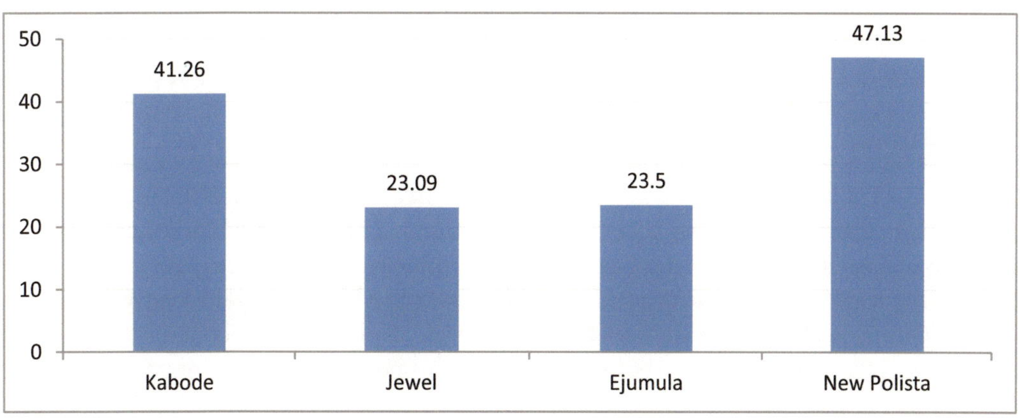

Figure 2. Proportion of farmers growing different varieties of sweetpotato: % (N = 732).

	Coeff.	*p*-value		Coeff.	*p*-value
atrho ejumula-kabode	0.444	0.000	rho ejumula-kabode	0.417	0.000
atrho jewel-kabode	0.313	0.000	rho jewel-kabode	0.303	0.000
atrho newpolista-kabode	0.278	0.000	rho newpolista-kabode	0.271	0.000
atrho jewel-ejumula	0.599	0.000	rho jewel-ejumula	0.537	0.000
atrho newpolista-ejumula	0.270	0.001	rho newpolista-ejumula	0.264	0.000
atrho newpolista-jewel	0.183	0.013	rho newpolista-jewel	0.181	0.011

Note: Likelihood ratio test of rhoejumula-kabode = rhojewel-kabode = rhonewpolista-kabode = rhojewel-ejumula = rhonewpolista-ejumula = rhonewpolista-jewel: Chi^2 (21) = 118.42; *p*-value = 0.000.

Table 2. Tests of correlations in decision to use different sweetpotato varieties.

results indicate that there is statistically significant and positive interdependence/correlation in the decision to choose among the orange-fleshed varieties and also between the orange-fleshed varieties and the white-fleshed New Polista. This finding indicates that estimating separate Probit or Logit regression models to assess the determinants of the decision to plant OFSP varieties would result in biased estimates and justifies the use of multivariate regression technique.

The results of the estimated multivariate probit model are presented in **Table 3**, by variety. We discuss the results by variety below.

4.1. Factors affecting the decision to grow Kabode

As hypothesized, results show that awareness of the nutritional benefits of OFSP and household food security status significantly affect farmer's decision to plant Kabode, an OFSP variety. The *p*-values for the two variables are both 0.0000 indicating that there is very strong evidence from the data to suggest that participation in the Marando Bora project (hence being aware of benefits of eating OFSP) and being food insecure affects the decision to plant Kabode.

Results also indicate that age and agroecology of the area affect the choice of variety planted. Specifically, age is negative and statistically significant indicating that older farmers are less likely to choose to grow Kabode. This finding is probably because older farmers are more used to the local varieties, thus find it difficult to switch to the orange-fleshed varieties. At the same time, aezP8, one of the variables included to capture the effect of agroecology on the choice of variety to plant, is both positive and strongly significant. Specifically, results indicate that farmers in areas falling within zone P8, which is less dry, are more likely to plant Kabode than those falling in the regions covered by zone W3 and P4 (i.e., aezP4W3, the base).

http://dx.doi.org/10.5772/67677

Variable	Kabode		Jewel		Ejumula		New Polista	
	Coeff.	***p*-value**	**Coeff.**	***p*-value**	**Coeff.**	***p*-value**	**Coeff.**	***p*-value**
Farmer specific variables								
intervened	6.949	0.000***	5.910	0.000***	5.893	0.000***	3.380	0.000***
foodsec	0.055	0.000***	0.048	0.000***	0.028	0.015**	0.013	0.300
gender	0.194	0.153	−0.087	0.516	0.214	0.113	0.047	0.728
lneduc	0.010	0.599	0.043	0.042**	0.253	0.209	−0.002	0.914
lnage	−0.486	0.040**	−0.330	0.163	−0.638	0.007***	−0.322	0.156
Farm specific variables								
valley	0.022	0.866	0.160	0.251	0.052	0.712	0.270	0.052*
lndistmkt	−0.023	0.603	−0.076	0.100*	−0.121	0.007***	0.049	0.750
lnusedfarm	0.001	0.998	−0.182	0.080*	−0.116	0.083*	−0.116	0.090*
Asset endowment variables								
lncropinc	0.006	0.491	0.018	0.028	0.019	0.026**	0.015	0.074*
credit	−0.083	0.514	0.003	0.979	0.179	0.127	0.021	0.849
group	0.208	0.110	0.249	0.066*	0.300	0.026**	0.057	0.658
Varietal trait variables								
moreyield	0.303	0.242	0.415	0.131	0.080	0.767	−0.302	0.214
sugary	−0.056	0.704	−0.064	0.660	0.193	0.216	0.331	0.031**
Agroecology variables								
aezP5N10	−0.128	0.455	−0.646	0.002***	−1.026	0.000***	0.248	0.158
aezP8	−0.520	0.000***	−0.068	0.614	−0.558	0.679	0.489	0.001***
_cons	−6.370	0.000	−8.780	0.000	−5.563	0.000	−1.956	0.039

Notes: *N*=732; Log pseudo likelihood = −1104.31; Wald chi^2 (64) = 6408.80; *p*-value=0.0000. Also ***, **, * indicate significance at 1, 5, and 10%, respectively.

Table 3. Factors influencing the use of sweet potato varieties: multivariate probit regression.

4.2. Factors affecting the decision to grow Jewel

The factors driving the decision to plant Jewel are presented in columns 4 and 5 of **Table 3**. As in the case of Kabode, we find, as hypothesized, a strong evidence that both participation in the project (a proxy for awareness of benefits of OFSP) and household food security status affect the decision to plant Jewel. Both variables have *p*-values of 0.0000 indicating that there is firm evidence from the data against the null hypothesis that awareness of the nutritional benefits of OFSP and food insecurity in the household have no effect on the decision to plant Jewel. The results also indicate that education increases the likelihood that a farmer adopts Jewel. This finding is in line with our priori expectations: more educated farmers are more likely to adopt an OFSP variety because education is associated with the demand for quality attributes (in this case the vitamin A content) of food [23, 24].

Results further show that farm-specific, asset endowment, and agroecological variables also affect the decision to plant Jewel. In particular, distance to the market (a proxy for transaction costs) and farm size both reduce the likelihood that a farmer chooses to plant Jewel. The finding that high transaction costs reduce adoption of OFSP variety is in line with the adoption literature which suggests that high transaction costs reduce the price farmers earn and hence dampen the incentives to invest in agricultural technology [25]. At the same time, the results indicate that being in areas under zone aezP5N10 and being a member of a farmer group increase the likelihood that a farmer will decide to plant Jewel. These results are as expected: moving from the less dry zone (i.e., aezP4W3) to the less dry (i.e., aezP5N10) provides more of the moisture needed to grow the less drought tolerant OFSP varieties such as Jewel. The finding that membership to a farmer group increases the likelihood of planting Jewel may be because such groups provide technical and social support to members as well as some value-addition activities [18, 26–28].

4.3. Factors affecting the decision to plant Ejumula

The factors affecting the decision to plant Ejumula, the final OFSP variety we examined in this study, are presented in columns 6 and 7 of **Table 3**. As in the two previous cases, the results indicate that benefit awareness and household food insecurity increase the likelihood that a farmer will grow Ejumula. The null hypothesis that knowledge of the benefits of OFSP and the household food insecurity have no effect on farmer's decision to plant Ejumula is rejected. Results also show that age affects the likelihood that a farmer plants Ejumula. Specifically, as in the case Kabode, the results indicate that older farmers are less likely to adopt Ejumula than younger ones.

Among the farm-specific variables, distance to market and size of farm are both negative and statistically significant suggesting that farmers that face higher transaction costs in the marketing of sweetpotato and those with large farms are less likely to adopt Ejumula. The finding relating the distance to the market (a proxy for transaction) supports our argument above that high transaction costs dampen incentives to grow OFSP. Asset endowment variables, income from crop sales and membership in a farmer group, also affect the decision to plant Ejumula. An increase in crop income and being a member of a group both increase the likelihood of planting Ejumula. The effect on crop income on the adoption of Ejumula is likely to be related to the financial requirements for labor use in the production of sweetpotato. Hired labor is one of the most expensive external inputs in the commercial production of vegetatively propagated crops [29]. Results also show that, among the agroecology variables, farmers in the less dry zone aezP5N10 are more likely adopt Ejumula compared to their counterparts in the drier zone aezP4W3 indicating that agroecology is important in the decision to adopt Ejumula.

4.4. Drivers of decision to adopt New Polista

The results of the factors affecting the decision to use the white-fleshed New Polista variety are presented in the last two columns of **Table 3**. Among, the farmer-specific variables, participation in the project (i.e., intervene) is the only variable that affects the decision to grow New Polista. Specifically, the results indicate that participation in the project increases the likelihood of planting New Polista. While this finding may appear to be contrary to expectations, it actually captures the way the project was designed. While the Marando Bora promoted awareness of the benefits of OFSP, it also promoted the growing of other popular local varieties such as New Polista for the food security purposes and as a source of income. Indeed, this is the reason why the project cleaned up the Polista variety, to remove viruses and to increase its yield potential. The results however do not find food insecurity a significant factor in the decision to grow New Polista.

Two farm-specific variables affect the decision to grow New Polista, namely having access to a valley bottom and size of land. The former increases while the latter decreases the likelihood of planting New Polista. The finding that access to valley bottom influences the decision to grow New Polista likely relates to the fact that access to land in such areas enables farmers to conserve planting materials (i.e., vines) during the dry periods. Results also show that crop income, taste (i.e., sugary), and being in less dry agroecological zone (aezP8) all increase the likelihood of growing New Polista. Notably, the results indicate that farmers who perceive New Polista to be sweeter (i.e., sugary) are more likely to grow it.

The results above have shown that agroecology and asset endowment play a major role in the decision to grow the various improved and cleaned up sweetpotato varieties, including the OFSP. To examine whether these variables jointly affect the decision to plant the four sweetpotato variables analyzed in this study, we conducted appropriate hypothesis tests for each. Following [18, 19], we also examined if the varietal traits affect the likelihood that a farmer will plant these improved varieties. Specifically, a Wald joint-exclusion test of the agroecology variables (proxied aezP5N10, aezP8) and access to the valley bottom, all of which are associated with moisture availability, yielded a Chi-square and p-value of 60.88 and 0.0000, respectively. This result indicates these variables jointly affect farmer's decision about the choice of sweetpotato varieties to plant. Thus, the null hypothesis that agroecology of the area has no effect on the choice of sweetpotato variety planted by the farmer is therefore rejected. On the other hand, a Wald test of nonsignificance of asset endowment variables (represented by asset-index, crop income, and size of land) yielded a Chi-square and p-value of 24.81 and 0.0158, respectively. This finding indicates that there is firm evidence from the data to suggest that farmers' endowment with physical assets (proxied by asset-index and farm size) and financial capital (proxied by income from previous crop) affect the decision about the sweetpotato variety grown. A Wald test of joint exclusion of the varietal attributes (proxied by moreyield and sugary) however finds no evidence that these variables jointly affect the choice of variety planted. The test yields a Chi-square and p-value of 10.68 and 0.2203.

5. Conclusions and lessons

This study examined the effect of awareness of the nutritional benefits of OFSP and food insecurity in the household on the decision to grow OFSP. The study used multivariate probit regression technique, which controls for interdependence/correlation in varietal adoption decisions, to test the effect of participation in the project (a proxy for awareness of nutritional benefits of OFSP) and food insecurity in the household on the decision to plant the three most important OFSP varieties.

The study finds a strong evidence that awareness of the nutritional benefits of OFSP increased the likelihood of a farmer deciding to plant OFSP varieties. It also finds that household food security status increased the probability that a farmer grows OFSP. Some other conditioning variables also affect the decision to plant improved sweetpotato varieties, including the OFSP varieties. In particular, access to agroecology of the area and endowment with financial and physical assets significantly increased the decision to plant improved sweetpotato varieties. This study therefore concludes that household food insecurity has a significant effect on the likelihood of farm households deciding to grow the OFSP varieties.

The findings of this study have several lessons for Sub-Sahara Africa (SSA) countries. First, they imply that interventions aimed at sensitizing farmers on the importance of OFSP need to be coupled with providing access to clean planting materials. In the Marando Bora project, these activities were coupled to ensure not only that farmers have access to better performing (i.e., higher yielding) clean planting material but also were aware of this as well as the nutritional benefits of the growing and consuming OFSP. Indeed, the finding shows that awareness of these benefits is instrumental in the decision to adoption OFSP.

Second, the study demonstrates that sweetpotato farmers are concerned about moisture availability when making the decision to produce OFSP. This finding is not new. Similar findings are presented in [30]. It, however, emphasizes one major challenge farmers' experience, namely, how to conserve planting material over the dry period for next season planting. Thus, efforts to promote the growing and consumption of OFSP need to train farmers on conservation of the planting material. Some of the strategies that can be used in this endeavor are discussed in Refs. [30, 31].

Another major lesson from this study relates to the finding on distance to market, a proxy for transaction costs, reduces the decision to grow OFSP. While this finding is expected, it implies the need to reduce the distances farmers have to access the market since it has implications on the commercialization of OFSP. Since distance to market was measured in terms of time taken to reach produce market, the lesson here is that local governments need to invest in improving the time farmers take to reach the market with their produce. Doing so may require simple improvement the state of the road rather than creating new physical markets in local communities.

The finding that food security status of the households affects the decision to grow OFSP also has implications for policy. In particular, this finding confirms the importance of sweetpotato as source of macronutrients (i.e., starch) and micronutrients (i.e., vitamin A). It therefore implies the need to continue the efforts to upscale the growing of sweetpotato by poor rural households who face the dual food security problem of access and nutrition and also do not have the means to afford food supplements.

Acknowledgements

Funding for this work was provided by the Sweetpotato Action for Security and Health in Africa project, financed by the Bill & Melinda Gates Foundation [OPP1019987], that also enabled the open access status of this chapter.

Author details

Julius J. Okello*, Kirimi Sindi, Kelvin Shikuku, Margaret McEwan and Jan Low

*Address all correspondence to: r.kakuhenzire@cgiar.org

International Potato Center, Sub Sahara Africa, Nairobi, Kenya

References

[1] Waized, B., Ndyetabula, D., Temu, A., Robinson, E. and Henson, S. 2015. Promoting biofortified crops for nutrition: lessons from orange-fleshed sweet potato (OFSP) in Tanzania (No. IDS Evidence Report; 127). Institute of Development Studies, Sussex, United Kingdom.

[2] Kirimi, L., Sitko, N., Jayne, T.S., Karin, F., Muyanga, M., Sheahan, M. and Bor, G. 2011. A farm gate-to-consumer value chain analysis of Kenya's maize marketing system. *Tegemeo Institute of Agricultural Policy and Development Working Paper*, 44.

[3] Stevens, R. and Winter Nelson, A. 2008. Consumer acceptance of pro-vitamin A biofortified maize in Maputo, Mozambique. *Food Policy*, 33:341–351.

[4] Hotz, C., Loechl, C., de Brauw, A., Eozenou, P., Gilligan, D., Moursi, M., Munhaua, B., van Jaarsveld, P., Carriquiry, A. and Meenakshi, J.V. 2012. A large-scale intervention to introduce orange-fleshed sweet potato in rural Mozambique increases vitamin A intakes among children and women. *British Journal of Nutrition*, 108:163–176.

[5] Hotz, C., Loechl, C., Lubowa, A., Tumwine, J.K., Ndeezi, G., Masawi, A.N., Baingana, R., Carriquiry, A., de Brauw, A., Gilligan, D. and Meenakshi, J.V. 2012. Introduction of β-carotene rich orange sweet potato in rural Uganda results in increased vitamin A intakes among children and women and improved vitamin A status among children. *The Journal of Nutrition*, 142(10):1871–1880.

[6] Mwanga, R.O.M. and Ssemakulla, G. 2011. Orange-fleshed sweetpotatoes for food, health and wealth in Uganda, *International Journal of Agricultural Sustainability*, 9(1):42–49.

[7] UNICEF and MI. 2004. Vitamin A and mineral deficiency: A global progress report: Micronutrient Initiative and the United Nations Children's Fund, New York.

[8] De Groote, H., Kimenju, S.C. and Morawetz, U.B. 2011. Estimating consumer willingness to pay for food quality with experimental auctions: the case of yellow versus fortified maize meal in Kenya, *Agricultural Economics*, 42(1):1–16.

[9] van Jaarsveld, P.J., Faber, M., Tanumihardjo, S.A., Nestel, P., Lombard, C.J. and Benadé. 2005. β-Carotene-rich orange-fleshed sweet potato improves the vitamin A status of primary school children assessed with the modified-relative-dose–response test. *American Journal of Clinical Nutrition*, 81:1080–1087.

[10] Arega, A., Yigezu, Y., Ndjeunga, J., Labarta, R., Andrade, R., Diagne, A., Muthoni, R., Simtowe F. and Walker, T. 2011. Measuring the effectiveness of agricultural R&D in Sub-Saharan Africa from the perspectives of varietal output and adoption. *ASTI/IFPRI-FARA Conference Working Paper, 7*. Available athttp://www.ifpri.org/publication/measuring-effectiveness-agricultural-rd-sub-saharan-africa-perspectives-varietal-output-?print

[11] Food and Agriculture Organization (FAO). 2002. The state of food insecurity in the world 2001. Rome, Italy.

[12] Hagenimana, V., Low, J., Anyango, M., Kurz, K., Gichuki, S.T. and Kabira, J. 2001. Enhancing vitamin A intake in young children in western Kenya: Orange-fleshed sweet potatoes and women farmers can serve as key entry points. *Food and Nutrition Bulletin*,22(4): 376–387.

[13] Chowdhury, S., Meenakshi, J.V., Tomlins, K.I. and Owori, C. 2011. Are consumers in developing countries willing to pay more for micronutrient-dense biofortified foods? Evidence from a field experiment in Uganda. *American Journal of Agricultural Economics*, 93(1):83–97.

[14] Mpogole, H. and Kadigi, R.M.J. 2012. Round potato (*Solanum tuberosum*) profitability and implications for variety selection in southern highlands of Tanzania. *Journal of Development and Agricultural Economics*, 4(9):258–267.

[15] Tecklewood, H., Kassie, M. and Shiferaw, B. 2013. Adoption of multiple sustainable agricultural practices in rural Ethiopia. *Journal of Agricultural Economics*, 64(3):597–623.

[16] Kassie, M., Jaleta,M., Shiferaw, B., Mmbando, F., and Mekuria, M. 2012. Interdependence in farmer technology adoption decisions in smallholder systems: Joint estimation of

investments in sustainable agricultural practices in rural Tanzania. Selected paper presented at the International Association of Agricultural Economists Triennial Conference, Foz du Iguacu, Brazil, 18–24 August 2012.

[17] Timu, A.G., Mulwa, M.R., Okello, J.and M. Kamau. 2012. The role of varietal attributes on adoption of improved seed varieties. The case of Sorghum in Kenya. *Selected Paper prepared for presentation at the Agricultural & Applied Economics Association's 2012 AAEA Annual Meeting, Seattle, Washington, August 12–14, 2012.*

[18] Otieno, Z., Okello, J.J., Nyikal, R., Mwang'ombe, A. and Clavel, D. 2011. The role of varietal traits in the adoption of improved dryland crop varieties: The case of pigeonpea in Kenya. *African Journal of Agricultural and Resource Economics*, 6, No 2, pp. 176–193.

[19] Jenkins, A., Velandia, M., Lambert, D.M., Roberts, R.K., Larson, J.A., English, B.C. and Martin, S.W. 2011. Factors influencing the selection of precision farming information sources by cotton producers. *Agricultural and Resource EconomicsReview*, 40(2):307–320.

[20] Greene, W. 2008. Functional forms for the negative binomial model for count data. *Economics Letters*, 99:585–590.

[21] Geweke, J. 1989. Bayesian inference in econometric models using Monte Carlo integration. *Econometrica*, 57:1317–1340.

[22] McCulloch, N. and Ota, M. 2002. Export horticulture and poverty in Kenya. Institute of Development Studies, University of Sussex, Brighton.

[23] Okello, J.J. and Swinton, S.M. 2011. International food safety standards and the use of pesticides in fresh export vegetable production in developing countries: implications for farmer health and the environment. InTech, Rijeka, Croatia - European union. DOI: 10.5772/14026.

[24] Regmi, A. and Gehlhar, M. 2005. Processed food trade pressured by evolving global supply chains. Amberwaves. February 2005 Issue. USDA/ERS. Washington, DC.

[25] Fafchamps, M. and Gabre-Madhin, E. 2006. Agricultural markets in Benin and Malawi. *African Journal of Agricultural and Resource Economics*,1(1): 67–94.

[26] Rehber, E. 1998. Vertical integration in agriculture and contract farming. Working Paper #46, Department of Agricultural Economics, Uludag University, Turkey.

[27] Anderson, E. and Gabrielsson, S. 2012. 'Because of poverty, we had to come together': collective action for improved food security in Kenya and Uganda, *International Journal of Agricultural Sustainability*, 10(3):245–262.

[28] Okello, J.J. and S.M. Swinton. 2007. Compliance with international food safety standards in Kenya's green bean industry: Comparison of a small and a large scale family farm producing for export. *Review of Agricultural Economics*, 29: 269–285.

[29] Shulte-Geldermann, E., Gildemacher, P.R. and Struik, P.C. 2012. Improving seed health and seed performance by positive selection in three Kenyan potato varieties. *American Journal of Potato Research*, 29:429–437.

[30] Okello, J. J., Sindi, K., Shikuku, K., Low, J., McEwan, M., Nakazi, F., Babu, A. and Mafuru, J. (2015). Effect of technology awareness and access on the conservation of clean planting materials of vegetatively produced crops: The case of sweetpotato. *Agroecology and Sustainable Food Systems,39*(9):955–977.

[31] Namanda, S., Gibson, R. and Sindi, K. 2012. Sweetpotato seed systems in Uganda, Tanzania and Rwanda. *Journal of Sustainable Agriculture,* 35(8):870–884.

Section 2

Health Issues

Chapter 3

Current Review of Medical Research in Developing Countries: A Case Study from Egypt

Sherif M. Shehata, Nehal M. ElMashad and
Azza M. Hassan

Additional information is available at the end of the chapter

http://dx.doi.org/10.5772/67282

Abstract

It is amazing to see how medical science has progressed. Medical research is now cross-national and cross-cultural, the relentless progress of globalization poses complex ethical questions for those wishing to do medical research in developing countries. In developing countries, poverty, endemic diseases, and a low level of investment in health care systems influence both the ease of performing and the selection of trials that can benefit the people of the countries. In this chapter, we present an overview of medical research situation in developing countries with critique of different clinical trials that was conducted in Egypt after review. Egypt has 41 universities and 94 health related medical schools. There are 24 faculties of medicine with up to 34 departments in each. Clinical research is an essential mandate for getting Master, Doctorate Degrees, and for promotion of faculty members. In Egypt, the Profession Ethics Regulations issued by the Ministry of Health (MOH) No. 238/2003 was endorsed and maintained in Law 71/2009. Beside these regulations, more than 56 Institutional Review Board (IRB) have been registered. The Egyptian Network of Research Ethics Committees (ENREC) was created in 2008. Yet, in the absence of robust legislative constraints, there is no clear way to avoid violations. Our experience in Tanta Faculty of Medicine is also highlighted in this chapter.

Keywords: medical research, medical ethics, developing countries, Egypt, Tanta Faculty of Medicine, Tanta REC

1. Introduction

It is amazing to see how medical science has progressed. It has only been a hundred years and the world has gone from the discovery of penicillin to the complete sequencing of the human genome. This is the "*Medical Research.*"

Many researches are driven by economic or academic interests that may or may not reflect the needs of the host country. One critic of such trials is the need to test new drugs for malaria, sleeping sickness, and Chagas disease that people in poor countries suffer from rather than on diseases of interest primarily to the developed nations.

There is also the delicate matter of double standards, which highlights the need to develop an ethical model for research and training partnerships between developed and developing countries employing an approach with long-term advantage for the latter or both partners at least in an equal manner.

2. Realities of medical research in developing countries

2.1. Historical background

The past 20 years have seen a considerable shift in the location of clinical drug trials sponsored by transnational pharmaceutical companies (TNCs) being conducted in low- and middle-income settings [1]. One of the primary obligations of the Declaration of Helsinki (DH) is to promote human well-being over the interest of science and society. According to DH, any medical study should provide every participant with the best proven diagnostic and therapeutic method [2]. The primary ethical commitment would be obtaining rapid, nonargued answers that may make researchers cross the line that forbids treating human subjects as a means to an end, leaving nothing to protect patients from underestimating their dignity, rights, and safety for the sake of research goals [3].

One of the great challenges in medical research is to conduct clinical trials in developing countries that benefit the citizens of these countries. After the textbook example of the unethical 40-year nontherapeutic study of 400 African American sharecroppers in "the Tuskegee Study of Untreated Syphilis" (TSUS), ethical concern stood on its head and led to the overhauling of federal guidelines for health research [4]. These reforms, however, do not extend to health studies conducted outside the United States [5].

Ethical review committees are present in developing countries in the form of research institutes or other scientific panels [6]. However, the reality is that these panels need to be independent and able to review clinical trials without prejudice. Also, the characteristics of many developing countries, which include population afflicted with life-threatening endemic diseases, poverty, and a low level of investment in health care systems, affect both the ease of performing trials and the selection of trials that can benefit the populations of the countries. Conflict of interest of physicians/researchers from developing countries is a detrimental factor in research bias. There are also some structural problems including the fact that operations of pharmaceutical research companies are not adequately controlled or authorities seem unwilling to address unethical drug testing [7].

There appears to be a general retreat from the clear principles enunciated in the Nuremberg Code and the DH as applied to research in the third world. Angell in 1997 wondered, "Why is that?!!" He attributed it to the differences in local standard of care or variation in diseases and their treatments in those regions, so that information gained in the industrialized world has no relevance making it a must to start from scratch [3].

2.2. International situation in developing countries

Indeed, the scale of the problem is unknown, because it cannot be estimated how many unethical clinical trials escape public attention and therefore remain unnoticed. Starting in 1996, TSUS-like scenario occurred in Pfizer's controversial Trovan clinical trials that took place in Kano over 200 persons, mostly children [8]. The new quinolone was tested without parents' informed consents; patients were unaware of the experiment and without an ethical review committee's approval of the trial in advance. Out of 190 children that were enrolled in the trial, five receiving the drug died while others suffered brain damage and paralysis. A panel of Nigerian medical experts reported that the trials had been illegal and exploitative and violated Nigerian law, the DH, and the UN Convention on the Rights of the Child. However, Pfizer denied that the drug trial was unethical [9].

One of the major examples of the Tuskegee-like trials in the third world is the regimens to prevent the vertical transmission of human immunodeficiency virus (HIV) [10]. According to CDC, 18 randomized, controlled trials of interventions to prevent perinatal HIV transmission were identified until 1997, 16 were conducted in developing countries in Côte d'Ivoire, Uganda, Tanzania, South Africa, Malawi, Thailand, Ethiopia, Burkina Faso, Zimbabwe, Kenya, and the Dominican Republic [11].

These trials involved a total of more than 17,000 women. In 15 of these trials, some or all of the patients were not provided with clearly effective zidovudine antiretroviral drug as they employ placebo-treated control groups. Failures to get patients' consent about changes in the experiment, administering wrong doses, serious problems in record keeping, delayed and underreporting of fatal and life-threatening problems, nondiscloser of thousands of side effects and adverse reactions, not following procedures for divulging Serious Adverse Events (SAEs), and destroying an early copy of the research reports are part of the violation of guidelines [10, 12].

Another same example was the dramatic Cariporide clinical trial applied in the Naval Hospital in Buenos Aires, Argentina to protect against heart damage after cardiac insult. Patients' consents were either faked or the patients did not know its contents. Thirteen patients died and at least three of them were considered murders. Data in medical records were changed and key documentation disappeared [13]. Although before 2005, the Schedule Y of the Indian Drug and Cosmetic Act prohibited clinical trials in India of drugs developed outside the country before Phase II trials were completed abroad, a review revealed that some illegal studies were conducted in 1999–2000. Phase III trials involving cilansetron, a new molecule of Solvay Pharmaceuticals for treatment for diarrhea from irritable bowel syndrome (IBS) [14], Pfizer's zoniporide trial that control perioperative cardiac events [15], nordihydroguaiaretic acid (NDGA) as treatment for oral cancer, and Otsuka's cilostazol trials for treatment of intermittent claudication were tested before the required animal experiments had been completed and serious adverse events were not reported [15, 16].

Between 2002 and 2006, the number of trials to compare antiretroviral standard continuous and intermittent therapies was conducted in Africa. The Development of Anti-Retroviral Therapy (DART) trial had recruited 3300 volunteers in Uganda and Zimbabwe [17]. Unfortunately, unethical trials continue to be conducted. One recent trial in India, reported in *The Lancet* in 2014, evaluated human-bovine (116E) vaccine for preventing a very common, potentially life-threatening viral infection "rotavirus" [18]. Two rotavirus vaccines have been available for the past decades that were proved to be highly effective in preventing rotavirus-induced gastroenteritis and the need for hospitalization. One of the unfair examples, despite the availability of these vaccines, more than 2000 children in the Indian trial received placebo injections of salt water rather than one of the available effective vaccines in a clinical trial funded by multiple private and government sources and enrolled approximately 6800 infants between 2011 and 2012 [18].

The central ethical question should be: why has not the successful intervention that is currently used as a matter of course in Western countries become the standard of care worldwide? Clinical trials have become a big business with many studies done in developing countries, as it is necessary to do quick work with minimal obstacles. Poverty and ignorance play a role in commercial industry like this. This does not suit the standards of the sponsoring countries and puts us not very far from Tuskegee even after more than 80 years [19]. This is a big concern for all of human race. Like Lurie and Wolfe [10], we need to redouble our commitment to the highest ethical standards, no matter where the research is conducted, and sponsoring agencies need to enforce those standards, not undercut them.

2.3. The case of Egypt: strength versus weakness

The contract research organization (CRO) Quintiles even recently advertised Russia, Turkey, and the Middle East and the Northern Africa MENA region as the "new darlings" in the world of biopharmaceutical sales [20]. According to the *ClinicalTrial.gov*, a service of the U.S. National Institute of Health (NIH), 1234 clinical trials were conducted in Egypt with the number of clinical trials nearly tripling between 2008 and 2011 making Egypt second only to South Africa on the African continent in terms of the number of TNC-sponsored studies [21, 22]. Based on the registry of clinical trials (CTs) in Egypt, treatment was the most common study purpose followed by prevention. Combined safety/efficacy was the most common endpoint followed by efficacy alone. For interventional studies, the most common intervention was drug use followed by procedure. The most common study phase was phase 3 followed phase 4 and phase 2. However, the output of the big number of health professionals and faculty members is definitely more than the registered studies, which, may be related to absence of Egyptian national trial registry and the national mandates for trial registration [23].

In February 2016, 21 international pharmaceutical and biotechnology companies were sponsoring active drug trials in Egypt. The two Swiss giants Novartis and Roche carried out the lion's share of trials. These trials took place at 131 sites spread over 9 cities in Egypt. Unsurprisingly, the majority was in Cairo (75), followed by Alexandria (31)—together accounting for about 81% of all sites. Over half of all international active drug studies in Egypt are cancer trials, followed far behind by infectious diseases (10%) and metabolic disorders (10%) [21].

An attractive research infrastructure, a fast-growing and largely treatment-naïve population, a mosaic panel of research areas, and incomparably low cost of living make Egypt among the most popular places in the MENA region for off-shoring medicine testing "pharmerging countries" [24]. Egypt has 41 universities and 94 health-related faculties and medical schools. There are 24 faculties of medicine with up to 34 departments in each faculty. There are more than 42,000 faculty members and 344,000 postgraduate students, 140,000 physicians, 18,200 dentists, 37,500 pharmacists, 176,000 nurses, and 35,000 physical therapists. Clinical research including clinical trials is an essential mandate for getting masters and doctorate degrees. Moreover, clinical research for publication is a mandate for promotion for faculty members according to the rules of the supreme council of Egyptian universities [23].

According to the Professional Ethics Regulations issued by the Ministry of Health (MOH) No. 238/2003, part four: "conducting medical research and experiments on human beings, any experiments for drugs and techniques on human beings prior to being endorsed by the competent quarters and acquiring a detailed study of the risks/benefits relationship are prohibited." The volunteers must comply in a clear way of the targets of the research, the research approaches, the benefits expected, the probable risks, and the extent of their effect on them with official written consent and/or approval of the official guardian or curator in the presence of a prosecution witness. The volunteers have the right to cease or withdraw from the research without sustaining any negative consequences. The researcher is required to submit a detailed and clear research targets report with justifications for conducting it on human beings to the approving authority for approval [25]. The same meaning was maintained in Law 71/2009 and a new draft law of 2014 [26, 27]. However, this draft caused much public concern because it contained an article allowing trials on children, pregnant women, drug addicts, detainees, and psychiatric patients. According to critics, it would have paved the way to experimentation of medicines on vulnerable people. Thus, this law has never seen the light of day [27].

The researcher is expected to discontinue any experiments on human beings if the accompanying risks exceed the benefits expected of the research and ensuring all preventive, diagnostic, and therapeutic methods for each patient for conducting the study. The draft of the national law on clinical trials driven from the constitution of Egypt that was leaked to the media in 2014 tried to lift those safeguards [27].

Besides these regulations, more than 56 RECs and Institutional Review Board (IRB) registered were designed in many health-related faculties, foundations, and institutes in Alexandria, Assuit, Aswan, BeniSuif, Benha, Fayoum, Giza, Ismailia, Mansoura, Minia, Sohag, Tanta, and Zagazig. Egyptian Network of Research Ethics Committees (ENREC) was created in 2008 to raise the harmonization between Research Ethics Committees, facilitate more uniform ethical review, and simplify REC procedures and standards [6].

Since there is no robust legislative constraints and clear guidance to charge entities or stakeholders involved in overseeing or executing clinical trials, concerns are increasingly being raised, whether ethical pitfalls of clinical research are adequately addressed, and whether the safety and the rights of subjects are constantly prioritized and maintained, leaving room for different interpretations and making it more difficult to identify violations and impose sanctions [28, 29]. Unlike other emerging countries, Egypt does not make it obligatory to have clinical trials conducted on their population before marketing approval is granted [30]. Moreover, there are concerns that RECs in Egypt may not be able to provide high standards of human subjects' protection due to its inadequate functioning ethics review system and reluctance of the national regulations and bureaucracy that occurs when they interact with the MOH [22, 31].

An extensive review carried out by multiorganizations, published in June 2016 and based on United Nation International Aid Program (UNIAID), Egyptian experts and clinical trial participants' interviewee and various media reports, many critics were assumed. Although they admit that the current requirements of Egypt's regulatory authorities that no clinical trial sponsored by a TNC can be conducted in Egypt unless the product being tested has been granted market approval in the originating country with several Egyptian experts interviewed during this research confirmed this prerequisite, they pointed to the absence of regulatory obligation to conduct clinical trials in the country before being able to request a license for the drug. This "conditional approval" may happen based on medical grounds such as genetic or disease specificities prevailing in Egypt [22].

Of the 57 international drug trials that were active in Egypt in February 2016, Declaration of Helsinki concluded that the vast majority are late-stage clinical trials related to products already licensed in high-income countries. However, 16% are Phase I and Phase II trials, raising ethical issues as to the relevance and benefit of these trials for the Egyptian population since tests on these medical products were completed elsewhere for marketing approval in a high-income country. These include cancer trials testing medicines that were not yet registered in high-income countries, off-label use, had no specific protection mechanism for vulnerable participants, and no posttrial treatment access mechanisms. International experts raised doubts about the scientific validity of the designs of several of these cancer trials [32].

- Kotb in 2012 recounts an incident that was under official investigation. The trials used drug ursofalk (ursodeoxycholic acid) that was conducted on children at one of Cairo University's hospitals, providing evidence that only 9% of the children improved while most of the cohort receiving treatment developed hepatic failure, lethal pneumonia, otitis media, and ascites with high incidence of death was uncovered [33].

- According to the Declaration of Helsinki Study, cancer trials described in Egypt were considered to be the clearest illustration of the vulnerability of trial participants and the profound inequality of their situation compared to cancer patients in wealthier nations. Due to the high prices of cancer treatments, experimental drugs may be the only medication that Egyptian cancer patient will receive. As such, they run an unknown risk of experiencing serious side effects while already suffering a serious disease [34].

- Egypt has the highest prevalence of viral hepatitis C in the world and was the first low- or middle-income country in 2014 to negotiate preferential pricing for the new direct acting antiviral (DAA) treatment sofosbuvir (Sovaldi) with manufacturer Gileadc [35]. However, the deal (US$ 300 per month of treatment instead of US$ 84,000 in the U.S.) was criticized

http://dx.doi.org/10.5772/67282

for its opacity. The "Sovaldi deal" generated diverging opinions among Egyptian experts as to whether the state-subsidized free treatment program is, in fact, a disguised clinical trial of national scale [36]. Given the absence of patent protection, several Egyptian companies were able to produce generic versions of DAAs for the market [32].

Ethics in health research is a collective consciousness and concerns of researchers, institutes, funders, medical journals' editors, regulatory agencies, and others. Ethical approval by one of these entities does not relieve others from responsibility. Egyptian authorities should develop a single, robust legislative framework with a functional independent control system that takes the DH and the Council for International Organizations of Medical Research (CIOMS) Guidelines as their reference point for ethical standards. Egyptian authorities should also create an online, regularly updated public registry of clinical trials conducted in Egypt. Ensuring access to information must be guaranteed, as it is a fundamental prerequisite to enable civil society to play its role in signaling, observing, auditing, and unveiling unethical clinical trials practices.

2.4. Tanta Faculty of Medicine model experience

University hospitals have their own in-house IRBs, which provide training to medical doctors and researchers participating in clinical trials. The only mechanism available to protect participants is the REC in the MOH, in the research centers, and in university hospitals [37].

To develop an educational and medical research policy in Tanta Faculty of Medicine, we plan the following standards to be on the track of international standards.

2.4.1. Research Ethics Committee

Research Ethics Committee (REC) plays a central role of ethical oversight of research involving humans or animals in our organization. REC reviews research proposals involving human or animal participants to ensure that they are ethically acceptable and in accordance with relevant standards and guidelines. Our REC includes institutional review board members and was organized and approved at the Faculty and University levels in June 2010.

In undertaking this role, REC is guided by relevant standards, which include those in the *International Statement on Ethical Conduct in Human Research* issued by CIOMS and WHO [38, 39]. Consequently, this Statement identifies the demands, principles, and values by which research should be designed and applied and to which HREC should refer when reviewing research proposals.

It also sets up requirements and responsibilities for:

- Researchers in submitting research proposals to REC.
- REC in:

(1) Considering and reaching decisions regarding these proposals and in monitoring the conduct of approved research plus to monitor and reporting any scientific misconduct.

(2) Developing awareness and teaching the ethics of scientific research for the faculty post-graduate and undergraduate students.

(3) Cooperation with the ethics committees of scientific research counterparts in Egypt, the Arab, and foreign countries.

2.4.2. Research plan

In general, the educational mission of the Faculties of Medicine is fortified by a highly successful research enterprise that includes widely varied scientific fields such as basic molecular and cellular biology and population health as well as hospital and community applied clinical researches.

Our institution's goal was to develop a plan to support research excellence in strategic areas, train the next generation of health researchers, and facilitate the translation of new knowledge into beneficial health outcomes for the patients, the population, and policy makers. Our Faculty has developed and established a strategic research plan in 2010. This plan was reviewed and modified according to Tanta University research plan and updated the paths proposed by the Ministry of Higher Education, then reapproved in June 2015. These plans are the outcome of an institutional planning committee after extensive consultation with all faculty departments.

2.5. The settled research priorities and guidelines of the ongoing plan are

Nine health-related areas of high priority were chosen guided by the international standards and based on the approved research plan of our university, mission, and vision of our faculty, needs assessment of the community at local, national and regional levels, interests and specialties of our staff members, available research resources including that supplied by scientific and health organizations with mutual interest, and the updates in science and medicine [40].

These research priorities are:

(1) Cancer research: to foster basic as well as clinical research in the field of early diagnosis, recent treatment modalities, and prevention.

(2) Emerging national health problems: The epidemiology, health effects, prevention, and eradication of emerging national health problems, e.g., hepatitis, H1N1, parasitic, and endemic diseases in our country.

(3) Organ transplantation and artificial prostheses.

(4) Obesity researches: causes, treatment, and prevention.

(5) Immunogenetic diseases: our vision is to implement research in biotechnology.

(6) Geriatric diseases.

(7) Regenerative medicine and stem cell therapy: Tanta Faculty of Medicine is catching up with the research in the area of tissue culture and application of the concept of stem therapy in medicine.

(8) Minimal interventional medicine and surgery (MIS).

(9) Emergency medicine.

Our REC has reviewed 2823 research protocols and project proposals in the last 6 years up to July 31, 2016. Note that 1705 proposals (60.4%) were accepted while 1118 (39.6%) needed modifications with rejection rate of 18% after corrections. The activity of REC has significant impact on our research. In 2011, Tanta Faculty of Medicine had about 140 international publication cited on PubMed, this number reached 616 at the beginning of 2016 with almost threefold increase in 5 years. Additionally, in an attempt to strengthen medical research, we established our official medical journal (Tanta Med J) as an online peer-reviewed journal published by Wolters Kluwer—Medknow. Since January 30, 2014, more than 200 articles were published in it apart from those cited in PubMed.

The REC committee has members from academic and clinical medical departments. They are selected based on their experience in different medical fields and their reputation for a term of 3 years. To insure its independence, our Faculty Dean and Vice deans were excluded from the committee board. The committee members also included representatives of the community: professor in Islamic religion, representative of the Orthodox Church, governor (or his representative), certified trainer in research ethics, certified trainer in human rights, and a judge as representative of the legal authority. Clear regulations were approved to support the committee's role. The number of the committee members range from 5 to 15 according to its regulations (in the current term there are 13 members), they meet on a monthly basis to discuss research proposals and to follow-up on approved projects. The committee pays members a very small incentive for each meeting and there are no fees charged for protocol review. IRBs face numerous obstacles to achieving their goals, as there is no law in Egypt that regulates the selection of members of IRBs. Other problems include budget constraints, inability to monitor approved protocols continuously, and a lack of national guidelines and accreditation mechanisms for IRBs. These points are our future concern to improve the performance of REC.

3. Background

Poverty accounts for almost one-third of the global burden of disease and there is a definite relationship between wealth/poverty and health/disease, although this relationship is not linear [41]. In "developing" countries, where cultural, linguistic, economic, and other barriers may prevail between researchers and subjects, it is especially important to ensure effective communication [42, 43].

The medical industry is not exempted from the development of globalization, and the number of medical research studies conducted in developing nations, instead of in Western countries, has rapidly increased to gain more financial and scientific benefits [44, 45].

3.1. Advantages of conducting medical research in developing countries

When the United States' National Bioethics Advisory Commission (US-NBAC) asked a pharmaceutical researcher why the industry seeks to conduct studies in developing countries, the answer was that the pharmaceutical industry is not a charitable business. It is a profitable Wall Street hard-core business [46]. There are several reasons that attract these companies to conduct their research in developing countries. Ruth Macklin divides these reasons into financial and scientific [45].

From sponsors' point of view, the main financial reasons are that the speed of research is faster in the developing country due to less oversight, thereby enabling the company gain approval for marketing and realize a profit sooner [46]. Research can often be done faster in those areas as time-consuming legislative requirements and local ethical review committees are not as well established in developing countries as in Western countries. Macklin points out that financially it is cheaper to carry out research in developing countries as they can offer lower costs for all of the ancillary goods and services necessary to set up and support the research, including labor costs for technical and scientific personnel [47].

Lack of awareness among participants about the methods and reasoning of research in healthcare may lead to therapeutic misconception as participants believe that the main goal of research is to provide them with therapy not to obtain information. For this reason, the US-NBAC recommended that investigators working overseas must indicate in their research protocols how they intend to minimize the possibility of therapeutic fallacy [48, 49].

3.2. Excellence in medical research

Regrettably, 50 years after the Nuremberg trials and the Nuremberg Code, unethical medical research on humans continues, even in highly privileged countries [50–52]. Similarly, the continuation of human and patient rights abuses for 50 years after the Universal Declaration of Human Rights, even in wealthy industrialized countries, illustrates how difficult it is to achieve such universal moral aspirations [53, 54]. How research be regulated to avoid the errors and indiscretions of the past and to avoid new forms of discrimination and victimization in the increasingly complex era of biotechnology?

Early in 1993, the Council for International Organizations of Medical Research (CIOMS) launched its guidelines endorsing that ethical values must reinforce respect for the dignity of research subjects and to minimize risk, maximize benefits, make convenient compensation for time, provide reparation for any damage occurring during the research, protect confidentiality, and avoid conflict of interest [55–60].

http://dx.doi.org/10.5772/67282

3.3. Methods to achieve universal standards

Universal ethical standards are still a debatable complex issue, which requires reflection on some issues. First, the best interests of subjects that may differ significantly according to personal and cultural priority and the magnitude of achievement in any situation. Second, what is considered truly universal? Third, is the entity of contextual issues that could be considered moral without resorting to ethical relativism [61–64]. Among those, recognition and dealing with contextual differences is a must to avoid both ethical imperialism and ethical relativism [65, 66].

3.4. International ethical guidelines

Different countries have different laws, different views on human rights, and different ethical principles. Most countries in the developed world have their own set of laws and regulations concerning research with human subjects. These laws and regulations emphasize the key principles of human research such as informed consent, risk minimization, reasonable risk-benefit ratio, and confidentiality [67].

Developing countries may not possess such regulations or if they do, the regulations are weaker. Additionally, there are no international laws on medical research that apply in all countries to which all researchers conducting studies in another country must follow. However, there are international ethical guidelines for conducting medical research that can be followed in order to design and conduct an ethical research in a developing country. The most widely accepted are the Nuremberg Code, the DH, and the guidelines developed by the CIOMS [67].

3.5. Research ethics committees in developing countries

In many developing countries, ethics has been paid insufficient attention. There is minimal similarity in the organization of research ethics committees (RECs) and little if any public responsibility. Existence of self-appointed private RECs lacking in expertise and liability, the absence of rational discourse, and possibilities of undeclared conflict of interest express most problems in some countries [59, 60].

3.6. Comprehensive guidelines for research ethics in developing countries

Many categories of issues require special consideration in formulating new guidelines for biomedical research on human subjects in "developing" countries. Incommensurable load of diseases aggravated by the extent of destitution and high levels of illiteracy is a major issue to be considered. Differences between patients' categories lead to added rights and ethical consideration in special groups by age or disease. Imbalance between the needed and actual resources available for research and basic health care with wide differences in access to health care is another important category. Finally, inadequate scientific and ethics infrastructures for the required reviewing process are a key issue [68, 69].

4. Concept of medical research

4.1. Value of medical research

Research is explained by Health Insurance Portability and Accountability Act (HIPAA) including the Privacy Rule and the Common Rule as "a systematic investigation, including research development, testing and evaluation, designed to develop or contribute to generalized knowledge" [70, 71].

Data analysis collected for either diagnostic or treatment purposes can be used for secondary research purposes. These purposes could be health services or public health research that include analysis of occurrences' patterns, determinants, natural history of disease, drug safety surveillance, and some genetic and/or social studies [72–74].

4.2. The importance of medical research

Medical research serves as sources of important information about disease outcomes, drift and risk factors, functional abilities, patterns of care, and health care costs. Clinical trials are sources of important notification about the efficacy and adverse effects of medical interventions by controlling the variables that could influence the study results [73, 74].

Food and Drug Administration (FDA) approval of a drug for a particular indication relies upon a series of controlled clinical trials. Guidelines for best practices with high-quality patient care can be achieved by recording and assessing experience in clinical practice [75]. Economists notice that medical research has a positive effect on human health and life span which in turn increase productivity that will be reflected on the national economy [76].

4.3. The globalization of medical research

Medical research goes globalization is a familiar term. Globalization has brought on economic benefits such as higher production rates, more efficiency, industrialization, and faster growing knowledge and innovation for those countries that are a part of it. We hear about poor working environment and low salaries in developing countries, a situation that Western companies have taken advantage of, which makes us think that everything that follows is not always morally justifiable [77].

The pharmaceutical industry is not exempted from globalization and has embraced it is as a core component of their business models, especially in the realm of clinical trials. Industry and government sponsors in wealthier countries move their research trials to less wealthy countries. The majority of medical research is currently sponsored and conducted by private pharmaceutical companies [78].

Medical research proved the fact that globalization of commerce, trade, industry, and travel means that diseases can spread easily across the globe. For example, HIV spread from Africa and around the world and each year a new strain of the influenza virus emerges in Southeast Asia and spreads throughout the globe. As diseases have become international, medical research should also become international [77].

4.4. The value and importance of medical information privacy

Medical privacy and confidentiality are vital to improving human health and health care. Protecting patients involved in research from harm or abuse and preserving their rights is essential to ethical research. Privacy has a value at the societal level as it permits complex activities, including research and public health activities to be carried out in ways that protect individuals' dignity without violating their rights [79].

4.4.1. *Value of privacy*

Privacy is simply used to designate different concepts as the right to body safety or to be free from supervision. All information being gathered, the intentions of the parties involved, as well as the politics and cultural probability [80, 81]. Privacy denotes those concerned with personal information collection, storage, and examine whether data can be collected either for primary or secondary purposes [82].

4.4.2. *The importance of privacy*

There are a variety of reasons for placing a high value on protecting the privacy, confidentiality, and security of health information [83]. Some theorists believe that respecting privacy (and autonomy) is a form of recognition of the attributes that give humans their moral uniqueness and part of human rights [84, 85].

Privacy facilitates and promotes other *fundamental values*, including ideals of personhood [86, 87] such as:

- Personal autonomy (the ability to make personal decisions)
- Individuality
- Respect
- Dignity and worth as human beings

Perceptions of privacy vary among individuals and various groups. Data that are considered intensely private by one person may not be by others [74].

4.5. Distinguish medical research from practice

Privacy rule can differentiate between medical research and similar health care practices as public health practice, quality improvement activities, and program evaluations [88] and writing reviews [76]. However, specifying which activities meet the definition of "research" is a major challenge for privacy boards [89]. Neither the regulations of investigators and health care practitioners nor their interpretations by HHS denote clear guidelines on how to distinguish research from activities that use similar techniques to analyze health information [90]. Unfortunately, failure to correctly denote an activity as research could potentially allow improper disclosure of personally identifiable health information without sufficient oversight [91].

4.6. Genetic information and the privacy rule

Research involving genetic information presents perhaps some of the most challenging areas for protecting the privacy of health information [92–94]. Recently, development makes it possible to learn a great deal about disease processes and individual variations in treatment effectiveness or susceptibility to disease from genetic analyses as the DNA sequences comprising a person's genome strongly influence a person's health.

Human genome knowledge, combined with advances in computing capabilities, can help decipher the roles that genetics and the environment play in the origins of complex but common human diseases as cancer. Patient samples stored in bio-specimen banks can provide a wealth of information for addressing long-standing questions about health and disease, and efforts are underway to create large genomic databases for that purpose [74, 94]. These data are of paramount importance for any community that could affect the national security. Based on the strict privacy rules inside the European Union than the United States, DNA is not direct identifier in Europe [95].

Genetic information does not itself identify an individual in the absence of other identifying information. Person's genetic code could be interpreted as a unique identifier and used to match a sequence in another databank, which includes identifiers [96, 97].

The NIH starts requiring data from the Genome-Wide Association Study in January 2008. That database became publicly accessible until August 2008 then NIH removed the database from the public Website regarding patient privacy [95, 98]. Those concerns stemmed from a study showing that a new type of DNA analysis could confirm the identity of an individual in a pool of similarly masked data if that person's genetic profile was already known [99]. NIH intends to move the aggregate genotype data to a secure, controlled-access database with policies for review and approval of data access requests in very strict manner [98].

5. International ethical standards in medical research

5.1. History and legal basis of research ethics

Research ethics is mostly developed as a concept in medical research, but the general principles apply for all fields of research. Informed consent and confidentiality are important for both sociological study and clinical research keeping both human and patient rights. As a reaction to malpractices that were revealed during the Nuremberg trials, the World Medical Association (established in Paris in 1947) adopted the DH in 1964, in Finland [100].

The DH stated that "for all research, the well-being of the individuals is the most important over all other interests and sets principles for medical research combined with medical care" [60].

5.2. The Nuremberg Code

The Nuremberg Code was the first international code of ethics for research on human subjects, introduced in 1947 after WWII, when the Nazi's outrageous experiments on human subjects were revealed to the world. The Nuremberg Code focused on medical research, consisting of only 10 rules which indicated the most basic and essential principles [101]. In fact, the Nuremberg Code has had a major influence on human rights law and medical ethics. In contrast, while the previous ethics codes focused on the obligations of the investigator toward the research subjects, the Nuremberg Code reverses that logic: The rights are directly awarded to the research subjects who is actually revolute to the view on research ethics [102].

5.3. The Declaration of Helsinki (DH)

The World Medical Association (WMA) introduced the DH in 1964 to provide additional guidance for researchers beyond what was included in the Nuremberg Code [103]. Hence, the Declaration is longer and more detailed (37 articles) than the Nuremberg Code (10 articles). Since the publication of the DH, it has been amended nine times, most recently in October 2013 [104]. The DH is considered the best-known and most widely available guideline in medical research ethics [104].

The DH covers a broad assortment of topics such as privacy and confidentiality, research oversight, protocol development, protection of vulnerable subjects, publication, scientific design, the use of placebos, and access to treatments [104]. In many countries, the HD has been enacted as law (such as the Nuremberg Code in some U.S. courts), and adherence to its principles is a requirement of many national and international guidelines [105].

5.4. International Ethical Guidance from the Council for International Organizations of Medical Sciences (CIOMS)

The CIOMS was formally constituted by the WHO and the United Nations Educational, Scientific, and Cultural Organization (UNESCO) in 1949, and it still remains under the aegis of these two specialized UN agencies. In 1982, CIOMS proposed the International Ethical Guidelines for Biomedical Research Involving Human Subjects. The purpose of these guidelines was to indicate how the ethical principles that were set forth in the 1975 version of the DH could be effectively applied. Emphasis was on application in developing countries, given their socioeconomic circumstances, laws, regulations, and executive and administrative arrangements. The guidelines were revised in 1993 and in 2002 [106]. The CIOMS guidelines are more detailed than the DH. They consist of 21 articles with many commentaries for each article which explain in detail many different situations. The CIOMS guidelines have had covered the topics of ethical justification and scientific validity of research, ethical review committees, informed consent registration, susceptibility of individuals, risk/benefits relationship, choice of control in clinical trials, privacy, compensation for injury in research, and national capacity to provide healthcare services [107].

In the meanwhile, the agreement on Human Rights and Biomedicine or the Oviedo Convention, adopted by the Ministers of the Council of Europe in 1996, stated that there is a strong connection between research ethics and human rights [108–110]. Including the primacy of the interest and human well-being, informed consent, and privacy are the corners of the research. The agreement sets standards for the use of the human genome and human embryos research [111].

UNESCO's Universal Declaration on Bioethics and Human Rights and CIOMS International Ethical Guidelines for Biomedical Research Involving Human Subjects are all other important international declarations and agreement [112, 113].

Within the European regulatory framework, research ethics is based on the evident European commitment to human rights. Firmly enshrined in the treaties, compliance with human rights is fundamental for all European policy domains [114].

5.5. Informed consent and conflict of obligations

Informed consent constitutes the cornerstone of research ethics in human subjects. It is the most important to recognize that there are differences between informed consent for participation in research and informed consent for patient care. Its importance is to unravel the gray zone especially in vulnerable groups [115, 116].

A great problem occurred when the doctor is both the investigator and the provider of patient care [115, 116], especially in developing countries where it may be impossible to separate the roles of investigator and care giver. In this case, the conflict of interest in many occasions could be obvious concerning that in developing countries grossly inadequate health care resources and the pressures to enroll research subjects may concentrate more on patients' best interests [117].

Informed consent is basic requirement in research involving human being, research, genetic material or biological samples, and data collection. The rights and interests of the research subjects are fully respected especially during children research [117, 118], vulnerable adults (elderly, prisoners, mentally deficient persons, comatose, severely injured patients, and psychiatric patients), and people with certain cultural, religious, or traditional backgrounds [118].

There are various requirements for a valid informed consent that must be fulfilled, such as the four requirements that Jennifer S. Hawking explains per her quotation: "*First*, only those potential subjects who pass the requirements for decision-making competence should be asked to give consent (when it is necessary to enroll incompetent subjects an appropriate surrogate must give consent). *Second*, there must be full disclosure of all the relevant information, *Third*, the subject or surrogate must understand the information, and *Fourth*, he or she must then consent freely or voluntarily" [119].

Shamoo and Resnik specify three challenges of acquiring informed consent in developing countries. *First*, there is the possible presence of linguistic barriers that might make it difficult to acquire effective consent. It can be necessary to use interpreters in order to converse with subjects in their native language and translations of consent documents, and other material such as brochures, questionnaires, and visual aid must be produced. Some words may not translate easily into different languages which may affect interpretation of the text presented to the subjects. Furthermore, some populations may have no written language, so use of a consent form or other such document can be problematic [77]. The *second* challenge is that there can be conceptual or cultural obstacles to effective consent. People from developing and unindustrialized countries may have little comprehension of Western concepts such as disease, cause and effect, genetics/DNA, virus, bacteria, and so on.

In order to assure that the requirement of full understanding is met, it is necessary to adapt the form and content of procedures for obtaining informed consent to the educational level of the potential subjects of research [78]. *Third* and last, many African nations consist of tribal governance. The leaders of the tribe may need to give permission before any member of the tribe can be recruited into a study and the members may not believe they have any right to decide by themselves whether to participate or not. They may not even comprehend the notion of individual decision [77].

Ethical relativists have used cultural differences, like lack of understanding of the concept "individual consent," as a defense for departing from widely accepted ethical standards for informed consent. Furthermore, in developing countries, women are sometimes thought of as less than men and their husbands sometimes make all the decisions, even those that only affect their wife's health and her enrolment in medical studies [78].

5.6. Animal research ethics

In Europe, the Commission report estimates that over 12 million animals are used for experimental or other scientific purposes each year. The most common used animals for these purposes are rodents, rabbits, mice, and rats [120].

The European Convention for the Protection of Vertebrate Animals used for Experimental and Other Scientific Purposes, adopted in 1986, is the first important document protecting the animals used in experiments [114]. This directive since its application in 1986 is meant to ensure the protection of animals used in experiments or for other scientific purposes and sets standards for control on the use of laboratory animals, housing and care of the animals, and for the training of the personnel involved in the animal testing [114]. Apart from setting standards, the directive aims at reducing the numbers of animals used for experiments, following the concept of the "Three R's (replacement, reduction, and refinement)."

For the Ethics Review organized by the European Commission, the researcher should provide all the details of the species (and strains) used, justify why they are used, explain why the anticipated benefits of the research justify the use of animals, and why methods avoiding the use of animals cannot be used [114, 115]. National authorities are responsible for the implementation of the Directive on the Protection of Animals [114].

5.7. Twelve golden rules to ethical research conduct

According to the 12 golden rules, each researcher must ensure that his/her research will fulfill the following criteria [114, 121]:

Respects the persons before, during, and after the research, follow the "Do no harm" principle, realize the rights of individuals to privacy, personal data protection and freedom of movement, informed consent for human being research, treat animals with respect following the three Rs: Replacement, Reduction, and Refinement when designing animal research, never misuse terrorists or military organizations, respect integrity of an individual and that any modification (genetic or technological) does not interfere with this principle, always respect environment biodiversity, and finally build on the understanding that any benefits are for the good of the society [122–124].

6. Conclusions

The need for new and better treatment options for medical research continues unabated. As long as that need persists, medical trials are likely to continue. Many medical researches are driven by economic or academic interests that may or may not reflect the needs of the host country.

The pharmaceutical industry is not a charitable business but it is a profitable one. There are many reasons that attract these companies, researchers, and sponsors to conduct their research in a developing country.

Many moral lessons have been learnt from the history of medical research. Regrettably, 50 years after the Nuremberg trials and the Nuremberg Code, unethical medical research on humans continues.

Protecting patients involved in research from harm or abuse and preserving their rights is essential to ethical research. Human rights, health development, and medical research ethics can be gathered together when standards are followed with minimizing bias and conflict of interests. Informed consent and confidentiality are important for both sociological study and clinical research keeping both human and patient rights.

Human and animal rights should be preserved in all categories of medical research. Quality of research in the medical field will be reflected on the quality of health care and welfare of the community whether it is performed in developing or developed countries. The 3 R's: Replacement, Reduction, and Refinement have to be followed. International guidelines provided by WHO, DH, CIOMS, WMA, UNESCO, and Nuremberg Code need to be ascertained in research whether performed in developed or developing countries. Most, but not all developing countries, have ethical review committees in the form of research institutes or other scientific panels. However, the reality is that these panels need to be independent and able to review clinical trials without prejudice.

We do not want a scientifically neat study if it is ethically flawed, we need to redouble our commitment to the highest ethical standards, no matter where the research is conducted, and sponsoring agencies need to enforce those standards.

The Tanta experience can be taken as a role model in developing countries to initiate guidelines to standardize the ethics of medical research at national and regional levels.

Author details

Sherif M. Shehata[1]*, Nehal M. ElMashad[2] and Azza M. Hassan[3]

*Address all correspondence to: sherifshehata2001@yahoo.com

1 Department of Pediatric Surgery, Faculty of Medicine, Tanta University, Tanta, Egypt

2 Department of Medical Oncology, Faculty of Medicine, Tanta University, Tanta, Egypt

3 Department of Medical Microbiology, Faculty of Medicine, Tanta University, Tanta, Egypt

References

[1] Alahmad G, Al-Jumah M, Dierickx K. Review of national research ethics regulations and guidelines in Middle Eastern Arab countries. BMC Med Ethics 2012; 13: 34.

[2] Declaration of Helsinki IV, 41st WMA General Assembly, Hong Kong, September 1989. In: Annas GJ, Grodin MA, Eds. The Nazi doctors and the Nuremberg Code: human rights in human experimentation. New York: Oxford University Press, 1992:339–42.

[3] Angell M. The ethics of clinical research in the third word. N Engl J Med 1997; 337(12): 847–9.

[4] Caplan AL. Twenty years after: the legacy of the Tuskegee syphilis study. When evil intrudes. Hastings Cent Rep 1992; 22 (6): 29–40.

[5] Fairchild AL, Bayer R. Uses and abuses of Tuskegee. Science 1999; 284 (5416): 919–21.

[6] WHO. Clinical trials without ethical review under the spotlight. http://www.who.int/bulletin/volumes/82/4/ethics0404/en/print.html

[7] Del Río C, Kamarulzaman A, Schüklenk U. Ethics, economic realities and medical research in developing countries. Reproductive Health Matters 1998; 6 (11): 135–6.

[8] Aronson J. Dying for drugs. BMJ 2003; 326 (7396): 990.

[9] Uwugiaren L. Nigeria: Pfizer directors declared wanted. All Africa, 10 Jan 2008. http://allafrica.com/stories/200801100283.html

[10] Lurie P, Wolfe SM. Unethical trials of interventions to reduce perinatal transmission of the human immunodeficiency virus in developing countries. N Engl J Med 1997; 337: 853–6.

[11] United States Department of Health and Human Services. The conduct of clinical trials of maternal–infant transmission of HIV supported by the United States Department of Health and Human Services in developing countries. Washington, DC, July 1997.

[12] Lallemant M, Vithayasai V. A short ZDV course to prevent perinatal HIV in Thailand. Boston: Harvard School of Public Health, April 28, 1995.

[13] De Young K, Nelson D. Latin America is ripe for trials and fraud. Washington Post, Dec 21, 2000. http://www.washingtonpost.com/ac2/wp-dyn/A31027-2000Dec20

[14] Roberts J. Solvay Pharma suspends Cilansetron registration activities in the U.S. IBS, Nov 30, 2005. http://www.ibsgroup.org/forums/topic/48398-solvay-pharma-suspends-cilansetron-registration-activites-in-the-us/

[15] Gulhati CM. Needed: closer scrutiny of clinical trials. Indian J Med Ethics 2004; 12(1):4–5.

[16] Mudur G. Johns Hopkins admits scientist used Indian patients as guinea pigs. BMJ 2001; 323 (24): 1204.

[17] Philips A, van Oosterhout J. DART points the way for HIV treatment programmes. Lancet 2010; 375 (9709): 123–31.

[18] Bhandari N, Rongsen-Chandola T, Bavdekar A, John J, Antony K, Taneja S, Goyal N, Kawade A, Kang G, Rathore SS, Juvekar S, Muliyil J, Arya A, Shaikh H, Abraham V, Vrati S, Proschan M, Kohberger R, Thiry G, Glass R, Greenberg HB, Curlin G, Mohan K, Harshavardhan GV, Prasad S, Rao TS, Boslego J, Bhan MK; India Rotavirus Vaccine Group. Efficacy of a monovalent human-bovine (116E) rotavirus vaccine in Indian infants: a randomized, double-blind, placebo-controlled trial. Lancet 2014; 383 (9935): 2136–43.

[19] Bailey W, Cruickshank C, Sharma N. Make your move: taking clinical trials to the best location. https://www.atkearney.com/documents/10192/312631/EA+vol+IX+no+1-Make+Your+Move.pdf/bb05c14b-2709-4ff1-828f-8ef851f303de

[20] Misik V. Reaping Rewards in Russia, Turkey and MENA. Quintiles Blog, November 18, 2014. http://www.quintiles.com/blog/reaping-rewards-in-russia-turkey-and-mena

[21] NIH Clinical trials. https://clinicaltrials.gov

[22] Matar A, Silverman H. Perspectives of Egyptian research ethics committees regarding their effective functioning. J Empir Res Hum Res Ethics 2013; 8 (1): 32–44.

[23] Zeeneldin AA, Taha FM. The Egyptian clinical trials' registry profile: analysis of three trial registries (International Clinical Trials Registry Platform, Pan-African Clinical Trials Registry and clinicaltrials.gov). J Adv Res 2016; 7 (1): 37–45.

[24] IMS Institute for Healthcare Informatics. Global Medicines Use in 2020: Outlook and Implications, 2015. http://www.imshealth.com/en/thought-leadership/ims-institute/reports/global-medicines-use-in-2020

[25] Egyptian Medical Syndicate. The Egyptian Medical Code of Conduct issued by Ministerial Decree 238/2003, 2003.

[26] Khoweiled A, Amer D, Abed M, Refaat O, Goueli T, Hamdi E. The Egyptian law 71/2009 'Care of mentally ill patients' (knowledge and opinions of service providers, relatives, and patients with substance abuse). Egypt J Psychol 2012; 33 (2): 74–82.

[27] Arab Republic of Egypt. 2014. The Constitution of Egypt. Unofficial translation.

[28] London L. Ethical oversight of public health research: can rules and IRBs make a difference in developing countries? Am J Public Health 2002; 92: 1079–84.

[29] Killen J, Grady C, Folkers GK, Fauci AS. Ethics of clinical research in the developing world. Nat Rev Immunol 2002; 2: 210–5.

[30] Kandeel N, El-Nemer A, Ali NM, Kassem H, El-Setouhy M, Elgharieb ME, Darwish M, Awadalla NJ, Moni M, Silverman HJ. A multicenter study of the awareness and attitudes of Egyptian faculty towards research ethics: a pilot study. J Empir Res Hum Res Ethics 2011; 6(4): 99–108.

[31] Younis IM. Overview of research committees' status in Egypt: challenges aspirations and current situation. Account Res 2015; 22: 222–36.

[32] Declaration B, SOMO, Wemos, EIPR, SICHCS. Industry-sponsored clinical drug trials in Egypt. Ethical questions in a challenging context, June 2014. https://www.somo.nl/wp-content/uploads/2016/07/Industry-sponsored-clinical-drug-trials-in-Egypt.pdf

[33] Kotb MA. Molecular mechanisms of Ursodeoxycholic acid toxicity and side effects: ursodeoxycholic acid freezes regeneration and induces hibernation mode. Int J Mol Sci 2012; 13(7): 8882–914.

[34] Joffe S, Miller FG. Ethics of cancer clinical trials in low-resource settings. J Clin Oncol 2014; 31: 3192–7.

[35] Hep C Coalition. Gilead's license on hepatitis C drugs, Sofosbuvir and Ledipasvir: a fool's bargain–Myths and facts. Hep C Coalition website 2014. http://hepcoalition.org/advocate/advocacy-tools/article/gilead-s-license-on-hepatitis-c?lang=en

[36] Abaza D. One year after Sovaldi: Why Egypt needs billions to beat Hepatitis C. Al Ahram online, October 20, 2015. http://english.ahram.org.eg/NewsContent/1/151/161149/Egypt/Features/One-year-after-Sovaldi-Why-Egypt-needs-billions-to.aspx.

[37] Sleem H, El-Kamary S, Silverman H. Identifying structures, processes, resources and needs of research ethics committees in Egypt. BMC Med Ethics 2010; 11: 12.

[38] CIOMS. International Ethical Guidelines for Biomedical Research Involving Human Subject. http://www.recerca.uab.es/ceeah/docs/cioms.pdf

[39] WHO Publication. Operational Guidelines for Ethics Committees that Review Biochemical Research. Reference number: TDR/PRD/ETHICS/2000.1.2000.

[40] Regulations of the research ethics committee, Faculty of Medicine, Tanta University 2015; 1–14.

[41] Wilkinson R. Unequal societies: the afflictions of inequality. London: Rutledge, 1996.

[42] Marshall PA. The relevance of culture for informed consent in US funded international health research. Consultation Report for the President's National Bioethics Advisory Commission Volume 11 Ethical and Policy issues in international research: Clinical trials in developing countries. US National Bioethics Advisory Commission, 2001.

[43] Lindegger G, Richter L. HIV vaccine trials: critical issues in informed consent. S Afr J Sci 2000; 96: 313–7.

[44] Glickman SW, McHutchison JG, Peterson ED, Cairns CB, Harrington RA, Califf RM, Schulman KA. Ethical and scientific implications of the globalization of clinical research. N Engl J Med 2009; 360: 816–823. DOI: 10.1056/NEJMsb0803929

[45] Macklin R. Double standards in medical research in developing countries. New York: Cambridge University Press, 2004, 6–8.

[46] Kass N, Hyder AA. Attitudes and experiences of US and developing country investigators regarding US human subjects regulations. Ethical and policy issues in international research: clinical trials in developing countries, vol. II. Maryland: NBAC, 2001, B–31.

[47] Macklin R, Appropriate ethical standards. The Oxford textbook of clinical research ethics, edited by Ezekiel J. Emanuel, Christine Grady, Robert A. Crouch, Reidar K. Lie, Franklin G. Miller, and David Wendler. New York: Oxford University Press, 2008, 713.

[48] Sanchez S, Salazar G, Tijero M, Diaz S. Informed consent procedures: responsibilities of researchers in developing countries. Bioethics 2001; 15 (S16): 398–412.

[49] National Bioethics Advisory Commission (NBAC). Ethical and Policy Issues in International Research: Clinical Trials in Developing Countries: Recommendation 3.10, 2001.

[50] Katz J, Capron AM, Glass NS. Experimentation with human beings. New York: Russel Sage Foundation, 1972.

[51] President's Advisory Commission. The human radiation experiments: final report of the president's advisory commission. Oxford University Press, 1998.

[52] Brody BA. The ethics of biomedical research: an international perspective. New York: Oxford University Press, 1998.

[53] Amnesty International. United States of America: human rights for all. London, 1998.

[54] Cassese A. Inhuman states: imprisonment, detention and torture in Europe today. London: Polity Press, 1996.

[55] Council for International Organizations of Medical Research (CIOMS). Ethics and research on human subjects: international guidelines. Geneva, 1993.

[56] Royal College of Physicians. Guidelines on the practice of ethics committees in medical research involving human subjects, 3rd ed. London, 1996.

[57] South African Medical Research Council. Guidelines for the ethics of medical research, 3rd ed. Cape Town, 1993.

[58] Levine RJ. Ethics and the regulation of clinical research, 2nd ed. New Haven: Yale University Press, 1988.

[59] Emanuel EJ, Steiner D. Institutional conflict of interest. N Engl J Med 1995; 332: 262–7.

[60] Spece RG, Shimm DS, Buchanan AE. Conflicts of interest in clinical practice and research. New York: Oxford University Press, 1997.

[61] Wilson JQ. The moral sense. New York: The Free Press, 1993.

[62] Thomas L. Living morally: psychology of moral character. Philadelphia: Temple University Press, 1989.

[63] Nagel T. Ethics without biology. In: Mortal questions. Canto: Cambridge University Press, 1991.

[64] Macklin R. Against relativism. London: Oxford University Press, 1999.

[65] London AJ. Equipoise and international human subjects' research. Bioethics 2001; 15: 312–32.

[66] London AJ. The ambiguity and the exigency: clarifying standard of care arguments in international research. J Med Phil 2000; 25: 379–97.

[67] Annas GJ, Grodin MA. The Nuremberg Code. The Oxford textbook of clinical research ethics, edited by Ezekiel J. Emanuel, Christine Grady, Robert A. Crouch, Reidar K. Lie, Franklin G. Miller, and David Wendler. New York: Oxford University Press, 2008, 136–8.

[68] Tan Torres Edejer T. North South research partnerships: the ethics of carrying out research in developing countries. BMJ 1999; 319: 438–41.

[69] Macaulay AC, Commanda LE, Freeman WL, Gibson N, McCabe ML, Robbins CM, Twohig PL. Participatory research maximizes community and lay involvement. BMJ 1999; 319: 774–8.

[70] AMS (Academy of Medical Sciences). Personal data for public good: using health information in medical research, 2006.

[71] Baily MA. Harming through protection? N Engl J Med 2008; 258 (8): 768–9.

[72] Murphy K, Topel R. The economic value of medical research. Chicago, IL: University of Chicago Press, 1999.

[73] Lowrance WW, Collins FS. Identifiability in genomic research. Science 2007; 317: 600–2.

[74] Lowrance WW. Learning from experience, privacy and the secondary use of data in health research. London: The Nuffield Trust, 2002.

[75] Bates DW, Leape LL, Cullen DJ, Laird N, Petersen LA, Teich JM, Burdick E, Hickey M, Kleefield S, Shea B, Vander VM, Seger DL. Effect of computerized physician order entry and a team intervention on prevention of serious medication errors. JAMA 1998; 280 (15): 1311–6.

[76] Hatfield M, Sonnenschein HF, Rosenberg LE. Exceptional returns: the economic value of America's investment in medical research, 2001. http://www.laskerfoundation.org/advocacy/pdf/exceptional.pdf

[77] Shamoo AE, Resnik DB. Responsible conduct of research. New York: Oxford University Press, 2009.

[78] Macklin R. Global justice, human rights, and health. Global bioethics: issues of conscience for the twenty-first century, edited by Ronald Michael Green, Aine Donovan, and Steven A. Jauss. Oxford: Oxford University Press, 2008.

[79] Aggarwal CC, Yu PS, editors. Privacy-preserving data mining: models and algorithms. Boston, MA: Kluwer Academic Publishers, 2008.

[80] Nissenbaum H. Privacy as contextual integrity. Washington Law Rev 2004; 79: 101–39.

[81] NRC. Engaging privacy and information technology in a digital age. Washington, DC: The National Academies Press, 2007.

[82] Westin A. Privacy and freedom. New York: Atheneum, 1967.

[83] Pritts J. The importance and value of protecting the privacy of health information: roles of HIPAA Privacy Rule and the Common Rule in health research, Institute of Medicine, 2008.

[84] Moore A. Intangible property: privacy, power and information control. In: Moore A, editor. Information ethics: privacy, property, and power. Seattle, WA: University of Washington Press, 2005.

[85] NRC. Privacy and information technology in a digital age. Washington, DC: The National Academies Press, 2007.

[86] Post R. Three concepts of privacy. Georgetown Law J 2001; 89: 2087–9.

[87] Solove DJ. Taxonomy of privacy. Univ Pennsylvania Law Rev 2006; 154: 516–8.

[88] Grady C, Hampson LA, Wallen GR, Rivera-Goba MV, Carrington KL, Mittleman BB. Exploring the ethics of clinical research in an urban community. Am J Public Health 2006; 96 (11): 1996–2001.

[89] Herbst AL, Ulfelder H, Poskanzer DC. Adenocarcinoma of the vagina. Association of maternal stilbestrol therapy with tumor appearance in young women. N Engl J Med 1971; 284 (15): 878–81.

[90] Washington DC Institute of Medicine (IOM). Implications of genomics for public health: Workshop summary. The National Academies Press, 2005.

[91] HEW (Department of Health, Education and Welfare). The Belmont Report: Ethical principles and guidelines for the protection of human subjects of research, 1979.

[92] Bregman-Eschet Y. Genetic databases and biobanks: who controls our genetic privacy? Santa Clara Comput High Technol Law J 2006; 23: 1.

[93] Farmer Y, Godard B. Public health genomics (PHG): from scientific considerations to ethical integration. Genom Soc Policy 2007; 3: 14–27.

[94] Greely H. The uneasy ethical and legal underpinnings of large-scale genomic biobanks. Ann Rev Genom Human Genet 2007; 8: 346.

[95] Adams R. Progress vs. privacy. CQ Weekly. 2008 May 26, 1404.

[96] Lin Z, Owen AB, Altman RB. Genomic research and human subject privacy. Science. 2004; 305 (5681): 183.

[97] Malin B, Sweeney L. How (not) to protect genomic data privacy in a distributed network: using trail re-identification to evaluate and design anonymity protection systems. J Biomed Informat 2004; 37: 179–92.

[98] Zerhouni EA, Nabel EG. Protecting aggregate genomic data. Science. 2008; 322: 44.

[99] Homer N, Szelinger S, Redman M, Duggan D, Tembe W, Muehling J, Pearson JV, Stephan DA, Nelson SF, Craig DW. Resolving individuals contributing trace amounts of DNA to highly complex mixtures using high-density SNP genotyping microarrays. PLoS Genet 2008; 4(8): e1000167.

[100] World Medical Association, Declaration of Helsinki: ethical principles for research involving human subjects (2008), articles 1, 6, 11–30 and 31–35.

[101] Nuremberg Military Tribunals, Trials of War Criminals before the Nuremberg Military Tribunals under Control Council Law No. 10. Washington: U.S. Government Printing Office, 1949, 182–3.

[102] Shuster E. Fifty years later: the significance of the Nuremberg Code, the New England Journal of Medicine, Massachusetts Medical Society, 1997, 1436–40.

[103] Shamoo and Resnik. Responsible Conduct of Research, 1998, 324.

[104] World Medical Association. WMA Declaration of Helsinki—Ethical Principles for Medical Research Involving Human Subjects. Edited October 2013.

[105] All information on the subsequent reviews of the Declaration of Helsinki can be found on the website of the World Medical Association. http://www.wma.net/en/60about/70history/01declarationHelsinki/index.html

[106] Idänpään-Heikkilä JE, Fluss SS. International ethical guidance from the Council for International Organizations of Medical Sciences. The Oxford textbook of clinical research ethics, edited by Ezekiel J. Emanuel, Christine Grady, Robert A. Crouch, Reidar K. Lie, Franklin G. Miller, and David Wendler. New York: Oxford University Press, 2008, 168.

[107] International Ethical Guidelines for Biomedical Research Involving Human Subjects CIOMS (in collaboration with the World Health Organization), 2002.

[108] Convention for the Protection of Human Rights and Dignity of the Human Being with regard to the Application of Biology and Medicine: Convention on Human Rights and Biomedicine CETS No. 164, Oviedo, 4.4.1997. http://conventions.coe.int/Treaty/Commun/QueVoulezVous.asp?NT=164&CM=8&DF=04/02/2013&CL=ENG

[109] Convention for the Protection of Human Rights and Dignity of the Human Being with regard to the Application of Biology and Medicine: Convention on Human Rights and Biomedicine CETS No. 164, Oviedo, 4.4.1997, articles 2, 5–9 and article 10.

[110] Convention for the Protection of Human Rights and Dignity of the Human Being with regard to the Application of Biology and Medicine: Convention on Human Rights and Biomedicine CETS No. 164, Oviedo, 4.4.1997, articles 11–14 and article 18.

[111] Biomedicine and Human Rights—The Oviedo Convention and its additional protocols, 2010, pp. 5–6.

[112] United Nations Educational, Scientific and Cultural Organization, Declaration on Science and the Use of Scientific Knowledge (adopted by the World Conference on Science), 1999. http://www.unesco.org/science/wcs/eng/declaration_e.htm

[113] United Nations Educational, Scientific and Cultural Organization, Universal Declaration on Bioethics and Human Rights, 2005. http://www.unesco.org/new/en/social-and-human-sciences/themes/bioethics/bioethics-and-human-rights/

[114] Directive 2010/63/EU of the European Parliament and of the Council of 22 September 2010 on the protection of animals used for scientific purposes, Off J Eur Union (20.10.2010) No. L 276/33–79, articles 7–8.

[115] Levine RJ. Informed consent in research and clinical practice: similarities and differences. Arch Intern Med 1983; 143: 1229–31.

[116] Taylor KM. Informed consent: the physician's perspective. Soc Sci Med. 1987; 24: 135–43.

[117] Hardy E. Factors often not considered before a multicenter trial is started. Clin Pharmacol Therapeut 1996; 60: 121–3.

[118] Informed consent is explicitly mentioned as a principle in article 7 of the International Covenant on Civil and Political Rights (1966), a United Nations Treaty. http://www2.ohchr.org/english/law/ccpr.htm

[119] Hawkins JS. Research ethics, developing countries, and exploitation: a primer. Exploitation and developing countries, edited by Jennifer S. Hawkins and Ezekiel J. Emanuel. New Jersey: Princeton University Press, 2008, 22–23.

[120] Sixth report on the Statistics on the number of animals used for experimental and other scientific purposes in the member states of the European Union, Brussels, 30.9.2010, COM(2010) 511 final, SEC (2010) 1107.

[121] International Ethical Guidelines for Biomedical Research Involving Human Subjects. Published 2003 (Archived 5th of November 2014). http://www.cioms.ch/publications/guidelines/guidelines_nov_2002_blurb.htm

[122] Germenis AE. Beyond the Ingelfinger Rule: the intellectual property ethics after the end of biomedical journals' monopoly. Med Inform Internet Med 1999 Jul–Sep: 24 (3); 165–70.

[123] Rice S. Policing the ethics police. Research review boards face scrutiny as feds propose new rules. Mod Health 2015 Dec 14; 45 (50): 18–20.

[124] Capron AM. Henry Knowles Beecher, Jay Katz, and the transformation of research with human beings. Perspect Biol Med. 2016; 59 (1): 55–77.

Chapter 4

Comparing GDP Health and Military Expenditure, Poverty and Child Mortality of 71 Countries from Different Regions

Colin Pritchard and Steven Keen

Additional information is available at the end of the chapter

http://dx.doi.org/10.5772/67120

Abstract

Child mortality rates (CMR) indicate how a nation meets the needs of its children, so relative to their region, do some countries 'neglect' their children? Using William Penn (1693) statement 'It's *a reproach to religion and government to suffer so much poverty and excess*' to judge nations CMR from three world regions within the context of poverty, health and military gross domestic product (GDP) expenditure data. **West (*n* = 21)**: USA, New Zealand and Canada are a *reproach*—Sweden, Japan Finland and Norway are *commended*. **Asia (*n* = 17]**: Pakistan, Myanmar and India are a *reproach*. Singapore and Thailand *commended*. **Sub-Saharan Africa (*n* = 33)**: Relative to their region, Madagascar and Namibia are commended. Twelve countries failed the United Nations (UN) target, including the relatively rich Nigeria and South Africa. Poverty and higher CMR are linked in all three regions. Relative poverty and military expenditures correlated in the West but not in the other regions. In the pursuit of social justice, societies need to be alerted to the extent of the impact of poverty on child mortality even though some countries will find this challenging.

Keywords: child mortality, poverty, health, military expenditure

1. Introduction

In terms of the well-being of children, there are profound implications in the United Nations Children's Fund (UNICEF)'s statement '*that in the last analysis child mortality rates are an indication of how well a nation meets the needs of its children*' [1]. Parents who relatively fail to meet the *needs* of their children can be described as 'neglecting'; can the same be said of nations?

Poverty is the context in which child mortality rates (CMR) have been analysed in this chapter. Therefore, this study assesses the relationship between poverty and CMR in 71 countries from three world regions, the West, Asia and Sub-Saharan Africa (SSA) and how successful they have been in reducing mortality rates over time relative and comparative to their region. There are, of course, many interrelated social policy factors that influence CMR reflecting differing political priorities so included is a comparison of health and military expenditure to reflect what in fiscal terms are competitive concerns [1–5].

Bringing together markedly different socio-economic regions has its problems, but it has been argued that in a globalised world the concept of developed and underdeveloped nations is redundant and countries should be seen along a continuum of socio-economic development [6]. This juxtaposition of three regions provides a comparative perspective of what is happening to children, in the context of poverty, within a regional perspective. Although the socio-political and economic make up of these regions varies considerably, all 71 countries under review are signatory to the United Nations millennium goals aspiration of reducing under-five CMR by 2% per annum [7, 8].

The importance of the poverty dimension originates from the seminal work of Wilkinson and Pickett who highlighted the significance of income inequality, a measure of relative poverty relevant to Western societies [4]. Income inequality is linked with a range of negative outcomes such as poorer employment, education, crime, housing and health outcomes as detailed in numerous Western 'clinical' studies [9–14]. International comparisons of CMR are problematic and more so when contrasting three world regions. However, as each nation is assessed, within its own region, against itself over time, it becomes is its own control, enabling us to judge how successful it has been in reducing CMR relative to its region [12–15].

In analysing mortality rates, it is easy to forget the emotional impact of the death of a child. This is epitomised in the lament of the octogenarian Elizabeth Barraclough who said *'I've lost a husband, mother and father, brothers and sisters but nothing, nothing is more bitter than losing a bairn'*. This would be true of any parent in any society in any region, so we also consider the impact that disproportionate levels of child mortality have upon societies. This is the first-ever known comparative study of societies' responses to children in three world regions and draws upon a range of recent and new research specific to this chapter.

2. Method

There are inherent methodological problems with international comparisons of mortality but the following method has sought to minimise them, as utilised in a number of comparative international studies covering healthcare, suicide, child-abuse-related deaths, cancer and neurological disease [15–18]. Nonetheless, there can be limitations linked to the accuracy of mortality data in less industrialised nations [1, 8, 19].

2.1. Mortality data

Two types of mortality data have been used: confirmed and estimated figures. The World Health Organisation (WHO) provides *confirmed* annual deaths for babies (<1 year) and infants (1–4 years) in the 21 Western and five of 17 Asian countries [20]. From these figures, under-five

(0–4 years) child mortality rates (CMR) per million (pm) of population have been calculated. Since1968, annual WHO mortality data were collected from member states though the data are invariably 4–5 years behind the year of publication. Whilst probably never entirely accurate, they are the most consistently reliable available international data for mortality [20].

UN Millennium Goals Indicators (UNMGI) and the UN Statistics Division provide *estimated* levels of child mortality from intra-country expert committees [8, 18] but have been criticised because of the discrepancies between them [21]. Inevitably, there are variations between WHO, UNICEF and United Nations Millennium Development Goals (UNMDG) data for the same years. For instance, a brief inspection of UNMGI data for the UK in 2010 gives a mortality estimate of 5.2 per thousand live births, equivalent to 5200 pm, but WHO data yield a confirmed rate of 4464 pm [20]. Although WHO rates are invariably lower than UNICEF-estimated data, UNICEF results are generally closer to WHO figures for the West and the industrialised Asian countries and therefore UNICEF data [8] have been used for societies without WHO information, as indicated in the tables.

As CMR varies on an annual basis, a 3-year baseline average (1988–1990) is contrasted with a 3-year index average (2008–2010) and a percentage of change calculated. As also indicated in the tables, WHO data for China were available until 1994, based upon a 10% sample of population (running into the tens of millions), but UNICEF data are used for 2008-2010. Index data for Canada and New Zealand is only available from 2007–2009 and Germany, Portugal and Spain have slightly later baseline years of 1990–1992 and is noted in the table.

2.2. Poverty data

There is a long-standing debate about definitions of poverty, crucially between 'relative' poverty in Western countries and 'absolute' poverty in the developing world [22–25]. Recently, the World Bank highlights that whilst there is no internationally agreed definition of poverty, in effect each country determines a 'relevant welfare measure' juxtaposed against a selected poverty line for that country to report poverty in relation to its total population [26]. The Western concept of relative poverty is usually proportionate to national average income, so a family income 60% below the average is designated as in relative poverty [26–28].

For Western countries, a ratio of income inequality is used, that is, the gap between the top and bottom 20% of incomes used by Wilkinson & Pickett [4], alongside gross national income (GNI) data [29] as indicated in the tables. The benefit of using this ratio is that it is country specific, thereby reflecting the relative positions of poorer families within that society but avoiding the blurring of average incomes. As previously noted, income inequalities have been found to be associated with a wide range of poorer outcomes in education, crime, unemployment and health [2, 4, 30–33].

As no comparable income inequality data exist for Asian countries, GNI figures by purchasing power parity (PPP) have been used [34]. PPP is the estimated value of the local currency converted into US dollars sufficient to obtain basic foodstuffs but does not demonstrate the income gaps that exist in that society. Absolute poverty relates to an individual surviving on $1–2 a day [24, 25]. GNI is the total national income divided by total population, adjusted for PPP and so provides a global indication of parity of income to show relative gaps between the West and other regions [29]. The problem of an average income figure is that it obscures variations between groups. For example, the UK's average income is £28,000, yet 60% of the population receive under £18,000 p.a. indicating the mode income is far lower than the average [35].

Recent World Bank data has been published that includes 30 of the 33 SSA countries (Anglo, Congo (Kinshasa) and Somalia were not available) and so matching GNI data are reported for 2010 [28]. SSA data are available for 2015, but over 5 years, there was virtually no difference between the countries ranking, hence CMR and 2010 GNI are also correlated to explore any link between CMR and poverty.

2.3. Socio-economic, health and military expenditure

The different socio-economic backgrounds of these regions are recognised but to an extent both Asian and SSA societies from the former British Empire have faced similar postcolonial struggles [36]. Comparisons of countries since their independence *within*, not *between* regions, are therefore considered reasonable.

Although Angola, China, Nigeria, Somalia, South Africa and Yemen are considered developing countries, they are among the world's top 20 producers of minerals and oil [34]. It is also noted that 14 of the 33 SSA countries have endured serious civil conflict over the period under review.

An important policy priority context is what percentage countries spend of their national wealth (gross domestic product, GDP) on health and military. World Bank data are extrapolated as a percentage of GDP for health and military expenditure from which a military to health expenditure ratio is calculated [37]. This ratio reflects national priorities and is likely to be influenced by local/regional political history as regimes change over time and respond to their sense of threat from their regional perspective. This is exemplified by the long-standing tension between India and Pakistan, Greece and turkey. Hence the military and health ratios can be sen as broad indicators of policy proirities.

2.4. Statistical analysis

Spearman rank order (Rho) correlations have been used to determine any association between regional CMR and poverty, that is, GNI, military and health data. Standard deviations (SD) of CMR in each of the regions have been calculated and 1 SD above or below the regional average is the measure used to assess whether a nation merits a *reproach*, using the words of William Penn (1693), or a *commendation*. 'It is a reproach to Government and Religion t Suffer such Poverty and Excess' [38]

3. Identifying countries of reproach and commendation

3.1. The West

Socio-economic data: **Table 1** lists Western socio-economic data. The USA has the widest income inequality, as their top 20% of salaries are 8.5 times that of the bottom 20% followed by Portugal (8 times) and the UK (7.2 times). The narrowest income inequalities are, apart from Japan (3.4 times), seen in European nations, for example, Finland (3.7 times), Norway (3.9 times) and Sweden (4 times). Switzerland has the highest GNI ($47,100) followed by the USA ($45,640), down to the lowest figures in Portugal ($24,080) and Spain ($31,490). Based upon 18 countries (owing to missing data from three countries), the Western GNI average is $35,662 per person; the UK figure lies just above this at $35,860 (see **Table 1**).

Health and military expenditure: **Table 1** also lists the West's health (GDPHE) and military expenditure (GDPME) as a percentage of total GDP.

Country	Income inequality	GNI $ average per person	%GDPEH 2010–2013	% GDP military expenditure	Military:health ratio
1. USA	8.5	45,640	17.1	3.3	1:5.2
2. Portugal	8.0	24,080	10.2	1.9	1:5.4
3. UK	7.2	35,860	9.2	1.9	1:4.8
4. Australia	7.0	38510	9.0	2.0	1:4.5
5. New Zealand	6.8	n/a	10.0	1.2	1:8.3
6 Italy	6.7	31,870	9.3	1.3	1:7.2
7. Greece	6.2	28,800	9.6	2.6	1:3.7
8. Ireland	6.1	n/a	8.9	0.4	1:22.3
9. Switzerland	5.7	47,100	11.2	0.7	1:16.0
10. Canada	5.6	37,280	11.0	1.0	1:11.0
11. Spain	5.6	31,490	9.3	1.2	1:7.8
12. France	5.6	33,950	11.6	2.1	1:5.5
13. Netherlands	5.3	37,940	12.4	1.2	1:10.3
14. Germany	5.2	36,850	11.3	1.2	1:9.4
15. Austria	4.8	31,900	11.0	0.7	1:15.7
16. Belgium	4.5	36,610	10.8	0.9	1:12.0
17. Denmark	4.3	32678	10.9	1.2	1:9.1
18. Sweden	4.0	38,050	9.6	1.1	1:8.7
19. Norway	3.9	39,869	9.4	1.5	1:6.3
20. Finland	3.7	n/a	9.1	1.3	1:7.0
21. Japan	3.4	33,440	10.1	1.0	1:10.1
Mean average	5.6	35,662	10.5	1.4	1:7.5

n/a, not available.
Income inequality and high military expenditure Rho = +0.4748 $p < 0.025$.

Table 1. Western countries: Income inequality and gross national income (GNI) by purchasing power parity (PPP) & average 2010–2013 GDP expenditure on health (GDPEH) and GDP military expenditure (sources World Bank): A military: health ratio [Source: World Bank, [37].

The average health expenditure in the West is 10.5% of GDP; therefore, out of every $100 of a nation's wealth, $10.50 is, on average, spent on health. Figures range from 17.1% in the USA and 11.6% in France down to 9% in Australia and 8.9% in Ireland. The average military expenditure in the West is 1.4% of GDP. Figures range from 3.3% in the USA followed by Greece at 2.6%, down to 0.7% in Austria and 0.4% in Ireland.

Military: Health ratios are narrowest in Australia 1:4.5, the UK 1:1.4.8 and the USA 1:5.2, the West's average being 1:7.5; ratios are widest in Ireland 1:22.3, Switzerland 1:16.0 and the Netherlands 1:10.3; reflecting different political priorities, which according to Nye Bevan is the essence of politics (Foot, 1978)

Child-mortality-rates: **Table 2** shows the top-six highest CMR (0–4 years) are from English-speaking nations led by the USA at 1503 per million (pm), New Zealand at 1308 pm, Canada at 1189 pm, UK at 1113 pm, Australia at 1030 pm and Ireland at 947 pm. Nations with the lowest CMR, apart from Japan at 663 pm, are from Europe: Sweden at 624 pm, Finland at 632 pm and Norway at 691 pm.

Country by CMR rank (latest years)	CMR baseline pm (1988–1990) [20]	CMR index pm (2008–2010 unless stated) [20]	% of change
1. USA	*2420*	*1503*	*–38*[#]
2. New Zealand (2007–2009)	*2361*	*1308*	*–45*
3. Canada (2007–2009)	*1740*	*1189*	*–32*[#]
4. UK	1929	1113	–42
5. Australia	1886	1030	–45
6. Ireland	1659	947	–43
7. Switzerland	1783	944	–47
8. Austria	1944	939	–52
9. Netherlands	1729	906	–48
10. Belgium	2013	886	–56
11. France	1740	876	–50
12. Germany	1611	838	–48
13. Italy	1895	822	–57
14. Spain	1790	820	–54
15. Denmark	1993	813	–59
16. Greece	2039	792	–61
17. Portugal	3019	782	–74
18. Norway	2005	691	–64
19. Japan	*1218*	*663*	*–46*
20. Finland	*1463*	*632*	*–57*
21. Sweden	*1520*	*624*	*–59*
Mean average	*1893*	*910*	*–51*

1 SD = 216 pm.
[#]Failed to meet Millennium target of reducing CMR by 2% p.a. (UN [39, 7]).

Table 2. West child mortality rates (0–4 years) per million (pm) and % of change (1988–1990 v 2008–2010) [Source WHO, [40]].

The USA, New Zealand and Canada merit a relative *reproach* as their CMR are 1 SD above the Western mean; Canada and the USA also failed to meet the UN millennium target of reducing CMR by 2% per annum. Conversely Sweden, Finland, Japan and Norway merit a *commendation* as their CMR is 1 SD below the Western mean. Portugal and Greece previously had the highest CMR but, at the index years, achieved the largest reductions (74%) over the period. Eleven other countries had falls in their CMR of 50% or more; the UK's rate fell by 42%, lower than the average Western reduction of 51% over the period.

CMR—poverty, health and military associations: There is a positive significant correlation between higher CMR and GNI (Rho = +0.6416; $p < 0.005$) confirming that at national levels there is an association between relative poverty and child mortality. Whilst there was no significant correlation between CMR and health and military expenditures, there was a significant correlation between higher military expenditure and worse relative poverty as measured by income inequality (Rho = +0.4758; $p < 0.025$).

3.2. ASIA

Socio-economic data: **Table 3** shows Singapore's and Hong Kong's GNI at $49780 and $44540, respectively; they hold the second and fifth highest GNI figures within the three regions, well above the average of the industrialised Asian countries at $38,750 and the West's average of $35,662. Conversely, GNI in non-industrialised Asian countries runs from $1180 in Nepal, to $1559 in Bangladesh and $6890 in China. So, the Western GNI average, based upon the US dollar's PPP, is nearly eight times higher than the non-industrialised Asian country average of $4460.

Health and military expenditure: The average expenditure on health as a percentage of GDP is 7.4% for industrialised and 4.4% for non-industrialised Asian countries (see **Table 3**). Figures range from 10.5% in Japan, followed by 7.5% in Cambodia, 6% in Nepal and Vietnam, down to 3.1% in Indonesia, 2.8% in Pakistan and 1.8% in Myanmar.

The average expenditure on the military is 2.6% for Asian countries. Figures range from 3.6% in Pakistan, followed by 3.4% in Myanmar and 3.2% in Singapore, down to 1% in Japan and 0.9% in Indonesia. The narrowest military to health ratios are in Myanmar (1:0.5) and Pakistan (1:08), as they spent more on their military than health expenditure.

Child mortality rates: Pakistan has the highest CMR of *non-industrialised* Asian nations at 87,000 pm and alongside Myanmar and India merit a *reproach* as their CMR are 1 SD above the regional non-industrialised mean (see **Table 4**).

China's (WHO) data from 1994, based upon urban and rural 10% samples, averaged CMR of 9394 pm. Yet, UNICEF data estimate a total mortality rate of 48,000 pm in 1990 reducing by 62% to 18,000 pm by 2010. CMR in Thailand is 1 SD below the non-industrialised Asian mean of 39,000 pm and merits a *commendation* alongside Singapore. Sri Lanka and China narrowly missed a *commendation* with current CMR of 17,000 and 18,000 pm respectively. Malaysia, with CMR *estimated* at 6000 pm, achieved a remarkable 67% reduction over the period. CMR in non-industrialised Asian countries are more than 40 times higher than the Western average. All industrialised Asian countries' CMR are lower than the Western average (910 pm) with remarkable lows of 522 pm in Singapore and 663 pm in Japan [20]. South Korea is likely to have suffered from the problem of diminishing returns [41] and also merits a *reproach* because its rate of 842 pm is above 1 SD above the industrialised mean; it also failed to meet the UN target.

Country and GNI rank	$ GNI average per person	GDPEH % 2014	% GDP military	Health:military ratio
1. Singapore	49,780	4.6	3.2	1:1.4
2. Hong Kong	44,540	n/a	n/a	n/a
3. Japan	33,440	10.5	1.0	1:10.5
4. Korea South	27,240	7.2	2.6	1:2.8
Industrialised average	**38,750**	**7.4**	**2.7**	**1:2.7**
5. Malaysia	13,710	4.0	1.5	1:2.7
6. Thailand	7640	4.6	1.5	1:3.1
7. China	6890	5.6	n/a	n/a
8. Sri Lanka	4720	3.2	2.2	1:1.5
9. Indonesia	3720	3.1	0.9	1:3.4
10. Philippines	3540	4.4	1.3	1:3.4
11. India	3280	4.0	2.4	1.1.7
12. Vietnam	2790	6.0	2.4	1:2.5
13. Pakistan **27**	2680	2.8	3.6	1:0.8
14. Cambodia	1820	7.5	n/a	n/a
15. Bangladesh	1550	3.7	n/a	n/a
16. Nepal	1180	6.0	1.5	1:4.0
17. Myanmar	n/a	1.8	3.4	1:0.5
Non-industrialised average	**4460**	**4.4**	**2.5**	**1:1.8**

n/a, not available.

Table 3. Asian countries: gross national income (GNI) by purchasing power parity (PPP) and % GDP expenditure on health (GDPEH) % GDP military (source World Bank) and health to military ratio [Source World Bank [37]] .

CMR—poverty, health and military associations: The correlation between CMR and GNI is highly statistically significant (Rho = +0.9323; $p < 0.001$) again confirming the statistical link between relative poverty and child mortality. There is no correlation between CMR and military and health expenditures. However, mention must be made about Myanmar and Pakistan, whose disproportionate high military to health expenditure proved to be the biggest distortion of all 71 countries reviewed.

Country by CMR Rank	CMR baseline pm (1988–1990)	CMR index pm (2008–2010)	% of change
Non-industrialised			
1.Pakistan	124,000	87,000	–30[#]
2. *Myanmar*	112,000	66,000	–41
3. India	115,000	63,000	–45
4. Cambodia	121,000	51,000	–58
5. Nepal	141,000	50,000	–64
6. Bangladesh	143,000	48,000	–66
7. Indonesia	85,000	35,000	–59
8. Philippines	59,000	29,000	–51
9. Vietnam	51,000	23,000	–55
10. China (WHO 1994)	9390	n/a	n/a
10. China	48,000	18,000	–62
11. Sri Lanka	32,000	17,000	–47
12. Thailand	32,000	13,000	–59
13. Malaysia	18,000	6000	–67
Average	**88,000**	**39,000**	**–56**
Industrialised			
14. Korea South 2007–2009 (WHO)	1220	840	–31[#]
15. Hong Kong (WHO)	1550	808	–48
16. Japan (WHO)	1218	663	–46
17. Singapore (WHO)	1598	552	–67
Industrialised average	**1397**	**715**	**–49**

Non-industrialised 1 SD = 23,000 pm.
Industrialised 1 SD = 116 pm.
n/a, Not available.
[#]Failed to meet Millennium target of reducing CMR by 2% p.a. (UN [39, 7]).

Table 4. Industrial and non-industrialised Asian countries CMR (0–4 years) per million (pm) and % of change (1988–1990 v 2008–2010) [Sources WHO [40]].

3.3. Sub-Saharan Africa

Socio-economic data: GNI data are available from World Bank [29] for 30 of the 33 SSA countries, as shown in **Table 5**. Gabon ($16,350), Botswana ($15,110) and South Africa ($12,350) hold the highest GNI figures in this region. The Democratic Republic of Congo, Liberia and Malawi and Niger have the lowest figures ranging from $630 to $880. Bearing in mind these figures denote average income per person, this means that a considerable proportion of SSA populations must be living in *absolute poverty* on less than $1 or $2 per day [25]. Although the SSA GNI average of $3,833 is similar to the non-industrialised Asian countries average of $4,460, the Western ($35,662) and industrialised Asian ($38,750) averages are around 10 times higher.

Health and military expenditure: No data were available for six SSA countries (see **Table 5**). The average expenditure on health as a percentage of GDP is 6.6%, well below the West's figure (10.5%) but above Asia's average (4.6%). There are marked variations led by Lesotho at 11.5%, Rwanda 11.1% and Liberia 10%, down to 5% in Zambia, 4.2% in Madagascar and 3.6% in Chad.

The average military expenditure in SSA countries is 1.5% of GDP. Again, there are marked variations ranging from 4.8% in Namibia and 3.5% in the Democratic Republic of Congo to 0.5% in Ghana and 0.4% in Nigeria. The average military to health ratio is 1:4.4. The narrowest is a 1:1 ratio in the Democratic Republic of Congo; Lesotho has the highest ratio of 1:16.

Child mortality rates: **Table 6** lists CMR for SSA nations. Only South Africa has WHO [20] data; UNICEF estimates are used for the remaining countries. Highest CMR are in Somalia at 188,000 pm, followed by Burkina Faso 176,000 pm, Sierra Leone 174,000 pm, Chad 173,000 pm, Democratic Republic of Congo 170,000 pm and 161,000 pm in Angola. These six countries are classed as a relative *reproach* as their figures are 1 SD above the regional mean; they also failed to meet the UN millennium goal target of reducing CMR by 2% per annum. Somalia, Zimbabwe and South Africa increased their rates over the period.

Countries with the lowest regional CMR include Namibia at 40,000 pm, Botswana at 48,000 pm and Madagascar at 62,000 pm, all of whom are 1 SD below the mean meriting a relative *commendation*. Botswana's commendation is tempered by the fact that they had a 19% reduction in CMR over the period thereby failing to achieve the UN target of a 2% reduction per annum and with a GNI by PPP figure four times the regional mean.

The average reduction in CMR was 33% and 16 SSA countries reduced their CMR by more than 35%; 12 achieving the millennium goal. Therefore, 21 (including South Africa) SSA countries failed to meet the UN target of a 2% reduction in CMR per annum, though five countries came close with falls of more than 30%. Fourteen SSA countries have been in civil conflict situations in the last 20 years; paradoxically Ethiopia, Liberia, Madagascar, Rwanda and Yemen managed to reduce their CMR by more than 40% over the review period. Compared to Nigeria who had the sixth highest income and equal seventh highest CMR, surely meriting a reproach.

Out of the 33 SSA counties, 21 (including South Africa) failed to meet the UN target of a 2% per annum reduction in CMR, although 5 came close with falls of more than 30%.

Perhaps the biggest surprise relates to figures from South Africa. Under the apartheid regime in 1990, WHO data yielded CMR of 6431 pm, but this might be a serious underestimation as child mortality in rural areas could have gone unreported. The first available WHO data for the post-apartheid regime (2002–2004) records a rate of 10,410 pm, equivalent to a 62% increase. Taking only post-apartheid WHO data, the latest index years 2007–2009 figure of 11,245 pm points to a rise in CMR of 8% over 7 years. However, South Africa's annual figures vary widely from year to year, for example, in 2009, the WHO reported rate fell to 9158 pm.

http://dx.doi.org/10.5772/67120

This variation is also reflected in the UN Statistics Division data where for the baseline years (1988–1990) CMR is estimated at 61,000 pm, 59,600 pm and 58,500 pm, respectively, averaging 59,700 pm. For the years 2008–2010, CMR estimates went from 69,300 pm, down to 53,200 pm and 47,500 pm, averaging 56,700 pm—a 5% reduction, yet well below the millennium target.

SSA country	GNI by PPP $average p.p	% GDP on health	% GDP military4	Military: health ratio
1 Gabon	16,350	3.8	1.2	1:3.2
2. Botswana	*15,110*	*5.4*	*2.8*	*1:1.9*
3. South Africa	*12,350*	*8.9*	*1.1*	*1:8.1*
4. Namibia	9380	7.7	4.8	1:1.6
5.. Swaziland	7450	8.4	1.8	1:4.7
6. Nigeria C	5380	3.9	0.4	1:9.8
7. Ghana C	3850	5.4	0.5	1:10.8
8. Sudan C	3810	6.5	2.1	1:3.1
9. Yemen C	3650	5.4	n/a	n/a
10. Zambia	3580	5.0	1.7	1:2.9
11. Lesotho	3280	11.5	0.7	1:16.4
12. Cote d' Ivory C	2890	5.7	1.5	1:3.8
13. Kenya	2820	4.5	1.5	1:3.0
14. Cameroon	2780	5.1	1.0	1:5.1
15. Senegal	2,210	4.2	1.6	1:2.6
16. Sierra Leone C	*2210*	*11.8*	*0.8*	*1:14.8*
17. Chad C	*1980*	*3.6*	*2.0*	*1:1.8*
18. Uganda	1680	9.8	1.3	1:7.5
19. Zimbabwe	1610	n/a	2.7	n/a
20. Gambia	1600	6.0	0.8[#]	1:7.5
21. Burkina Faso	*1560*	*6.4*	*2.2*[#]	*1:2.9*
22. Rwanda C	1,540	11.1	1.2	1:9.3
23. Madagascar C	*1370*	4.2	*0.6*	*1:7.0*
24. Ethiopia C	1370	5.1	0.7	1:7.3
25. Guinea	1140	4.7	n/a	n/a
26. Mozambique	1060	6.8	1.0	1:6.8
27. Niger	880	6.5	n/a	n/a
28. Malawi	760	n/a	0.7	n/a
29. Liberia C	710	10.0	0.7	1:14.3

SSA country	GNI by PPP $average p.p	% GDP on health	% GDP military4	Military: health ratio
30. Dem Republic Congo	*630*	*3.5*	*3.5*	*1:1.0*
31. Tanzania	*n/a*	*7.3*	*1.1*	*1:6.6*
32. Angola	*n/a*	*n/a*	*n/a*	*n/a*
33. Somalia	*n/a*	*n/a*	*n/a*	*n/a*
SSA average	*3833*	*6.6*	*1.5*	*1:4.4*

n/a, Not available.
#Military expenditure from 2000.
C, Civil conflict over the period.

Table 5. Sub-Saharan African countries: gross national income (GNI) by purchasing power parity (PPP) and health and military expenditure on health (GDPEH) 2014 [Source World Bank [37]] #indicates 2000 military GDP.

SSA country	CMR Baseline pm	CMR index pm	% of change	Lowest GNI: rank
1. Somalia C	*180,000*	188,000	*+4 #*	*n/a*
2. Burkina Faso	*205,000*	176,000	*−14 #*	*10*
3. Sierra Leone C	*276,000*	174,000	*−37 #*	*15=*
4. Chad C	*207,000*	173,000	*−16 #*	*14*
5. Dem Republic Congo C	*181,000*	170,000	*−6 #*	*1*
6. Angola C	*243,000*	161,000	*−34 #*	*n/a*
7. Nigeria C	213,000	143,000	−33 #	25
8. Niger	311,000	143,000	−54	4
9. Cameroon	137,000	136,000	−1 #	17
10. Mozambique	219,000	135,000	−38 #	5
11. Guinea	229,000	130,000	−43	6
12. Cote d' Ivory C	151,000	123,000	−19 #	19
13. Zambia	183,000	111,000	−39 #	21
14. Ethiopia C	184,000	106,000	−42	7=
15. Sudan C	125,000	103,000	−18 #	23
16. Liberia C	227,000	103,000	−55	2
17. Uganda	175,000	99,000	−43	13
18. Gambia	165,000	98,000	−41	11
19. Congo (Kinshasa) C	116,000	93,000	−20 #	n/a
20. Malawi	222,000	92,000	−59	3
21. Rwanda C	163,000	91,000	−44	9
22. Lesotho	89,000	85,000	−4 #	20

SSA country	CMR Baseline pm	CMR index pm	% of change	Lowest GNI: rank
23. Kenya	99,000	85,000	−14 #	18
24. Zimbabwe	78,000	80,000	+3 #	12
25. Swaziland	96,000	78,000	−19 #	26
26. Yemen C	128,000	77,000	−46	22
27. Senegal	139,000	75,000	−46	15=
28. Ghana C	122,000	74,000	**-39** #	**24**
29. Gabon	93,000	74,000	−20 #	30
30. Madagascar C	159,000	62,000	*−61*	*7=*
31. Botswana	59,000	48,000	*−19 #*	*26*
32. Namibia	73,000	40,000	**−45**	27
33. South Africa (*WHO 2002–2004–2007–2009)*	*10,410*	11,245	*+8 #*	*28*
Averages: SSA (excluding S. Africa)	**164,000**	**110,000**	−33 #	
Non-industralised Asia	**88,000**	**39,000**	**−56**	
Industralised Asia	**1397**	**715**	**−49**	
Western	1893	**910**	**−52**	

Highest CMR and lowest GNI Rho= +0.5132 $p = 0.005$.
1 SD 39,000 pm.
n/a, Not available.
#Failed to meet Millennium target of reducing CMR by 2% p.a. (UN [39, 7]).
C, Civil conflict over the period.
No GNI rank for Anglo, Congo (Kinshaha) and Somalia.

Table 6. Sub-Saharan Africa CMR (0–4 years) per million (pm), % of change (1988–1990 v 2008–2010) and lowest GNI rank.

CMR—poverty, health and military associations: The rank order of the lowest GNI with the highest child mortality rates was significantly and positively correlated (Rho = +0.5204; $p = 0.005$), thus across the three regions, there are positive and significant statistical associations with CMR and 'poverty' however defined, reflecting the truism that poverty, even relative poverty, is linked to the deaths of children throughout the world.

When looking at SSA nations, those with the highest GNI figures such as Cameroon and Nigeria, against expectations, had higher CMR, whilst poorer countries such as Madagascar and Zimbabwe had lower CMR, suggesting major differences in policy in these societies in relation to child health. To explain this more fully would require country-specific research. Remembering that GNI is adjusted for PPP in comparative terms, we in the West probably cannot conceive what such low levels of effective income mean for these societies. Again, perhaps counter intuitively, there was no correlation between the health, military expenditures and CMR.

4. Discussion

Limitations: The biggest limitation of this study relates to the necessity of using two different datasets—confirmed WHO data and UNICEF estimates of CMR, with the inevitable acknowledged inconsistencies [8, 20]. The biggest data inconsistency, however, concern South Africa, for example, UN-estimated data that far exceeded WHO rates were available. Self-evidently, we are not in a position to state which figures are the most reliable; WHO data appear to hold a greater degree of internal consistency as, for example, UN rates compared to WHO data when available always show WHO rates as lower. The marked increases, based upon South Africa's 1990 WHO figure of 6431 pm, raise the question of the accuracy of earlier pre-1994 apartheid regime figures. It *may* be that the former regime would have been less likely to include rural Black deaths. This in part *might* account for some of their rises though there have been increases in treatment-resistant TB and HIV/AIDS deaths in the country, which may have contributed to real rises in CMR [42–44]. Conversely, the increases could be due to more accurate reporting systems yet only country-specific research could confirm this. Another limitation is that 14 of the SSA countries faced civil conflict during the period, which is very likely to have affected those countries ability to meet the UN millennium goal, although five of these countries, for example, Liberia and Ethiopia, did meet the target.

These limitations mean that these results cannot be definitive. Rather, they are indicative of changes found in other studies of non-Western societies such as Islamic, Latin American and former Warsaw Pact countries related to suicide and child-abuse-related deaths, where data accuracy has been found to be problematic because of cultural and political taboos [15–17]. Nonetheless, despite these limitations, this first-ever comparative study of societies' response to children in three world regions provides significant indicators of those meriting a relative regional *reproach* or *commendation*. More importantly, these results provide a baseline for future comparative studies and how well or otherwise these societies are meeting the needs of their children.

4.1. The West

Most Western governments can be congratulated on the impressive reduction in mortality rates, but the *USA, New Zealand and Canada* are classed as a *reproach* for having CMR 1 SD above the regional mean. Are these countries relatively neglecting the needs of their children? As far as the UK is concerned, it had the fourth highest CMR of the 21 countries alongside the third highest income inequality figure; it has been found that British children, in regard to poverty and health expenditure, are significantly disadvantaged compared to other Western societies [13, 45]. The fact that the six highest CMR occurred in English-speaking countries suggests that, despite major reductions, there are cultural factors influencing CMR. Are English-speaking societies less child-focused than other Western nations?

Relative poverty and higher CMR are significantly correlated, which is seen in the fact that the five Western countries with the highest CMR occupied the six widest income inequalities positions. Conversely, countries with the narrowest income inequalities have the lowest

CMR, that is, Sweden, Finland, Japan and Norway, meriting their *commendation,* as well as *Greece* and *Portugal,* who had the biggest CMR reduction in the region.

4.2. Asia

There is a very strong correlation between CMR and relative poverty in Asian countries. Whilst *Hong Kong and Singapore* have lower CMR than the West's average, seven non-industrialised Asian countries had impressive reductions (more than 40%) in their CMR. *Singapore and Thailand* with their relatively high GNI figures and CMR 1 SD below the mean merit a *commendation*. However, *Pakistan, India and Myanmar* are a relative *reproach.*

4.3. Sub-Saharan Africa

Even acknowledging the incredible poverty of Africa compared with much of Asia and the West, the levels of CMR are overwhelming. Averaging 3.1% of all under-fives dying, surely this is a continent of hidden and silent sorrows. However, it is noted that some SSA countries, such as Nigeria, Angola and South Africa are among the top 20 oil-producing and mineral-supplying nations [28] yet all failed the UN challenge. Against expectations, some relatively richer countries, for example, Nigeria have higher CMR, whilst lower income countries such as Madagascar have lower figures. Further country-specific research is required to explain these apparent anomalies.

4.4. Governments

What also has to be recognised is that globally *the rich are getting richer*. Inequality continues to widen in such countries as the UK [46] and according to Credit Suisse, 0.7% of the world's population has increased its wealth holding to 44% of global wealth and 8.6% of the world's population now own 85% of the world's wealth [47]. The authors of this Credit Suisse Report argue that rapid increases in income inequality often lead to economic recession and in view of the current global economic situation, this gives further impetus to consider not only the current situation of children, but if these inequalities continue what will the outcome be? Therefore, when we see evidence of the social consequences of not achieving the UN goal of reducing child mortality, with its statistical link to poverty in Western, Asian and African societies, we should speak out. The UN millennium aspiration is essentially a campaign for social justice and we need to highlight the very corrosive effect of poverty and its impact upon children in *every continent,* for to be respectably silent is surely not an option. Hence, we have an obligation to hold our individual societies and governments to account, especially to those societies who merited a *reproach.*

When exploring the percentage of GDP on military expenditure, it was significant that the higher military expenditure in the West was statistically linked with worse income inequality, but not in the other regions. However, when considering the comparison of health and military expenditure ratios in Asia and Africa, we are ill-equipped to comment, in part because of unavailable data and the various countries perceived security threats. However, we recall the valedictory address of President Eisenhower, America's top general and commander-in-chief of the Allied war in Europe, who warned of the inherent socio-economic-political dangers of the 'military industrial complex'.

> *We have been compelled to create a permanent armaments industry of vast proportions.................. We annually spend on military security more than the net income of all United States corporations.*
>
> *This conjunction of an immense military establishment and a large arms industry is new in the American experience. The total influence -- economic, political, even spiritual -- is felt in every city, every State house, every office of the Federal government. We recognize the imperative need for this development. [But]*
>
> *In the councils of government, we must guard against the acquisition of unwarranted influence, whether sought or unsought, by the military-industrial complex. The potential for the disastrous rise of misplaced power exists and will persist. [48] [Our preposition].*

When discussing CMR, in one sense, using rates distances us, but rates are statistics, numbers are real children. One practical feature must be the accumulative societal impact of high child mortality as bereavement itself is damaging to family health [49, 50]. Losing a child must be one of the worst and bitter tragedies for any parent in whatever world region and should be a focus of future research. So what do these rates mean in terms of relative excess' deaths of children? The USA and UK, who claim to be the mature and greatest democracies, have somewhat distorted political priorities, not only warned of by President Eisenhower, but former Chief of Staff General Colin Powell, who complained the US military was out of tilt and distorting the US economy [51]. Yet the US and the UK have the higher military to health expenditure ratios, reflecting their priorities. Does this influence the conjugation that if the UK and USA had the same current CMR of Portugal, who had been the highest Western country in 1989–1991, then there would be 850 fewer dead children in Britain and 13,591 fewer American grieving parents, more than four times the worst ever terrorist atrocity. Indeed, both countries' CMR substantially exceeded that of Hong Kong, Singapore and South Korea. It might be argued that for every bullet, plane and tank manufactured, potentially it is taking the sustenance from children in need, not only in the West but also in the other two regions.

One excuse for SSA is they only have imperfect or new democracies, which we do not accept as apartheid ended 26 years ago and forthcoming research over a similar period of the former Warsaw Pact countries, shows that eight of them now have lower CMR than the USA, so with such considerable improvement, we should have greater expectations for post-apartheid Africa.

In all three regions, there seem to be questionable priorities: countries with narrow ratios, narrower than the average, such as Greece, Australia, UK and the USA, all less than 1:5.5, should be challenged as to the rationale in relation to their CMR. In Asia, except Japan, they have a far 'worse' health to military ratio, averaging 1:2.3. Again, surely this should raise questions as to their priorities—especially Myanmar and Pakistan, who spend more on military than on health and who have the highest CMR in Asia. In view of India's economic success, their ratio of 1:1.7 in part may be a reaction to their neighbour's military expenditure, but again should be challenged.

Finally, on the 'government' side of Penn's dictum, Sub-Sahara-Africa military: health ratios vary considerably, averaging 1:4.4. However, for 12 of the 27 SSA countries for whom we have data are below the 'average' and in view of CMR toll is of itself a reproach. For in the last analysis, every gun, tank and plane manufactured is competing for feeding and providing adequate healthcare for their children. This is reported with great sadness, but we must never

http://dx.doi.org/10.5772/67120

be afraid to report what we find even if it can inadvertently be re-framed as racist, as politicians over the centuries have used patriotism as the last refuge for the political scoundrel.

4.5. Religion

William Penn (1693) condemned both government and religion [38], however. Christianity and Islam, the main religions in the West, Asia and Africa, hold strong socially positive messages about the care of children. Both condemn child neglect and abuse in the strongest terms. For example, Jesus of Nazareth, also revered in Islam, denounces those who actively or passively neglect and abuse children:

> *but whosoever shall hurteth one of my little ones, it were better for him that a millstone were hanged about his neck and that he were cast into the depth of the sea (Matthew 18.v 6).*

From the Qur' an, there are clear obligations concerning how to treat and give priority to children, for example; *'He who treats the orphan with harshness and does not encourage feeding the poor so woe be to such praying ones, who are unmindful of their prayers!'* (Chapter 107 Al-Maum: 2-5). Those who ignore the poverty issue related to children are particularly condemned:

> *Nay but you do not honour the orphan Nor do you urge one another to feed the poor and love wealth with exceeding love (Chapter 89 Al-Fajr: 17, 18).*

Therefore, these two faiths come together to reinforce Penn's (1693) message that *'it is a reproach to religion and government to suffer so much poverty and excess'.*

5. Implications

The professions and those academics in universities concerned with children should not be afraid to highlight the United Nations declaration of the Rights of Children. At times of limited resources for services and research, some organisations may be afraid of their staff appearing 'political' or to offend powerful vested interests. Yet the inherent independence of the professional and academic ethos means we have a responsibility to 'tell it as it is' based upon the best available evidence. Therefore, whilst some countries can be commended for the progress they have made, these results should be a spur to the other to match the best or better in their regions. Here is evidence that is a challenge to all societies to honour its obligation to children in the constant pursuit of social justice, especially those societies of *reproach* who need to hear the silent sorrows of bereaved parents who have no voice.

Author details

Colin Pritchard* and Steven Keen

*Address all correspondence to: cpritchard@bournemouth.ac.uk

National Centre for Post-Qualifying Social Work & Professional Practice, Faculty of Health & Social Sciences, Bournemouth University, Royal London Senior Lecturer House, Christchurch Road, Bournemouth, UK

References

[1] UNICEF (2001). Child Deaths by Injury in Rich Nations. Innocenti Research Centre, Florence, Italy.

[2] Feinstein, L., Hearn, P., Renton, Z., Abrahams, C., & Macloed, M. (2007). *Reducing Inequalities: Releasing the Talents of All.* London: National Children's Bureau.

[3] House, JS., Schoeni, RF., and Pollack, H. (2009). *The Health Effects of Social and Economic Policy*. Washington, DC: National Poverty Centre.

[4] Wilkinson, R., & Pickett, K. (2009). *The Spirit Level.* London: Allen.

[5] Ponnambalam, L., Samavedham, Lee, H.R., & Ho, C.S. (2012). Understanding the socio-economic heterogeneity in healthcare in US countries: the effect of population density, education and poverty on H1N1 pandemic mortality. *Epidemiology and Infection,* 140, 803–812. doi: 10.1017/S0950268811001464.

[6] Rosling, H (2014). *Worldwide child mortality down to 1 in 20.* August 2016. Retrieved from: http://www.gapminder.org/factpod/worldwide-child-mortality-down-to-1-in-20/

[7] UNMDG (2009). *The Millennium Development Goals Report*. New York, United Nations.

[8] UN Children's Fund. (2015). *Levels and trends in child mortality report 2015. Estimates developed by the UN inter-agency group for child mortality estimation.* Geneva: UN. Retrieved from: http://www.childmortality.org/files_v20/download/IGME%20report%202015%20child%20mortality%20final.pdf

[9] Burchinal, M., McCartney, K., Steinberg, L., Crosnoe, R., Friedman, S.L., McLloyd, V., Pianta, R., & NICHD Early Child Care Research Network (2011). Examining the Black-White achievement gap among low-income children using the NICHD study of early childcare and youth development. *Child Development,* 82, 1404-1420. doi: 10.1111/j.1467-8624.2011.01620.x.

[10] Freemantle, N., Wood, J., Griffin, C., and MacArthur, C. (2009). What factors predict differences in infant and perinatal mortality in primary care trusts in England? A prognostic model. *British Medical Journal,* 339, 287–292. doi: http://dx.doi.org/10.1136/bmj.b2892

[11] Wang, C., Guttman, A., and To, T., (2009). Neighbourhood income and health outcomes in infants: How do those with complex conditions fare? *Archives of Pediatric and Adolescent Medicine,* 163, 668–670.

[12] Pritchard, C., Williams R., & Wallace, M.S. (2011). Comparing the USA, UK and 17 Western countries' efficiency and effectiveness in reducing mortality. *Journal of Royal Society of Medicine* Shorts, 2, 1–10. doi: 10.1258/shorts.2011.011076

[13] Pritchard, C., & Wallace, S. (2015). Comparing UK and other Western countries' health expenditure, relative poverty and child mortality: Are British children doubly disadvantaged? *Childhood & Society,* 29, 462–472. doi: 10.1111/chso.1279

[14] Pritchard C & Keen S (2016). Child Mortality and poverty in three world regions 1988–2010: Evidence of relative intra-regional neglect? *Scandinavia Journal Public Health*, 44;734–741.

[15] Pritchard, C., & Mirza, S. (2016). Under-fives child mortality and child-abuse-related-deaths in the former USSR: Is there an under-reporting of abuse-related deaths. *Child Abuse Review*, 25, 218–229. doi: 10.1002/car.2355

[16] Hansen, L., & Pritchard, C. (2008). Consistency in suicide rates in twenty-two developed countries by Gender over Time 1874-78, 1974-76 and 1998-2000. *Archives of Suicide Research*. 12, 251–262. doi: 10.1080/13811110802101153

[17] Pritchard, C., & Amanullah, S. (2007). An analysis of suicide and undetermined deaths in 17 predominately Islamic countries contrasted with the United Kingdom. *Psychological Medicine*. 37, 421–430.

[18] Pritchard, C., Hickish, T., Rosenorn-Lanng, E (2016). Comparing UK and 20 Western countries adult (55–74) cancer and total mortality rates 1989–2010: Cause for cautious celebration. A population based study. *Journal of Royal Society of Medicine Open*, doi:10. 1177/20542704166350364.

[19] UN Statistics Division. (2016). *Millennium development goals indicators*. August 2016. Retrieved from: http://mdgs.un.org/unsd/mdg/data.aspx

[20] WHO (World Health Organisation). (2012). *World health statistics*. August 2016. Retrieved from: http://www.who.int/gho/publications/world_health_statistics/2012/en/

[21] Alkema, L., & You, D. (2012). Child mortality estimation: A comparsion of UN IGME and IHME estimates of levels and trends in under five mortality rates and deaths. *PLoS Med*, 9, e1001288. doi: 10.1371/journal.pmed.1001288

[22] Gordon, D., Levitas, R., Pantazis, C, Patsios, D., Payne, S., Townsend, P., Adelman, L., … Williams, J. (2000). *Poverty and Social Exclusion in Britain*. York: Joseph Rowntree Foundation. August 2016. Retrieved from: https://www.jrf.org.uk/sites/default/files/jrf/migrated/files/185935128x.pdf

[23] IRP (Institute for Research on Poverty). (2009). *How many children are poor?* August 2016. Retrieved from: http://www.irp.wisc.edu/faqs/faq6.htm

[24] Laderichi, C.R., Saith, R., and Stewart, F. (2003). Does it matter that we do not agree on definitions of poverty? A comparison of 4 approaches. *Oxford Development Studies*, 31, 253–274. DOI: http://dx.doi.org/10.1080/1360081032000111698

[25] USDHHS. (2009). *The HHS Poverty Guidelines. One version of the U.S. Federal Poverty Measure*. Washington: U.S. Department of Health and Human Services. August 2016. Retrieved from: https://aspe.hhs.gov/2009-hhs-poverty-guidelines

[26] World Bank (2016). *Measuring Poverty*. August 2016. Retrieved from: http://go.worldbank.org/MJO6SB4JQ0

[27] Economist Editorial (2011). Measure by measure. The world's richest countries try to count its poor. *The Economist*, 20th January, p 1.

[28] US Census Bureau. (2012). *How the census bureau measures poverty*. August 2016. Retrieved from: *https://www.census.gov/hhes/www/poverty/about/overview/measure.html*

[29] World Bank (2016a). *GNI per capita, PPP*. August 2016. Retrieved from: http://data.worldbank.org/indicator/NY.GNP.PCAP.PP.CD

[30] Martorell R., & Zongrone, A. (2012). Intergenerational influences on child growth and under-nutrition. Paediatric *Perinatal Epidemiology*, 26, s1, 302–314. doi: 10.1111/j.1365-3016.2012.01298.x

[31] Hanf, M., Nacher, M., Guihenneuc, C., Tubert-Bitter, P., Chavance, M. (2014). Global determinants of mortality in under 5's: 10 year worldwide longitudinal study. *British Medical Journal*, 347:f6427. doi: http://dx.doi.org/10.1136/bmj.f6427

[32] Unger, A. (2013). Children's health in slum settings. *Archives of Diseases of Childhood*, 98, 799–805. doi: 10.1136/archdischild-2011-301621

[33] Lomazzi, M., Borisch, B., Laaser, U. (2014). The millennium development goals: Experiences, achievements and what's next. *Global Health Action*, 7, 23695. doi: http://dx.doi.org/10.3402/gha.v7.23695

[34] US Bureau of Statistics. (2012). *Statistical abstract of the United States*. August 2016. Retrieved from: https://www.census.gov/library/publications/2011/compendia/statab/131ed.html

[35] ONS (Office of National Statistics). (2015). *Annual survey of hours and earnings*. August 2016. Retrieved from: http://www.ons.gov.uk/employmentandlabourmarket/peopleinwork/earningsandworkinghours/bulletins/annualsurveyofhoursandearnings/2015provisionalresults

[36] Kwarteng, K. (2011). *Ghosts of Empire*. London: Bloomsbury.

[37] World Bank (2016). *GDP on military expenditure*. August 2016. Retrieved from: http://worldbank.org.military.expenditure.NY.

[38] Penn, W. (1693). Some fruits of solitude in reflections and maxims. Part 1: no.52. Oxford: Oxford University.

[39] United Nations (2000). The Millennium Goals: Reducing Child Mortality. Geneva, UN.

[40] WHO (2015). Annual Health Statstics. http://www.who.int/whosis/mort/table. Agust 2016.

[41] Murphy, K. & Topel, R. (2003). Diminishing Returns. The costs and benefits of improving health. Perspective Biological Medicine, 46; 108–128.

[42] Crump, J.A., Ramadhani, H.O., Morrissey, A.B., Saganda, W., Mwako, M.S.,…Bartlett, J.A. (2012). Bacterial disseminated tuberculosis in Sub-Saharan Africa: A prospective cohort study. *Clinical Infectious Diseases*, 55, 242–50.

[43] Heeren, G.A., Jemmott, J.B., Tyler, J.C., Tshabe, S., Ngwane, Z. (2011). Cattle for wives and extra-marital trysts for husbands? Lobola, men and HIV/STD risk behaviour in Southern Africa. *Journal of Human Behaviour and Social Environment, 21*, 73–81. doi: 10.1080/10911359.2011.534903

[44] Mudenda, V., Lucas, S., Shibema, A., O'Grady, J., Bates, M., Kapata, N., Schwank, S., Zumla, A. (2012). Tuberculosis and tuberculosis/HIV/AIDS associated mortality in Africa: the urgent need to expand and invest in routine and research autopsies. *Journal of Infectious Disease,* 15, s2, 340–346. doi: 10.1093/infdis/jir859

[45] Pritchard, C., & Williams, R., & Wallace, M.S. (2015) Child mortality and poverty in the Western nations 1980-2010: Are English-Speaking-Countries' children disadvantaged? *Childhood,* 22, 138–144. doi: 10.1177/0907568213513308

[46] Milburn, A. (2014). *The second State of the Nation Annual Report from the Social Mobility and Child Poverty Commission.* August 2016. Retrieved from: https://www.gov.uk/government/publications/state-of-the-nation-2014-report

[47] Davies, J., Lluberas, R., Shorrocks, A. (2014). *Global Wealth Report 2014.* Geneva: Credit Suisse. August 2016. Retrieved from: http://economics.uwo.ca/people/davies_docs/credit-suisse-global-wealth-report-2014.pdf

[48] Eisenhower (1960). Presidential State of the Nation Address. wikopedia.

[49] Espinosa, J., & Evans, W.N. (2013). Maternal bereavement: The heightened mortality of mothers after the death of a child. *Economics & Human Biology,* 11, 371–381.

[50] Rostila, M., Saarela, J., & Kawachi, I. (2012). Mortality in parents following the death of a child: A nationwide follow-up study from Sweden. *Journal of Epidemiology and Community Health,* 66, 927–933. doi: 10.1136/jech-2011-20033

[51] Powell, C. (1995). *A Soldier's Way: An Autobiography*. London, Hutchinson.

Section 3

Rural Development

Chapter 5

Spot Improvement of Rural Roads Using a Local Resource-Based Approach: Case Studies from Asia and Africa

Yoshinori Fukubayashi and Makoto Kimura

Additional information is available at the end of the chapter

http://dx.doi.org/10.5772/66109

Abstract

Rural roads in developing countries continue to be in poor condition despite multiple interventions. To provide access to markets, hospitals and schools for rural communities, capacity building has been conducted, enabling rural communities to participate in road projects. This process has included the transfer of Do-nou technology, which is appropriate for spot improvement using a local resource-based approach. The goal has been to transform the road projects implemented through community initiatives, maximizing their effectiveness and practicality, and thus improving the conditions of rural roads. Case studies have been conducted in Myanmar, the Philippines and Kenya. They demonstrate that spot improvement and the use of locally available materials can provide socioeconomic benefits to communities. Designs based on this approach have been developed for the construction of base courses, retaining walls and causeways. These designs can be applied over wide areas and modified to reflect the unique conditions of each project area. The experience gained in community mobilization and stakeholder involvement, which is essential in the proposed approach, can serve as a guide when applying the approach in new areas.

Keywords: rural roads, accessibility, spot improvement, local resource-based approach, community initiatives, capacity building, developing countries

1. Introduction

In this chapter, we discuss one of the key measures for improving rural roads and extending socioeconomic benefits to rural communities in developing countries. The key challenge is the improvement of rural roads under circumstances in which financial and technical constraints dominate.

Spot improvement was conceived as one of the solutions. This method involves a local resource-based approach in which community initiatives are transformed into practical interventions. Specifically, Do-nou technology [1], which is a Japanese term for a type of soil bag, became recognized as a means of building unpaved roads [2], retaining walls, and other road structures using the geotextiles available in developing countries. Only simple skills and labour are required, which fosters community initiatives for the improvement of rural roads. This approach has been introduced in both Asia and Africa.

Figure 1 shows a schematic view of the road network in a developing country. Road classification schemes vary from one country to another, but in general, road networks consist of trunk/regional, rural, rural access and unclassified roads. The trunk/regional roads are grouped as major roads, while the remainders are classified as rural.

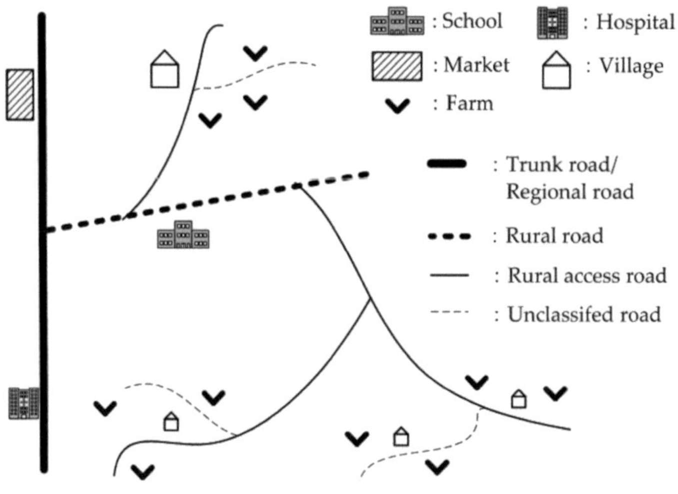

Figure 1. Schematic view of road network.

The road networks in developing countries have been developed through a combination of local government institutes efforts and assistance from donor agencies. Interventions have prioritized the major road networks, given their capacity to accelerate the growth of the market economy, the scale of their impact, and the efficiency of investment. Because the limited financial resources are mainly given to building, rehabilitating, and maintaining major roads, the rural roads in developing countries remain in poor condition.

While rural roads carry only low volumes of traffic, they are vital lifelines for people who live along them, offering access to markets, schools and hospitals. The inaccessibility of many rural roads isolates the local population from socioeconomic benefits (**Figure 2**). Thus, the poor state of rural roads can be identified as a significant cause of poverty in rural areas [3].

Figure 2. Ambulance stuck on an unpaved road in Papua New Guinea.

On 25 September 2015, the 2030 Agenda for Sustainable Development called Transforming our World was adopted by the United Nations Sustainable Development Summit [4]. The new targets that were set were referred as to Sustainable Development Goals (SDGs) and had the aim of ensuring that no one would be left behind. The ninth goal was to build resilient infrastructure, promote inclusive and sustainable industrialization and foster innovation. Research initiatives and case studies on ways of improving rural roads through the development of appropriate technologies and by equipping rural communities to use them are in line with this international development goal.

In this chapter, we present case studies of capacity building to enable rural communities to tackle the rural road problem through spot improvement using local resource-based approaches. We discuss the following issues:

1. The conventional approach to rural road improvement and its limitations;
2. The characteristics of the proposed local resource-based approach to rural road improvement;
3. Case studies from Asia and Africa;
4. Lessons to be learned from the case studies.

2. Conventional approach to rural road improvement and its limitations

2.1. Labour-based technology (LBT) favours government institutions

Since the 1970s, a number of projects have been conducted with the purpose of improving the capacities of local government institutions, enabling them to deliver rural infrastructure services effectively in developing countries [5]. Labour-based technology (LBT) has been mainstreamed in these projects. The key to this approach is the use of locally available resources such as labour, tools, and light equipment, combined with good workmanship and high quality standards. The definition of LBT varies from one country to another. However, from the view point of the authors, the following definition of LBT accurately describes its real implementations. LBT optimises the use of productive labour and complements the use of labour with the equipment that is essential to meet specified technical and engineering standards [6]. LBT is more appropriate for road projects that are executed by local government institutions, rather than those achieved through community initiatives.

2.1.1. Design standards

In LBT projects, unpaved roads are designed in accordance with the geometric and structural standards specified in the current design manual for low-volume gravel roads, and these are prepared by local government institutions [7, 8]. To comply with these standards, it is necessary to procure specified materials such as gravel with an appropriate grain size contributions, plasticity, and CBR value. It is also necessary to use equipment that can meet the specified technical and engineering standards. Tractors, trucks, and compact rollers are needed for hauling gravel, watering, and compaction (**Figure 3**).

To make this equipment available, LBT requires contractors who are capable of owning, or at least operating and maintaining it, while the communities living along the road can find only employment as labours.

While such a design policy ensures that the roads selected for the projects are of high quality and meet the standards, the unit cost is increased. As a result, the length of the improved road that can be achieved is limited.

Figure 3. Road rehabilitation work in Timor Leste, using the equipment required for LBT.

2.1.2. Basic rule for available road budget allocation

Any roadwork programme conducted by a local government institution has as its basic rule the protection of earlier investment. The available funds are therefore allocated firstly to routine maintenance, secondly to periodical maintenance and thirdly to rehabilitation [5]. In the case of a road on which some sections have fallen into total disrepair, it may be judged that there is no point in providing further maintenance. Instead, the appropriate approach would be to undertake extensive reconstruction or rehabilitation works before the road is once again included in the maintenance scheme.

On this basis, and due to the limited budgets available, badly degraded rural roads with lower traffic volumes may receive no intervention over long-time periods (**Figure 4**).

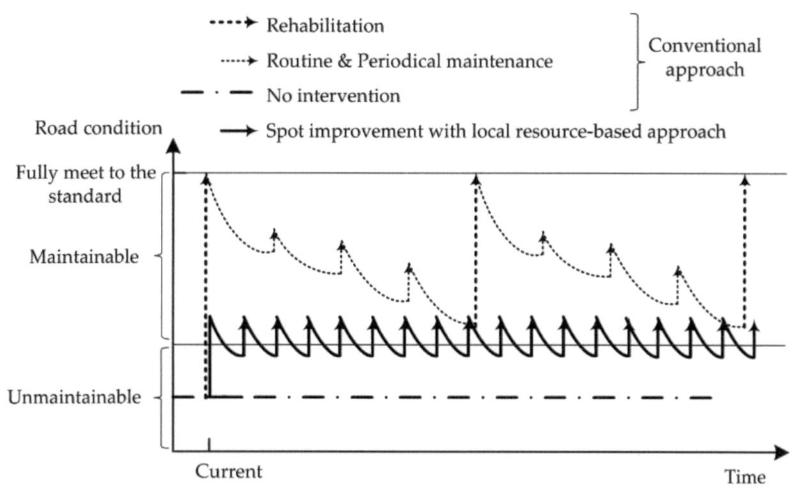

Figure 4. Road condition and interventions over time.

2.2. Limitations of the conventional approach

In Kenya, where the LBT approach has been applied to rural road projects since the 1970s, 31% of classified roads and 72% of unclassified roads were evaluated as being in poor condition in surveys conducted between 2007 and 2009 [9]. It is claimed that the government needs urgent additional funding to restore the network to a maintainable condition. However, it is difficult to envisage the government allocating such additional funding, considering the history of LBT in Kenya. A new approach is therefore needed to improve Kenya's rural road network.

Spot improvement using a local resource-based approach, which can be applied to road works through community initiatives, is considered be one of the measures that could be used to improve rural roads, in tandem with government road projects. In contrast with LBT, the proposed approach uses community initiatives to undertake practical road projects, thus improving access to markets and social services and accelerating development.

3. Spot improvement using a local resource-based approach

3.1. Objectives

If road projects conducted through community initiatives can achieve satisfactory quality, rural roads that government institutes cannot improve because of budget limitations can be improved instead by communities themselves, or by collaboration between the local government and community.

In such road projects, the community itself must manage the selection and procurement of base materials and the compaction of the base and wearing course materials. At this point, geotextile technology can be applied to reinforce the shear strength of the soil material through manual compaction. This method has been applied to rural road infrastructure.

The technology should use local resources and be labour intensive, and simple, enabling community members to perform all aspects of the improvement work. Thus, spot improvement methods using local resources have been developed to promote community participation. Specifically, Do-nou technology has been applied to rural road infrastructure.

3.2. Methods and implementation

Matsuoka and Liu [1] found that quality-controlled soil bags, here called Do-nou, have high-bearing capacities and developed both a theoretical model and a practical formula for calculating their capacities. This theory enabled the authors to identify the plastic bags used for crops, fertilizer, sugar, etc. in rural areas of developing countries to be used as Do-nou bags, thus serving as geotextiles for reinforcing the shear strength of the soil material.

3.2.1. Base course built through manual compaction

3.2.1.1. Structural design

The structural design of a base course consisting of Do-nou is shown in **Figure 5**.

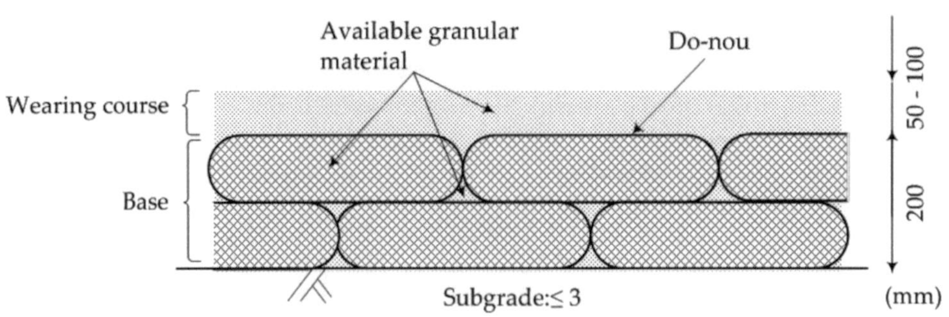

Figure 5. Structural design of road built with Do-nou.

Figure 6. Practical manual compaction method for community work.

Layers of Do-nou filled with locally available gravel form the base, bearing the traffic load and reducing deformation, and thus protecting the subgrade from excessive stresses. The wearing course in turn prevents the Do-nou from being exposed, whilst providing a smooth and durable road surface. The thickness of the compacted wearing course layer is 50–100 mm, which is appropriate under circumstances in which only manual compaction with hand rammers of small mass is available, and in which the cost of transporting the wearing course material needs to be minimized. This thin wearing course requires frequent but simple maintenance, including filling to restore the gravel lost through erosion due to weather and traffic.

3.2.1.2. Manual compaction

For civil projects initiated and completed by communities in the poor rural areas of developing countries, the most widely available, efficient, and practical compaction method is the use of a hand rammer with a mass of approximately 10 kg and a base area of approximately 0.04 m^2 (for example, a square of 0.2 m per side). Such rammers are dropped from a height of approximately 0.6 m and accelerated manually (**Figure 6**).

When building a base course using Do-nou technology, the confinement of the soil material in bags makes this manual compaction method satisfactory for the base course. The manually compacted Do-nou layer can provide a firm platform for the later compaction of the wearing course.

3.2.1.3. *High bearing capacity of Do-nou*

The tensile strength of the bags enclosing the soil material increases through this compaction process (**Figure 7a**). The soil inside the bag becomes denser, while the bags themselves become taut (**Figure 7b**). When traffic passes across the road surface, the soil material is subjected to passive shear (**Figure 7c**). The stress conditions are shown in **Figure 7d**. According to Matsuoka and Liu [1], the major principal stress σ_{1f} at failure can be calculated as follows:

$$\sigma_{1f} + \frac{2T}{B} = K_p\left(\sigma_{3f} + \frac{2T}{H}\right) \tag{1}$$

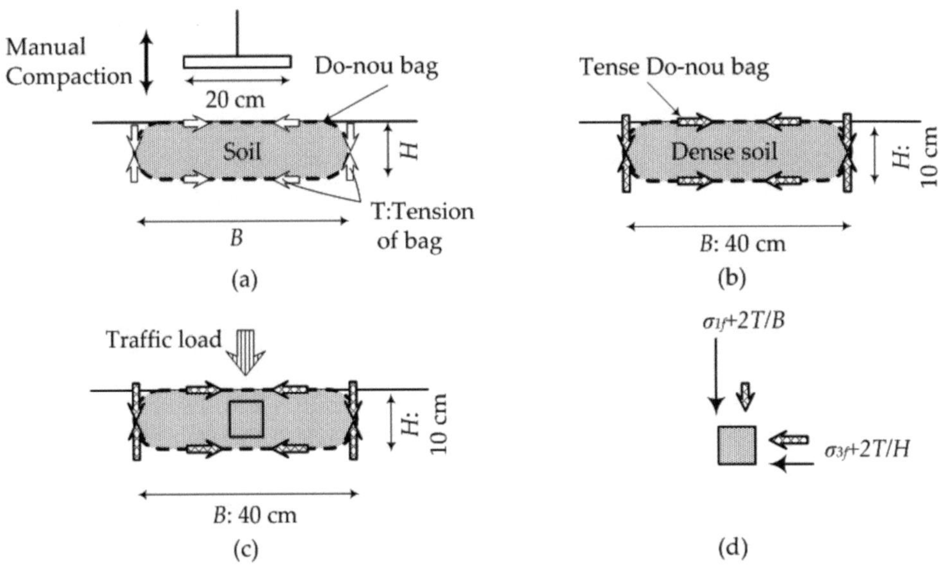

Figure 7. Mechanism that generates the bearing capacity of Do-nou: (a) Do-nou subject to manual compaction; (b) Do-nou after compaction; (c) Do-nou under traffic load; (d) stress condition of the soil material inside Do-nou at passive failure.

Therefore,

$$\sigma_{1f} = \sigma_{3f}K_p + \frac{2T}{B}\left(\frac{B}{H}K_p - 1\right) \tag{2}$$

where T is tensile strength, and B and H are the width and height, respectively, of the Do-nou. $K_p = (1 + \sin \emptyset)/(1 - \sin \emptyset)$ is the lateral earth pressure ratio in the passive state and $\emptyset$ is the internal friction angle of the soil material inside the bag. The bearing capacity of each Do-nou can be calculated by multiplying σ_{1f} times the area of the Do-nou, $B \times L$, where L is the length of the Do-nou.

As the Do-nou undergo compaction, the effective vertical and horizontal stresses on the soil material inside the bags increases. Compared to the loose soil incurred in the case of conventional designs but no compaction with equipment, the shear to which the material inside the Do-nou is subjected is confined. Moreover, the tensile strength *T* generated in each bag also increases its capacity, as shown by Eq. (2). Thus, by confining the soil in bags, the base course consisting of Do-nou achieves a higher bearing capacity. The bags act as a geotextile, increasing the shear strength of the soil.

Equation (2) shows that the bearing capacity of each Do-nou increases as the tensile strength of the textile that makes up the Do-nou bag increases, and as the ratio of *B*/*H* and $K_p = (1 + \sin \emptyset)/(1 - \sin \emptyset)$ becomes larger, where K_p is a positive function of $\emptyset$. Thus, bags with higher tensile strengths and granular soil materials with higher internal friction angles are preferred in Do-nou applications.

3.2.1.4. Do-nou bags

It was found that bags woven from either polypropylene or polyethylene could be utilized. Such bags are widely used in developing countries for crops, sugar, seeds, and fertilizers. Tensile strength tests confirmed that the fabric used in bags designed to hold 25 kg had sufficient ductility and tensile strength to bear traffic loads [2]. Two widely recognized tensile strength criteria are that a bundle of 1000 bags of width 45 cm and length 60 cm should have a mass of more than 45 kg, and that the fabric should have more than 10 woven threads per inch. Used empty bags represent a geotextile resource that is widely available in the rural communities of developing countries, and these can be employed for road intervention using the Do-nou technology.

The procedures introduced to fill and compact the Do-nou mean that each compacted Do-nou reaches a width and length of 40 cm, a thickness of 10 cm, and a mass of about 20 kg. The Do-nou then resembles a boulder in size and weight and is easily to handle. The Do-nou is laid uniformly on the subgrade to form the base course.

3.2.1.5. Gravel

Gravel road design manuals usually specify the base and wearing course material in terms of particle size distribution, strength, and plasticity, taking account of climate factors. The thickness of the base course is specified for each type of material based on the strength of the subgrade and the traffic load over the design lifetime, which is generally 5–10 years. Since Do-nou technology increases the density and bearing capacity, poorly graded and weaker types of gravel with higher plasticity can be used in base courses at the similar thickness specified in the manuals. Material confined within the Do-nou bags can be used to fill the spaces between the laid and compacted Do-nou, as shown in **Figure 5**. The Do-nou approach therefore widens the range of materials that can be used as the base course.

		Do-nou technique application	Design manual in Ethiopia [7]	Design manual in Kenya [8]
Traffic range (number of vehicle per day)		<100	<75	50–150
Envisaged compaction means		Hand rammer with a mass of around 10 kg	Roller with a mass of 5 tons	
Base	Material	Available granular and sandy material & Do-nou bags	Specified gravel • Soaked CBR ≥15 • Swelling ≤1.5% • Plasticity index <12 • Grading coefficient G_c 16–34[b]	Specified gravel • Soaked CBR ≥20 • Plasticity index 5–20 • Well-graded[e]
	Thickness (mm)	200	200	500
Wearing course	Material	Available granular and sandy material[a]	Specified gravel • Maximum grain size 37.5 mm • Soaked CBR ≥15 • Grading coefficient G_c 16–34[b] • Shrinkage product S_p 100–365[c] • Treton impact value TIV (%) 20–65[d]	Same material as base
	Thickness (mm)	50–100	150	150

[a]Since there is no reinforcement, it would be preferable that the material would comply with the specification as wearing course material in the design manual.

[b]'Well-graded' specified in terms of G_c = (Percent passing 26.5 mm—percent passing 2.0 mm) × percent passing 4.75 mm/100.

[c]Appropriate plasticity specified in terms of S_p = Linear shrinkage [7] × percent passing 0.425 mm sieve.

[d]Appropriate coarse particle hardness specified in terms of TIV, TIV <20 means the material is too hard to be broken with a grid roller, while TIV >65 is too soft to resist excessive crushing under traffic.

[e]Specified in terms of grading curve envelop as shown in **Figure 8**.

Table 1. Minor gravel road design for a subgrade where the soaked CBR value is <3 in a wet climate.

For Do-nou applications, the percentage of angularly shaped particles that can be retained on a 37.5 mm sieve should be minimized, to avoid tearing or puncturing the bags during compaction.

The authors applied the Do-nou technology to an actual construction project, working with the local community and monitoring the conditions after the work was completed. Minor gravel road design for a subgrade where the soaked CBR value is <3 in a wet climate is shown in **Table 1**. For comparison, the conventional designs based on the design manuals used in Ethiopia [7] and Kenya [8] are also presented. Uniform sand and sandy gravel with the grading curves shown in **Figure 8** were used in the Do-nou base, even though they fell outside the specified grading curve envelope. Further research is ongoing to extend the method to use of silty clay.

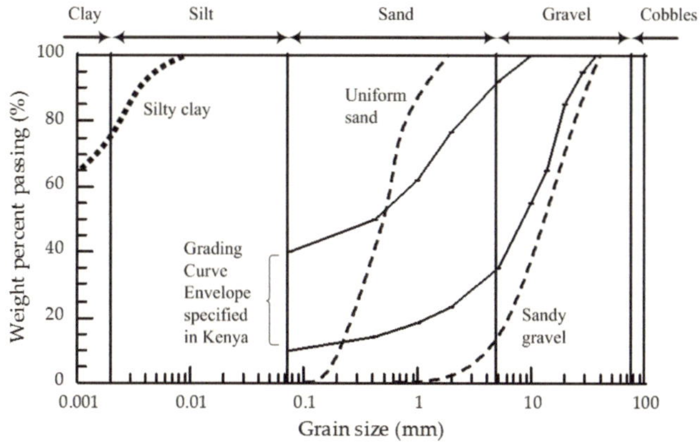

Figure 8. Grain size distribution curves of the specified gravel and others.

3.2.1.6. Practical construction procedures for communities

These procedures were designed to be practical for use in community road initiatives. Efforts are needed to control the moisture content of available granular material and to optimize the wearing course for compaction. Assessment on optimum moisture can be performed visually by observing a sample of the material that is tightly squeezing in the hand. However, access to the water needed to wet the material is sometimes challenging in the field.

The bags are filled with the granular material using a measurement container of 0.016 m^3. The open end of each bag above the fist is then tied with nylon string. These procedures (**Figure 9**) ensure that all of the Do-nou has the same size and weight, making it easy to lay them uniformly with minimum space between the adjacent Do-nou.

Figure 9. Procedures for filling the Do-nou bags with granular material: (a) Measurement container; (b) transferring material to bag; (c) open end of the bags above the fist; (d) tying with nylon string; (e) Do-nou filled with granular material.

Each Do-nou is then compacted with 15 strokes of a hand rammer. When well compacted, the dimensions of the Do-nou should be 40 cm × 40 cm × 10 cm. Any remaining space between the compacted Do-nou is then filled with available gravel material, and the next layer is laid on top.

The wearing course material is spread with a near-optimum moisture content and is first compacted manually with a hand rammer, then by passing the traffic-like gravel transportation trucks on the road. Since no specialized compaction equipment is available, the compacted lift thickness cannot be greater than 50 mm.

3.2.2. Retaining wall built with unskilled labour

Rural road projects often require the constructions of structures such as culverts, bridges and retaining walls [5]. This construction is normally performed using a mix of skilled and unskilled labour and some equipment. When choosing the most appropriate technology for this type of work, it is important to select materials that are locally available and to reduce the amount of materials that need to be transported over long distances.

Retaining walls are normally built using boulders, sand and cement by the worker groups supervised by stonemasons. This process requires the timely delivery of the various materials in appropriate quantities and masonry skills (**Figure 10a**, **b**), putting the construction of retaining walls beyond the resources available to many local communities.

(a) (b) (c) (d)

Figure 10. Construction of retaining wall: (a) Material for retaining wall with masonry; (b) construction of retaining wall by masonry; (c) construction of retaining wall with Do-nou; (d) torn bags and cemented material inside bags.

http://dx.doi.org/10.5772/66109

Do-nou technology, in contrast, increases the range of work that can be undertaken by communities themselves, using only unskilled labour.

When there is no source of stones or boulders within a reasonable distance of the construction site, Do-nou filled with *in-situ* soil can be utilized as an alternative.

Unlike boulders, all Do-nou are rectangular, with uniform dimensions and weights, which make them simple to lie uniformly and to interlock. (**Figure 10c**). Uniform dimensions of Do-nou minimize the space between adjacent Do-nou, which can then be filled with mortar.

To address the vulnerability to ultraviolet light of Do-nou bags woven from polypropylene or polyethylene, the soil in the bags is mixed with cement. Initially, the soil and cement mix is confined tightly, with tensile strength generated through manual compaction. The mixture solidifies before the Do-nou bags become prone to tearing (**Figure 10d**).

3.3. Strengths and limitations

As discussed in Sections 3.1 and 3.2, spot improvement using local resource-based approach empowers communities living near rural roads to undertake their own improvements. The use of Do-nou technology in road building and structural work supports this approach. The strengths and limitations are summarized below.

Strengths:

- Compaction of soil material for building the base course can be performed manually;
- Gravel that does not exactly comply with specifications for the road base can be utilized;
- Where boulders and stone are not available, retaining walls can be built from *in-situ* soil, using Do-nou bags and cement;
- Since masonry is not essential, unskilled workers can build road structures, such as retaining walls;
- Communities can develop skills in road improvement and apply these continuously and sustainably (**Figure 4**).

Limitations:

- Roads constructed or repaired using this approach do not always meet the prescribed standards;
- More frequent maintenance is required than when conventional approaches are used;
- Although the use of locally available material is maximized, non-local materials are still required, such as Do-nou bags with required number, soil or gravel to fill the Do-nou bags, wearing course material, cement, etc.;
- Collaboration is necessary with other stakeholders, such as government institutes, NGOs, and private companies;

- Improving the most problematic road sections is only a partial solution;
- The community must be motivated to improve the roads by themselves and must be organized to work together productively.

4. Case studies from Asia and Africa

4.1. Applications in rural road improvement projects with community initiatives in Myanmar

4.1.1. Application at flooding area

4.1.1.1. Site selection

In Kayin State of Myanmar, following the recommendations of the Department of Rural Development, village Y was selected for a rural road improvement project. Through meetings with the leader and members of the community and a field survey, a 120-m length of road prone to flooding, in which the maximum water level was more than 1 m above ground level, was identified for improvement. When flooded, the community must use small boats to gain access to schools, hospitals, and markets. Accidents have occurred, and two school-age children were killed in past floods.

4.1.1.2. Design

To raise the road surface above the maximum water level, an embankment with a Do-nou retaining wall was designed, as shown in **Figure 11**. The existing ground surface was protected with single-column Do-nou layers filled with soil mixed with cement. The embankment was supported with double-column Do-nou layers, the inner filled with *in-situ* soil and the outer with soil mixed cement. The *in-situ* soil was judged appropriate for mixing with cement for use as filling material into Do-nou bags and use as the embankment material. The column of Do-nou layers was <1.5 m in height, and the slope ratio was rise of 1 over run of 0.5. Trials of the mixing ratio of cement and *in-situ* soil identified an appropriate ratio of 1:10 by volume.

4.1.1.3. Construction

Construction was performed during the dry season, from March to April in 2014, with 49 villagers working 5–6 h/day. With these resources, the length of 120 m was completed, with an embankment and Do-nou retaining wall (**Figure 12**).

http://dx.doi.org/10.5772/66109

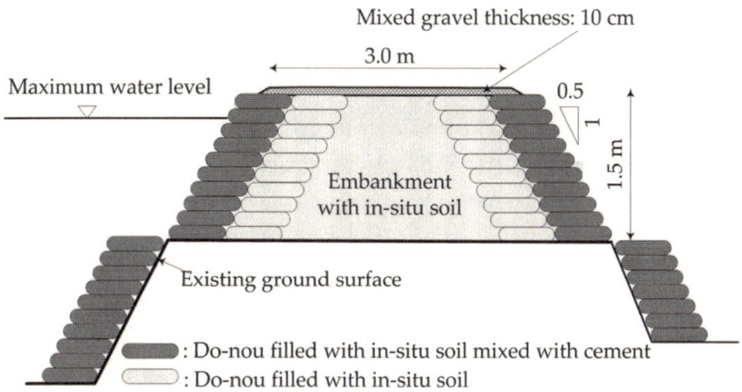

Figure 11. Design of road embankment with Do-nou retaining wall.

Figure 12. Construction of road embankment with Do-nou retaining wall: (a) Before construction; (b) construction of the embankment with Do-nou retaining wall; (c) after construction.

The cost of construction is summarized in **Table 2**. The largest element was the cost of cement, at 36.6% of the total, followed by the cost of Do-nou bags, and the transportation of tools and materials. The labour fee was not concern of the community members, and thus, this sum was paid into the Community Fund after construction was completed.

Item	Quantity	Unit	Cost (USD)	%	Note
Gravel	125.4	m^3	245.18	4.5	
Sand	4.6	m^3	16.40	0.3	Mixed with gravel for grading of grains
Cement (50 kg)	600	Bag	1992.60	36.6	
Do-nou bags	17,000	Bag	1717.90	31.6	
Tools	–	–	432.22	7.9	
Transportation	–	–	624.68	11.5	For tools and material
Labour fee	–	–	410.00	7.5	
Total			5438.98	100.0	

Table 2. Cost of construction.

4.1.1.4. Impact

One year later, an assessment was made of the construction site during the rainy season. This assessment confirmed that conditions remained good, as shown in **Figure 13**. The inhabitants of village Y subsequently applied the Do-nou retaining wall construction method to other sections of road, after the project ended. The work was initiated by the community leader, and the material and transportation costs were covered by the Community Fund.

Interviews with villagers revealed the following positive impacts of the project:

- During the rainy season, boats are no longer needed to move around the village;
- Students can attend schools from their home even during the rainy season, thus the absence from class is decreased;
- Patient can be transported to hospital more safely and quickly;
- Crops can be transported before spoiling;
- The community knowledge of Do-nou technology enables continuous maintenance to be conducted;
- The community has become better organized through the experience of working on the project.

Figure 13. Road condition 1 year after the completion, during rainy season.

4.1.2. Application at delta

4.1.2.1. Site selection

Ayeyarwady region of Myanmar is located at delta of the river. The sedimentary clay is prevailing. Following recommendations of a local NGO, village K in Ayeyarwady region was selected for a rural road improvement project. The people were used to construct their access roads by spreading the *in-situ* clay dug out from the adjacent rice paddy. During rainy seasons, the surface becomes muddy so that even bikes and bicycles are not passable, while during the dry season, the road surface becomes firm but rough so the traffic has to pass slowly. Due to the inaccessibility of roads, during rainy seasons, children have to be absent from their classes. In order to enable the access to the neighbouring village all the year, a 1200-m length of the existing road was targeted for improvement.

4.1.2.2. Design

Considering the current major traffic means in village K, that are bikes and bicycles, concrete pavement with 10 cm in thickness was constructed on the existing road surface as shown in **Figure 14**. In order to enable those traffic loads to go by each other, the two lanes with 60 cm in width were built. To protect the embankment from erosion caused by going up and down of the water level surrounding, Do-nou filled with *in-situ* clay were laid along the slope. Here, to address the vulnerability to ultraviolet light of Do-nou bags, Do-nou laid at 45° gradient was covered with the cohesive *in-situ* clay soil. The vegetation occurs from the attached clay and the root spreads, which stabilize the slope without confinement effect generated from the bags.

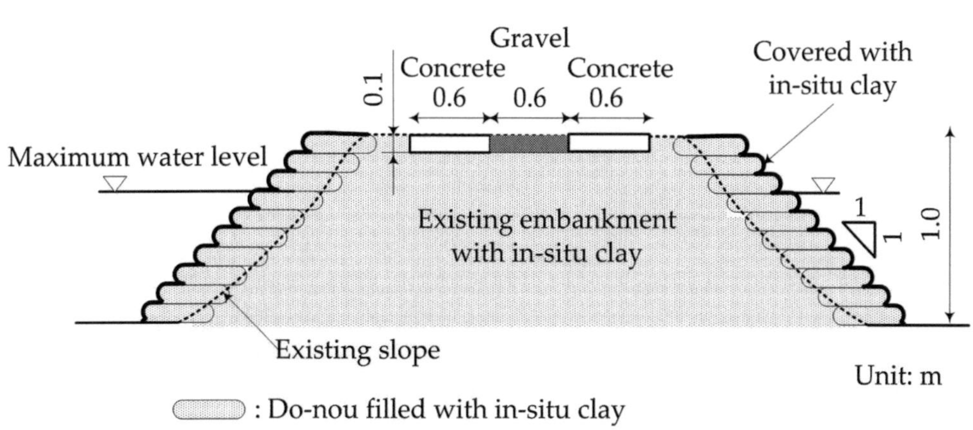

Figure 14. Design of concrete pavement and Do-nou retaining wall.

4.1.2.3. Construction

Construction was performed during the dry season, from January to May in 2014, with 20–50 villagers working 6 h/day. During the hottest season from March to May, the community managed to work at night, from 6 o'clock to midnight to avoid the heat (**Figure 15**). With these resources, the length of 1200 m was completed, with the concrete pavement and Do-nou retaining wall.

The cost of construction is summarized in **Table 3**. The unit cost per m with the cross section as shown in **Figure 14** is USD 12.32. The largest element was the cost of gravel, at 27.7% of the total, followed by the cost of cement, and tools. The labour fee was paid for the skilful workers who assisted concrete pavement work. The community members participated in the road works have no concerns on their labour fee, thus this sum was paid into the Community Fund after construction was completed.

(a) (b) (c)

Figure 15. Construction at village K: (a) Covering Do-nou with clay; (b) working at night; (c) bucket brigade for casting concrete.

Item	Quantity	Unit	Cost (USD)	%	Note
Gravel	212.2	m^3	4088.60	27.7	
Sand	85.0	m^3	401.80	2.7	
Cement (50 kg)	845	Bag	3440.31	23.3	
Do-nou bags	18,000	Bag	1697.40	11.5	
Tools	–	–	3309.18	22.4	
Transportation	–	–	1031.64	7.0	
Labour fee for skilful worker	60	Person day	217.79	1.5	Supervisor: 4.10 USD/day Assistant: 3.28 USD/day
Labour fee for participants			354.24	2.4	Sum amount agreed with the community, paid to the Community Funds
Others	–	–	242.26	1.7	
Total			14,783.22	100.0	

Table 3. Cost of construction.

4.1.2.4. Impact

From the assessment one year after the completion, it was confirmed that conditions remained good, as shown in **Figure 16**. The interviews with villagers revealed the following positive impacts of the project:

- The time to send children to schools is shortened and the parents spare time for other works;
- Children can attend the class even during rainy seasons;
- Bike taxi businesses are established;
- The community knowledge of Do-nou technology enables continuous maintenance to be conducted;

(a) (b)

Figure 16. Road condition: (a) Before construction; (b) condition 1 year after the completion.

On the other hand, as negative impact, the concerns on the increase in traffic accidents were raised. The training on traffic safety and installing the safety facilities, such as sign boards and bump, should be included in the project.

4.2. Construction of a vented ford in collaboration with the provincial/municipal government, community and NGOs

4.2.1. Vented ford construction site

In Nueva Vizcaya Province of the Philippines, the people of village C had suffered from flooding at the intersection of the river and the access road into the town during rainy seasons. Some sections of the road from the town to the village had been gradually paved with concrete by the provincial government, but no intervention had been made at the intersection with the river.

A Japanese NGO had trained the people of village C on the cultivation and marketing of organic agricultural products for income generation. The project had been implemented in close collaboration with local NGOs and provincial/municipal governments. However, the access problem at the intersection had constrained the project, and improvement was beyond the resources of the local governments. Surveying and construction started after the NGO consulted with the authors to seek solutions to this problem.

4.2.2. Vented ford design

Following a field survey with the municipal engineers, a vented ford with concrete slabs 4.0 m wide and 30.0 m in length was proposed, as shown in **Figure 17**.

The structure followed the basic pattern in the LBT manual [5], with Do-nou filled with soil and cement substituted for masonry. The objectives were to promote participation by all of the community members and to shorten the construction time. The ratio of cement to gravel was 20% by volume. Layers of Do-nou were combined vertically with penetrating reinforcement bars. To bear the water pressure at the upstream side, the concrete was cast to form a 20-cm-wide wall between Do-nou columns serving form.

The reinforced concrete pipes were backfilled with river gravel and with Do-nou filled with gravel. Concrete pavement was constructed in accordance with the specifications for provincial roads in the Philippines.

Due to the land use near the intersection, the axis of the vented ford could not be made vertical to the river flow, but had to be slanted as shown in **Figure 17a**.

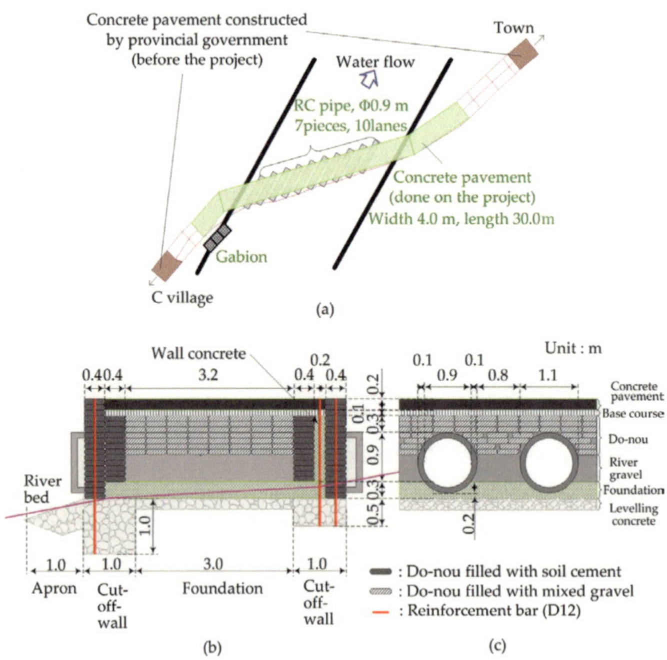

Figure 17. Plain and cross-sectional view of the vented ford: (a) Plain view; (b) longitudinal section view; (c) vertical cross-sectional view.

http://dx.doi.org/10.5772/66109

4.2.3. Collaboration with provincial/municipal government, community and NGOs

Three-way discussions were held between the local government, village C, and the authors' NGO to discuss the design and clarify the role of each through the facilitations of the local and the Japanese NGO. The roles were allocated as shown in **Table 4**, and **Figures 18** and **19**.

Party	Role	Contribution
Authors' NGO	Design Supervision Procurement of materials Payment to labourers	Fund for the entire construction
Local governments	Supervision	Transportation (trucks) Equipment (backhoe, transit mixer, roller) Gravel
Community	Mobilization of labour	Cooking of lunch and refreshment, available tools

Table 4. Role and contribution of each party.

(a) (b) (c)

Figure 18. Work items managed using equipment provided by local government: (a) Excavation of the cut-off-wall and foundation; (b) transit mixers and water pump during casting concrete; (c) compaction of base course with roller.

(a) (b) (c)

Figure 19. Work items managed by the community: (a) Leveling the concrete surface; (b) filling the gaps of RC pipes; (c) laying Do-nou.

The cost details prepared by the authors' NGO are shown in **Table 5**. For 48 days between March and April 2015, 20–30 people worked for 8 h/day on the project.

Item	Quantity	Unit	Cost (USD)	%	Note
RC pipe	70	pcs	3998.40	14.1	Inner diameter 0.9 m, thickness 0.1 m
Cement (40 kg)	1620	Bag	8527.68	30.0	
Do-nou bags	9300	Bag	3124.80	11.0	
RC bars	85	pcs	462.69	1.6	D10, D12, D16, 1 pcs = 6 m
Gabion net	28	pcs	1254.40	4.4	1 m × 1 m × 2 m
Fuel	1354	Litre	947.12	3.3	For equipment and truck
Tools	–	–	839.55	3.0	
Allowances	1380	Person day	7728.00	27.2	Minimum wage per day: USD 5.6
Lunch	1380	Person day	1545.60	5.4	USD 1.12 per person day
Gravel	217.00	m^3	–	–	Provided by municipal government
Stones	82.00	m^3	–	–	For foundation, collected on site
Transportation	–	–	–	–	Two trucks with drivers, provided by municipal government
Equipment	–	–	–	–	Excavator, loader, transit mixer, roller with operator, provided by municipal government
Total			28,428.24	100.0	

Table 5. Cost of construction.

4.2.4. *Maintenance by local governments and communities*

In October of 2015, the area was hit by the strongest typhoon in 15 years. The vented ford overflowed, and sediment was deposited at the upstream side. After the typhoon passed, it was observed that, although the ford was partially damaged, its stability was not affected. To restore the ford's functionality, the provincial government sent an excavator for emergency removal of the sedimentation (**Figure 20**). The neighbouring community voluntarily assisted with the emergency work.

The structure was confirmed to be stable even after the flooding, and the local government and communities took ownership of the ford.

(a) (b) (c)

Figure 20. Vented ford affected by a typhoon and emergency work done by the provincial government: (a) Overflowing; (b) deposited sedimentation; (c) removing the sedimentation by the excavator of the provincial government for emergency.

4.2.5. Impact

The access to the local town from village C has been improved drastically (**Figure 21**). Recognizing the effectiveness of vented ford, the provincial government adopted the structure and applied the same construction method at a nearby intersection of the same river and a provincial road.

(a) (b) (c)

Figure 21. Conditions at the intersection with the river before and after construction: (a) Before the construction; (b) after the construction; (c) the conditions one year after the construction.

4.3. Application to rural road improvement through capacity building of farmer/youth groups in Kenya

4.3.1. Rural road improvement and impact through capacity building of farmer and youth groups using Do-nou technology

Since 2008, Do-nou technology has been used in Kenya for spot improvement using the local resource base. The approach has been transferred to 125 farmer and youth groups (**Figure 22**). Training and demonstration groups have been held, generally involving 25 members over 10–15 days. These were organized at road sections identified as problematic by the group. Do-nou technology has been used to build base courses, retaining walls at both the inlet and the outlet of culverts, and abutments of wooden bridges, as shown in **Figure 23**. In most cases, the drainage system was also improved.

(a) (b)

Figure 22. Training/demonstration of spot improvement using Do-nou technology: (a) Training at road side; (b) demonstration on Do-nou technology.

Figure 23. Applications of Do-nou technology during training/demonstrations with farmer groups: (a) Before construction; (b) after the construction; (c) retaining wall at inlet of culvert; (d) Do-nou abutment of wooden bridge.

The training/demonstration sessions helped the trainees and neighbouring communities appreciate the benefits gained from the road works, such as better access to schools and hospitals throughout the year, reduction in public transportation fares and reduced loss of agricultural product.

However, after the training was completed, the groups were unable to continue the road projects by themselves, due to difficulties in collecting the necessary materials, in particular, granular soil for use in the bags and wearing course.

Cooperation with and supports from other stakeholders was therefore necessary to enable the community initiatives to continue. Do-nou technology and the concept of spot improvement using local resource-based approach must be understood by stakeholders such as government institutes and private road construction clients.

4.3.2. Dissemination of Do-nou technology in Kenya

Figure 24 shows the progress of the dissemination of Do-nou technology in Kenya.

Initially, to demonstrate improved access to markets of farmers, training and demonstrations were conducted with farmer groups on spot improvement using Do-nou technology. These training sessions, and the outcome of the technology, were reported to local authorities and to the Ministry of Agriculture, which was keen to promote market-oriented agriculture. However, little support or cooperation was gained to enable the road work to be continued.

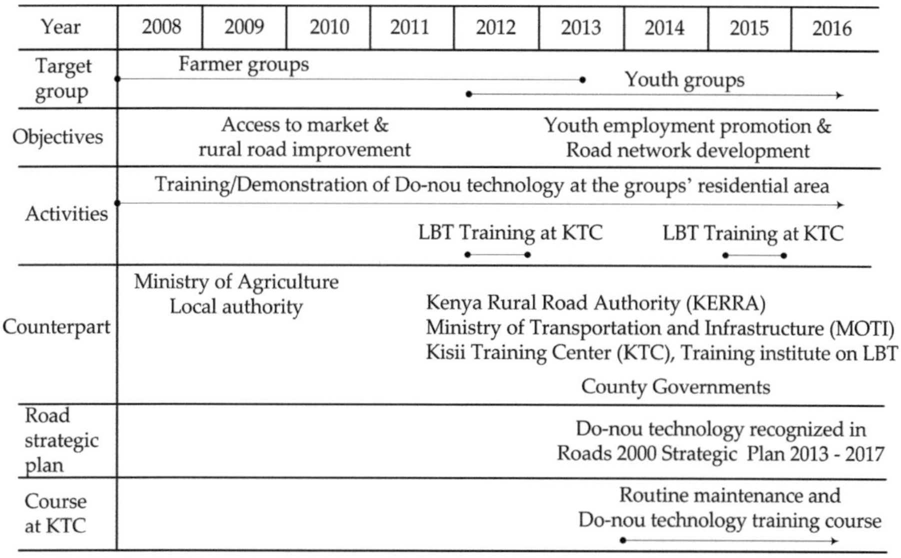

Figure 24. Progress of the dissemination of Do-nou technology.

Some of the farmer groups then established an association that undertook missions to improve rural access roads using their acquired knowledge of Do-nou technology. It was considered advantageous for the association to negotiate with stakeholders to gain their support and cooperation. However, opportunities for collaboration were limited and ad hoc, because the association was not a qualified contractor.

However, Do-nou technology was recognized by the Kenya Rural Road Authority following stakeholder meetings and field visits. The International Labour Organization funded a youth employment promotion project, in which youth groups were trained in Do-nou technology for spot improvement of their residential area. Their representatives participated in the training at the Kisii Training Center (KTC), which is the public training institute for LBT, for a six-week course on routine maintenance and business management. Ten of the 20 youth groups then established their own company, called Micro and Small Enterprises (MSEs), and began work. With the certification provided by the training course at KTC, the three companies registered as qualified contractors, allowing them to bid for government projects and thus expanding their business opportunities. Contracts for access road construction and other building works were also secured from other sectors apart from road administrators, such as health centers, schools, and churches.

In order to address the issue of youth unemployment meaningfully, the Kenyan government launched the policy, "Access to Government Procurement Opportunities", in which 30% of all government contracts were to be earmarked for youth, women, and persons with disability, without requiring competitive bidding against established firms [10]. The policy helped the youth groups that had learned Do-nou technology and joined the training course at KTC to further expand their businesses.

Do-nou technology was also recognized in the Roads 2000 Strategic Plan 2013–2017 [11], and a training course in routine maintenance and Do-nou technology was established in the KTC program.

In 2015, the Ministry of Transportation and Infrastructure (MOTI) allocated funds amounting to about USD 229,300 to train 120 youth members in the KTC course on routine maintenance and Do-nou technology. By May of 2016, about 30% of the graduates from the course had either established their own companies or registered as qualified contractors. MOTI is now planning to adopt a specification for Do-nou technology.

4.3.3. *Involving communities in road projects*

Based on the experience of capacity building in Kenya, four patterns for involving the local communities in road projects have been identified. These are summarized in **Figure 25**. Pattern A is the case of a conventional road project using LBT. Patterns B and C reflect the original

Pattern	A	B	C	D
Stakeholders involved	Government/ Private client ↓ *Contract* Contractor ↓ *Empoly as labour* Community	Farmer groups (Community)	Government/ Private client ↓ *Force account/ Contract* Association ⇧ *Registration* Farmer groups (Community)	Government/ Private client ↓ *Contract* Contractor *Contract* ↓ *Contract* Micro & Small Enterprises ⇧ *Training/Certificate/ Registration* Youth groups (Community)
Technology/skill to be trained to community	Road works of LBT Instructed by contractors	Spot improvement using Do-nou technology, Group management	Spot improvement using Do-nou technology, Group management	Spot improvement using Do-nou technology, Company registration, Routine maintenance, Business management
Objectives	Road network development	Access to markets and social services	Access to markets and social services	Youth employment promotion/ Road network development
Target road	Rural roads	Rural access roads/ Unclassified roads	Rural access roads/ Unclassified roads	Rural roads
Advantage	Rural road are improved to meet to engineering and technical standard.	Problematic portions communities suffered are improved. Only simple training is required.	Problematic portions communities suffered are improved. Only simple training is required.	Youth employment is promoted. Road network is maintained.
Disadvantage	A certain amount of budget is required.	Organized/self-reliant group (community) can apply. The scope of work is very basic. Support/ cooperation is required.	Cohesive association can apply. The scope of work is basic. Business chance is limited.	Comprehensive training is required. Establishment company, registration as contractors are necessary.

Figure 25. Patterns of involvement in road works.

purpose of developing and transferring spot improvement using a local resource-based approach, which was to provide access to communities excluded from conventional road projects executed by government institutes. Both patterns present challenges in the sustainability of road projects undertaken by communities themselves. The cohesiveness and self-reliance of the groups is key in these patterns. Support and cooperation in the provision of materials help to make the community road projects sustainable and to ensure the continuing accessibility of the rural roads.

In Pattern D, a combination of government policies on youth employment and Do-nou technology training forms the basis for helping youth launch businesses as contractors. Subsidization of the training fee (about USD 1500 per person) for a comprehensive training course on routine maintenance and business management is necessary. The commitment of those graduating from the course supports the establishment of MSEs and the registration of participants as contractor.

5. Lessons from case studies

In line with the SDGs goal of leaving no one behind, research was conducted on the provision of access to markets and social services for rural people in developing countries. Road projects executed both by government institutes and by local community initiatives were considered to be key measures for improving the conditions of rural roads. To enable work to be managed by the communities with unskilled workers, and with local resources, spot improvement using a local resource-based approach was applied. Do-nou technology was transferred to the communities and used in the improvement of problematic road sections in Asia and Africa.

In Myanmar, the road embankment and concrete pavement with retaining wall built with Do-nou were constructed. The design was intended to be the most practical for the communities and at the same time to make the portions passable all the year. For this case, not only Do-nou bags and soil, but also cement was required.

The communities were motivated with the simple but effective technology and working hard to acquire the technology and complete the road structure. The communities was well-organized and had mind-set of self-reliance so that they applied the technology to the other portion by procuring the necessary material by themselves.

The case in Myanmar demonstrates that communities that are organized and self-reliant can apply Do-nou technology sustainably, improving and maintaining their rural roads. This is a good example of the Pattern B shown in **Figure 25**.

In the case of the Philippines, funds, technical advice and mobilization of stakeholders were provided by NGOs, local governments and communities. By working together, they were able to solve the flooding problem at the intersection of a road and a river. Do-nou technology shortened the construction period and enabled all of the members to participate in the work. The NGOs played an essential role in ensuring the success of this collaborative project between government and community. Such projects can supplement government executed road projects, supporting the improvement of rural access roads.

In Kenya, government policy on youth employment promotion helped the technology gain recognition, and it was then adopted into the training courses run by KTC. Training in Do-nou technology provided the first step in converting unemployment youth into contractors. A specification for Do-nou technology is scheduled to be adopted by the Kenyan government. Adoption may increase the willingness of government or other stakeholders to provide support or to collaborate with communities that wish to improve their rural roads using Do-nou technology.

These case studies demonstrate that spot improvement and the use of locally available material approach can provide socioeconomic benefits to communities that have been isolated for years from the government and donor agency interventions in infrastructure development. Feasible designs have been developed, in accordance with the proposed approach, for the construction of base courses, retaining walls, foundations of bridges, bridges and causeways. These designs can be applied over wide areas and modified to reflect the unique conditions of each project area. The experience gained in community mobilization and stakeholder involvement, which is an essential in the proposed approach, can serve as a guide when it is applied in a new area.

In order to improve rural roads and make communities resilient to the road problem, Do-nou technology, as applied to spot improvement of rural roads using a local resource-based approach, has been transferred to 25 countries in Asia, the Pacific, Africa and Middle and South America. One of the solutions to long-neglected road problems in rural area has been developed. Research will continue to develop further appropriate technologies, accumulate and analyse cases of community mobilization, and collaboration between stakeholders and communities, and develop designs for structures under unique conditions using different types of local materials.

Acknowledgements

The case in Myanmar was implemented with the fund from Ministry of Foreign Affair of Japanese Government. The case in the Philippines was funded by the Japan International Cooperation Funds. The cases in Kenya were funded by Toyota Foundation, Ministry of Foreign Affair of Japanese Government and International Labour Organization. The authors would like to acknowledge those donors and all the people who are related to the projects.

Author details

Yoshinori Fukubayashi[1*] and Makoto Kimura[2]

*Address all correspondence to: yfukurin@gmail.com

1 Community Road Empowerment (INGO), Kyoto, Japan

2 Graduate School of Engineering, Kyoto University, Kyoto, Japan

References

[1] Matsuoka, H., Liu, S. New earth reinforcement method by soilbags ("DONOW"). Soils and foundations. 2003;43(6):173–188. doi:10.3208/sandf.43.6_173

[2] Fukubayashi, Y., Kimura, M. Improvement of rural access roads in developing countries with initiative for self-reliance of communities. Soils and Foundations. 2014;54(1): 23–35. doi:10.1016/j.sandf.2013.12.003

[3] Lebo, J., Schelling, D. Design and appraisal of rural transport infrastructure: ensuring basic access for rural communities. World Bank Technical Report. 2001;496: 96 p.

[4] The United Nations. Transforming our world: the 2030 agenda for sustainable development [Internet]. 2015/09/25. Available from: https://sustainabledevelopment.un.org/post2015/transformingourworld [Accessed: 2016/08/10].

[5] Johannessen, B. Building Rural Roads. Bangkok: The International Labour Organization; 2008. 466 p.

[6] ILO, Don Bosco. Manual, Labour-Based Technology for Rural Road Maintenance. 1st ed. Timor-Lestei: ILO & Don Bosco; 2014. 130 p.

[7] Ethiopian Roads Authority. Design Manual for Low Volume Road [Internet]. 2011/04. Available from: http://www.era.gov.et/Publications/ERAsManualsStandards/Design-Manuals.aspx [Accessed: 2016/08/10].

[8] Ministry of Transport and Communications. Road Design Manual Part III Materials and Pavement Design for New Roads. Kenya; 1987. 218 p.

[9] Kenya Roads Board. Road Conditions [Internet]. Available from: http://www.krb.go.ke/78-webcontent/87-road-conditions [Accessed: 2016/08/10].

[10] Access to Government Procurement Opportunities. Available from: http://agpo.go.ke/ [Accessed: 2016/08/10].

[11] Ministry of Road. Roads 2000 Strategic Plan 2013–2017. Kenya; 2012. 101 p.

Chapter 6

Natural Disaster and International Development

Luke Strongman

Additional information is available at the end of the chapter

http://dx.doi.org/10.5772/67063

Abstract

Recovery from natural disaster has for many years been seen in objective terms as simply the time taken to replace damaged infrastructure. Increasingly, however, social scientists are describing the large part that human capital plays in the recovery from natural disaster in the form of 'resilience'. The purpose of the chapter is to delineate, from a social scientific perspective, the main factors involved in disaster rehabilitation from a necessarily superficial but nevertheless accurate and useful viewpoint. The main areas to be considered are infrastructural impacts, psychological impacts and communication factors. The chapter concludes by defining various perspectives that contribute to the quality of resilience that underscores the investment in human capital in post-disaster zones.

Keywords: natural disaster, infrastructure, psychology, social networks, psychological effects, communication, resilience

1. Introduction

A natural disaster is a major adverse event resulting from natural processes of the earth. Natural disasters may have the properties of being environmentally disruptive (war, earthquake, flood), a hazard (major but temporary disruption to environment) and/or socially focused (no major impact on land or infrastructure but on a human populous). The classic definition of a disaster is of an 'occurrence causing widespread disruption or distress'. As Lindell points out, a disaster may be characterised by three temporal periods—pre-impact, trans-impact and postimpact; however, some disasters have multiple or secondary impacts [1]. Furthermore, disasters are sometimes identified by a series of impact zones which display irregularities in effect. In general, society tends to have more knowledge about what has gone wrong in natural disasters than what goes right in recovery [2]. Even today, relatively little is known about how quickly an area affected by natural disaster may be rehabilitated and in what circumstances and under what conditions. As the World Bank reported in 2014:

> *During the 1980–2012 period, estimated total reported losses due to disasters amounted is US$3.8 trillion.... Hydro-meteorological disasters accounted for 74% (US$2.6 trillion) of total reported losses, 78% (18,200) of total disasters and 61% (1.4 million) of total lives lost. Looking ahead, climate change will have major implications on global ecosystems, agriculture and water supply, sea level rise and storm surges [3].*

It can be argued that natural and human-made disasters that effect human populations are becoming more common worldwide due to a myriad of factors related to population growth and urbanisation. But in fact natural disasters are not becoming more prevalent; rather, there is increased reporting of them. In fact, as Lowrey et al. point out, of the 15,833 reported disasters worldwide from 1900 to 2006, over a third of these occurred between 2000 and 2006 [4]. Nevertheless, the prevalence of natural disasters themselves is unlikely to be much increasing, though the reporting of them is, but as Strömberg states, '... the average magnitude of the reported disasters has fallen' [5]. While more than half the globe becomes urbanised, the prevalence of the effect of natural disasters is greater than previously experienced, although due to increased technical know-how in building and in healthcare, the effects of natural disasters may be decreasing.

It is possible that prior to modernisation, urbanisation and globalisation, many events that could have been assigned the status of natural disaster remained unreported due to their geographical remoteness or the lack of impact on large populated areas. It is therefore not strange that the incidence of natural disaster causing events is increasing, though the impact of them has become more measured. In this context rehabilitation from natural disaster is a topic that increasingly necessitates a multidisciplinary approach to social scientific analysis.

Traditionally it was assumed that disaster recovery would be predicated on the extent of damage within a natural disaster zone. As Lindell points out, disaster effects may be determined by three pre-impact conditions: 'hazard exposure, physical vulnerability and social vulnerability—as well as three event-specific conditions—hazard event characteristics, improvised disaster responses and improvised disaster recovery' [6]. It is no longer necessarily the case that as Dacy and Kunreuther state that '[i]t just seems reasonable to assume that the speed of recovery following a disaster will be determined primarily by the magnitude of the physical damage' [7]. Rather, increasingly social networks and community resilience are shown to play a larger part in recovery from catastrophe than simply that measured by the restoration of infrastructure. The overcoming of catastrophe does not produce replacement communities; it produces reinvented, renewed and differently evolved communities. As Dynes has suggested, based on experiences of survivors in a number of disasters, social capital may be the basis for resilience as it provides information and resources at a critical moment [8]. However, as Aldrich relates, population density (the population per unit area) determines the rate of recovery, the greater the density the population conversely the more slowly it may recover due to the difficulty in providing permanent and temporary housing in the disaster period [9]. Consequently, rather than area damage, some social scientists have argued that population density—the population per unit area—alters the rate of recovery. Areas with greater population densities may recover more slowly because of the difficulty in providing temporary and permanent housing for displaced people during the post-disaster period. Nevertheless, there are behavioural typologies which do produce resilient and rehabilitated communities.

Structural vulnerability	Extreme stresses	High wind, seismic shaking
Physical vulnerability	Susceptibility to biological changes—casualties	Impacts on anatomical structures and physiological functioning
Social vulnerability	Limitations in physical assets	Buildings, contents
	Psychological	Knowledge, skills and abilities
	Social	Community integration
	Economic	Financial savings
	Political	Public policy resources

Table 1. Factors of vulnerability in disaster impacts (after Lindell [1, 6, 42]).

According to Aldrich, four factors are thought to influence the rate of recovery from disaster zones resulting from earthquakes. These are the amount of damage, the population density of the affected area, the efficacy of human capital and the amount of available economic capital [2]. As Ross and Carter explain, '[t]he spontaneous activation of "social capital"—bonds within and between social groups—has been impressive, a solace to those affected, as well as a huge practical and economic benefit. Organised volunteers, such as from the Red Cross, were the foundation of evacuation centres' [10]. However, Aldrich also notes that 'social capital', namely, the 'networks, norms and social trust that facilitate coordination and cooperation for mutual benefit' [11], best predicted a population recovery. 'Human capital' is the ability of people to remain cooperative and resilient in communities and to work in a coordinated way together on sustainable relief. This is a requisite of community rehabilitation from earthquakes. Finally, Lindell suggests that '[p]hysical impacts can be reduced by hazard mitigation practices and emergency preparedness practices, whereas social impacts can be reduced by recovery preparedness practices' [6]. This requires extensive pre-impact planning (see **Table 1**).

2. Factors in society for consideration for international development

2.1. Building and infrastructure

Arguably, permanence may be sacrificed for flexibility in earthquake environments when infrastructure is considered. Since at least 1751 and the devastation of the earthquake at Port-au-Prince in the Caribbean Haiti, it has been known that timber structures (houses and buildings) are able to withstand earthquakes more easily due to their flexibility of construction design [12]. Even in contemporary cities which are earthquake prone, buildings of mid-height (ten levels or under) built on base isolators which separate the motion of the building from the land underneath, or that have counterweights which control the extent of 'sway', perform best in earthquakes. So while a sense of relative permanence in built materials is sacrificed, nevertheless, in domestic architecture timber constructions are able to withstand many of the violent movements associated with earthquakes. The domestic built environment of colonial settlements was largely accomplished in timber constructions—that being the readily available material in comparison to stone used in public structures. Such domestic infrastructure could sustain rebuilding. But choice and style of rebuilding materials are not the only considerations in earthquake-zone rehabilitation.

2.2. Social networks

Motivation, empathy and communication play a tangible role in disaster rehabilitation as do resources required to rebuild infrastructure. Furthermore, social ties serve as informal insurance; people also network for financial, physical and logistical guidance. Networked communities are more politically active and better connected to overcome barriers to demand. Information sharing also increases with trust; however, embedded networks raise the cost of an 'exit' for individuals from a community (in terms of benefits forfeited). Furthermore, closely interlinked communities increase the probability that demands are articulated and obstacles are overcome. However, in communities with a comparatively higher level of social capital, individuals and groups can work towards a solution [13].

As the English Parliamentary Office of Science and Technology (2012) state:

> *Bangladesh is an example of a country where the spread of mobile phones and improved scientific understanding of natural hazards has helped reduce the number of deaths caused by annual flooding and more extreme hazards, such as cyclones. These advances have been exploited effectively through enhanced contingency planning and early warning systems. The mobile phone network does not reach everyone, but once the message is out, other solutions, like cyclists with megaphones, can be used [14].*

Sebag-Montefiore noted that after the quake and tsunami in eastern Japan in 2012, the disaster provoked an 'unprecedented mobilisation of volunteers, public outcry following the Fukushima cover-up…the stirrings of new construction and architectural ambitions [and a] prevalent feeling among the young [to] pave the way to discard the stifling traditions of the past, including the patriarchal customs of provincial cities' [15]. This includes artistic and artisan responses such as mural paintings and the remaking of 22.5 million tons of tsunami debris into furniture (an enterprise also featured in the response to the Christchurch earthquakes of 2010 and 2011). Thus, recovery from loss is a key motivational factor, along with self and other community rehabilitations and new business opportunities that evolve from adapting dislocated environments into restructured ones. However, natural disaster environments can also serve as nodal points for learning.

Olshansky outlines seven lessons learned from reconstructions following natural disasters. These are [16]:

- Economic and social networks are more resilient than buildings—recovery begins with people first.
- Taking time to plan to ensure full participation of stakeholders is necessary in reconstruction and is proportionate to speed of recovery.
- Bureaucracies tend to lack the flexibility for community-based organisations emerge.
- Areas with fewest resources get minimal attention from aid organisations.
- Relocation is resisted by citizens, but without citizen support, relocations often fail.

http://dx.doi.org/10.5772/67063

- Cities see some improvement after disasters but never as much as planners intend; improvement occurs over a longer-than-expected timescale.
- Setting funding priorities is a difficult part of recovery—money is always insufficient.

Consequently, recovery from natural disasters always takes longer than most initial planning indicates. Disasters radically alter community and societal equilibrium and create huge differentials in experiences which take a long time to readjust from.

2.3. Building and infrastructure: historical sources

Olshansky argues that lessons learned from the Kobe earthquake in Japan, in 1995, involve three main factors. These are, firstly, the development of a clear vision in post-disaster response; secondly, an emphasis on people (community, welfare, health and habitat) and, thirdly, thinking creatively about property—temporary and permanent housing facilities and new sustainable building designs and materials [17]. The maintenance of social networks is considered necessary. Relatedly, an historical example shows what can be accomplished by modernisation. A memorandum (termed the Dissertação) by Manuel da Maia who was responsible for the elaboration of proposals for the renovation of the lower area of Lisbon in the wake of the 1755 earthquake (and Reconstruction Plan of 1758) revealed a method for fair transfer of old properties into new ones with appropriate equivalent values. This was achieved by 'dividing the total new surface area created within the Plan by the total value of the old properties'. The result was uniformity of architectural facades and increased modularity [18]. One of the central features of the rebuild was a Property Register established after the earthquake and fire, in which a record of the ownership and state of buildings was maintained—surveying the dimensions of 'streets, squares, public and private building' [18]. Thus, modernism was progressed in large part on quantification of infrastructure relative to value.

2.4. Building and infrastructure: modern examples

In Christchurch, Canterbury, New Zealand, following the devastating earthquakes of 2010 and 2011, the Canterbury Earthquake Recovery Authority (CERA) divided its response plan into four strategic areas of social, economic, natural and built but also leadership and integration applying to the other areas; the CERA Act defines 'rebuilding' as pertaining to physical resources and communities as well as 'improvement' and 'enhancement' of the latter in the recovery [19]. In the post-disaster environment, opportunities become apparent to incorporate new sustainable building practices into redevelopments and to adapt and reinvent environments from relocated materials. Building innovations might include 'green' building (or building in sympathy with the natural environment) and designing for maximum efficiency, for example, by practices which involve renewable energy sources or insulation and adoption of technological innovations such as building information modelling. Eversely has argued that evidence from Haiti after the devastating 2010 quake near Port-au-Prince, '... the single most important resource in the hours and days immediately following such events, relevant knowhow and practical help will become vital too' [20]. According to Gill cited in Eversely, '[i]t also involves replacing or upgrading basic water and electricity infrastructure, providing immediate areas for markets and other informal trading and providing materials and on-site advice for early self-help reconstruction by Haiti: replacement housing needs to be resilient to future disaster risks families and small communities. Finally it calls for a focus for continuing governance' [20]. Clearly, for developing communities, commerce, trade, durable physical resources and human capital and organisation are critically important. However, time is another all important factor—and the recognition of a cityscape that is both pre- and post-quake. As Jonathan Ling, chief executive of Fletcher Building Ltd., the company appointed by the government as project manager for the reconstruction of homes damaged in the September 4, 2010 and February 22, 2011, quake, much of the Christchurch rebuild said, 'There will not be a finite day on which this is finished'. 'There will be new buildings going up' in the central business district, Mr. Ling said, 'on empty blocks probably for 10, 15 or 20 years' [21]. Some of the uninhabited blocks will change owners numerous times before they are eventually built on.

Three years following the Christchurch quakes, the inner-city landscape is denuded of building—over 1000 demolitions have taken place (1611 full or partial demolitions were scheduled in total). The atmosphere is one of floating shells of building amid the dissolving remnants of built space. Familiar landmarks remain, but they are sighted from unfamiliar angles. Thus, the imagined pace of a rebuilt Christchurch assumes its shape progressively, incrementally amid the barren spaces of urban renewal. Amid the hiatus in construction plans stands the Spartan and surprisingly uniform and unornamented remnants of a built cityscape. The predominant remaining buildings are 1970s concrete multistoreys (under ten storeys), indicating there must have been an engineering practice in reinforced concrete introduced during this era that made these buildings more resilient to the movement that causes earthquake damage. While the vast majority of community aid following disaster is based on infrastructure rehabilitation, social networks are also an important aspect of rebuilding and the nurturing of social networks develops trust and interconnectedness [22]. However, it is the social effect of the trauma of earthquake, or constant demolition, or the large rents in the fabric of the built form that has characterised Christchurch's citizen's everyday lives that also demands the most attention. Trauma is partly characterised as 'loss of communality' [23]. The effect of trauma on the psychology of the earthquake survivors cannot be underestimated and ameliorative processes are regarded to be 'restoring connectedness, social support and a sense of collective efficacy' [24]. If there is one concept that summarises the requisites for survival during and after natural disaster, it is resilience. As Smith et al. explain, '[r]esilience is the ability of an individual or group to carry on and solve problems so that survival of hard times is more likely' [25]. Furthermore, resilience is a protective factor that describes an ability to rebound, make improvements in physical or psychosocial conditions and to recover from loss or illness [26]. Resilient behaviours include motivational contributions to others' lives, strengthening of coping skills, improving knowledge about caring activities and encouragement with nurturing activities [27]. People with higher health ratings report lower depressive symptom scores but higher resilience scores [27]. This is consistent with people enjoying good health having a higher band of tolerance for minor negative health problems.

2.5. Psychological effects

As Somasundaram and Sivayokan observe, both natural and man-made disasters are recognised as causing a variety of 'psychological and psychiatric sequelae' [23]. Sometimes, people at risk from natural disaster don't prepare for its eventuality because to acknowledge the need for preparation creates anxiety. Montgomery and Morris (n.d.) point out that people at risk have two choices—either to behave in ways that reduce risk or to discount the risk [28]. Thus, taking precautions to prepare for a disaster also needs people to manage their anxiety. Three orders of response are possible. These include adaptive and resilient coping responses, nonpathological distress and maladaptive behavioural patterns to diagnosable psychiatric disorders [23]. Collective traumatisation may result for large groups of effected people and 'loss of community' but is also best addressed by community interventions along the dimensions—economic development, social capital, information and communication and community competence [29]. However, after large-scale natural disasters, the effects of community disturbance may be prolonged. As Gordon and Fleming state, 'In the third year after a disaster the immediate crisis has passed. International experience shows that in most cases people have confirmation of their personal situations—problems and opportunities—and can begin to heal' [30]. In any context health is seen as '… complete physical, mental, familial, social, cultural, spiritual and ecological well-being and not merely an absence of disease or infirmity' (WHO) (see **Figure 1**) [31] [24].

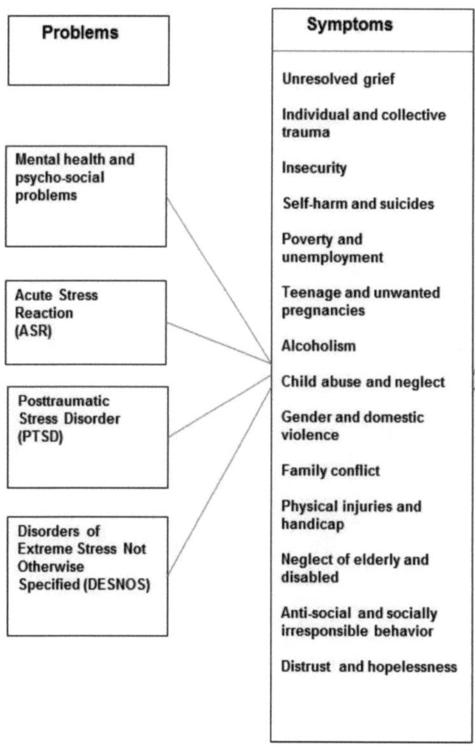

Figure 1. Problems, symptoms and protections of mental health issues in disaster zones.

Norris et al. identify higher rates of anxiety following disaster and depression. They identify five main effects in the post-disaster scenario. These are non-specific distress, health problems or concerns (somatic complaints and medical conditions, quality of sleep), chronic problems in living (interpersonal relationships, occupational stress and financial stress, ecological stress), psychosocial resource loss (perceived social support, social embeddedness, self-efficacy, optimism) and problems specific to youth (clinginess, dependence, loss of sleep, aggressive behaviour, separation anxiety) [32]. As Weine points out, it is only comparatively recently that scholars have integrated 'social capital measures into a quantitative study of rehabilitation' [33]. Social capital is defined as the 'networks, norms and social trust that facilitate coordination and cooperation for mutual benefit' [11]. Quantitative study of rehabilitation has tended to focus on the restoration of infrastructural facilities and the capital input in so doing as opposed to the human causal linkages that bring such restoration into effect. Relatedly, areas with larger population density recover after disasters more slowly because of the difficulty in providing temporary housing. However, the traditional formula for the recovery rate is provided by Dacy and Kunreuther who argue that 'the speed of recovery following a disaster will be determined primarily by the magnitude of physical damage' [7]. It was thus thought that the amount of damage would determine the rate of recovery, but more recent research has turned instead to community regeneration through the resilience of social capital in post-crisis recovery [34]. As Weine also suggests, social ties form a kind of 'informal insurance' of ready-made support networks—providing information, financial and administrative support and guidance. Politically active communities can present demands and extract resources better. Trustworthy neighbours share information, prevent duping and looting and maintain the relative integrity of community relations [35]. Furthermore, embedded networks raise the costs of 'exit' for individuals—as networks carry latent effects which benefit individuals in a shared community. Such networked neighbourhood (rich in human capital) is more likely to articulate community needs to authorities and work together to overcome obstacles [36]. Thus, it stands to reason, if, following catastrophe efforts and made to strengthen social networks, leading to a better chance of recovery. There is a second reason why social capital is a constituent factor for community resilience and urban renewal and that is because it enables the mobilisation of information and resources at critical moments [37].

2.6. Communication factors

Lien et al. state that survival in post-disaster zones is most likely if people (trapped by building collapses in earthquakes) are rescued within 72 h [38]. Survival tolerance probably diminishes after 3 days. The question then becomes what are effective communication practices for post-disaster zones. As Quintanilla states, 'It is critically important that affected communities know how, when and where aid services can be accessed, what's going on around them and how they can connect with aid providers' [39]. The need for information increases and the availability and clarity of information decreases. In terms of hardware requirements for communication after natural disasters, in developed societies where information and computer technology (ICT) is prevalent, the environmental constraints for a disaster area may include temporary Internet links, unavailability of servers and limited or no Internet access. However, where broadband computing is available through relief or remaining facilities, communication is improved when devices with simple interfaces are used, Wi-Fi notebook formats are popular and where power generation is also available [40]. New technologies—mobile, SMS, social media—increase the ability to access quality information [41]. Reliability and trustworthiness of information is deemed critical. Information-sharing networks can quickly disseminate news, for example, via mobile phone texting or the Twitter service. In this context, peoples' responses to disaster are not always that of panicked confusion; rather, there is an adaptive response termed normalcy bias that provokes 'confirmation' prior to remediation or protective action [42]. As Aldrich relates, '[i]f social networks prove to be an important part of the rebuilding process, then aid givers should allocate resources to ensure that social structures are not damaged in the evacuation and resettlement processes' [43]. In post-disaster environments, most people respond by texting or tweeting about uncertain or precarious conditions if they are in densely populated areas, while those in remote areas will communicate whether or not they are safe; as Longstaff and Yang state in an immediate post-disaster situation such as an earthquake, individuals and organisations require an ability to receive (and transmit) information in secure trustworthy routes (to report damage and rehabilitation needs) and in the absence of such systems, panic may ensue [44]. Therefore, information sharing through effective communication systems is a form of investment in social capital, or 'safety valve', which helps to strengthen community resilience. As Quintanilla suggests, '... communication itself is a form of aid' [45]. Secondary communication issues include mitigation of real threats companies might suffer to their operational abilities; these might include collapse of the share price, serious legal claims, loss of credit, possible bankruptcy, damage to the company's image or reputation, loss of employees and possible closure [46]. Mitigation is best achieved through planning. However, communication in a crisis needs clarity and conciseness; it needs logical progression, a focus on the facts and the avoidance of jargon [47].

3. Conclusion: resilience in disasters

History has shown that while natural disasters are by definition, devastating, survivors can rebuild their lives given the opportunity. In combination with the complex rebuilding of infrastructure in post-disaster zones, social scientists and human resource practitioners are increasingly advocating that a psychology of resilience is necessary for community rebuilding. Resilience is defined by Norris as 'A process linking a set of adaptive capacities to a positive trajectory of functioning and adaptation after a disturbance' [48]. Longstaff and Yang observe that resilience is the 'capacity of a system to absorb disturbance, undergo change' yet still functions in the same way [49]. Thus, resilience is the ability of a system to recover from setback with no major change in its form or functioning. Norris also defines five dimensions along which resilience may be enhanced by 'networked adaptive capacities'. These are, firstly, developing economic resources—reducing inequities; secondly, enhancing social capital through minimising harm through damage mitigation; thirdly, adaption and utilisation of pre-existing organisational networks; fourthly, protecting naturally occurring social supports and, fifthly, community planning [48]. Consequently, central planners engaged in community rehabilitation strategies should look to strengthen these community functions in post-catastrophe environments. Hence, resilience may refer to adaptive governance 'across spatial scales (local to national) and between sectors (government, community)'; it may refer to knowledge, communication and social learning; maintaining a positive outlook and drawing on social networks for support [10]. Surviving a natural catastrophe and rebuilding a community after it require the investment in human capital which has the quality of being able to be self-sustaining by exhibiting resilience.

Author details

Luke Strongman

Luke.Strongman@OpenPolytechnic.ac.nz

Social Sciences, Open Polytechnic of New Zealand, Lower Hutt, New Zealand

References

[1] M. K. Lindell, Disaster studies. *Current Sociological Review*. 61, 5–6, 797 (2013).

[2] D. P. Aldrich, Social, not physical, infrastructure: the critical role of civil society after the 1923 Tokyo earthquake. *Disasters*. 36, 3, 398 (2012).

[3] The World Bank, Managing Disaster Risks for Resilient Development. Retrieved from: http://www.worldbank.org/en/results/2013/04/12/managing-disaster-risks-resilient-development (2014, April 10).

[4] W. Lowrey, W. Evans, K. K. Gower, J. A. Robinson, P. M. Ginter, L. C. McCormick and M. Abdolrasulina, Effective media communication of disasters: pressing problems and recommendations. *BMC Public Health*. 7, 97, 2 (2007).

[5] D. Strömberg, Natural disasters, economic development and humanitarian aid. *Journal of Economic Perspectives*. 21, 3, 202 (2007).

[6] M. K. Lindell, Disaster studies. *Current Sociological Review*. 61, 5–6, 799 (2013).

[7] D. C. Dacy and H. Kunreuther, *The Economics of Natural Disasters: Implications for Federal Policy*. (New York, NY: The Free Press, 1969). p. 72.

[8] R. R. Dynes, The dialogue between Voltaire and Rousseau on the Lisbon earthquake: the emergence of a social science view. *University of Delaware Disaster Research Center Preliminary Paper*. 293, 399–400 (1999).

[9] D. P. Aldrich, Social, not physical, infrastructure: the critical role of civil society after the 1923 Tokyo earthquake. *Disasters*. 36, 3, 399–400 (2012).

[10] H. Ross and R. W. Carter, Natural disasters and community resilience. *Australasian Journal of Environmental Management*. 18, 1, 2 (2011).

[11] R. Putnam, Bowling alone: America's declining social capital. *Journal of Democracy*. 6, 1, 67 (1995).

[12] J-F. Mouhot, History matters. The tragic annals of Haiti. *History Today*. 60, 4 ,3 (2010, April).

[13] D. P. Aldrich, Social, not physical, infrastructure: the critical role of civil society after the 1923 Tokyo earthquake. *Disasters*. 36, 3, 401 (2012).

[14] The Parliamentary Office of Science and Technology, Resilience to Natural Hazards in Developing Nations. *Postnote* 402. Retrieved from: www.parliament.uk/briefing-papers/POST-PN-402.pdf (2012).

[15] C. Sebag-Montefiore, Tradition, washed away. *New Statesman*. 141, 5095, 14 (2012, 5th March).

[16] R. Olshansky, San Francisco, New Orleans: lessons for rebuilding. *Social Policy*. 36, 2, 17 (2005–2006).

[17] R. Olshansky, San Francisco, New Orleans: lessons for rebuilding. *Social Policy*. 36, 2, 18 (2005–2006).

[18] R. Dos Santos, M. Helena, S. I. Trias and T. S. I. Ferran, Trading properties after the earthquake: the rebuilding of eighteenth-century Lisbon, *Planning Perspectives*. 26, 2, 302 (2011).

[19] V. Smith, C. Hart and S. Oliver, What CERA did. *Planning Quarterly*. Issue 183, 27 (2011).

[20] J. Eversely, RTPI News. Post-earthquake rebuild underlines need for professions' joint approach. *Planning Issue*. 1854, 24 (2010).

[21] J. Ling cited Chris Bourke, Christchurch Faces 20-Year Post-Quake Rebuild, Fletcher CEO Says. Bloombergo.com (April 26, 2011)

[22] S. M. Weine, Developing preventive mental health interventions for refugee families in resettlement. *Family Process*. 50, 3, 412 (2011).

[23] D. Somasundaram and S. Sivayokan, Rebuilding community resilience in a post-war context: developing insight and recommendations – a qualitative study in Northern Sri Lanka. *International Journal of Mental Health Systems*. 7, 3, 2 (2013).

[24] D. Somasundaram and S. Sivayokan, Rebuilding community resilience in a post-war context: developing insight and recommendations – a qualitative study in Northern Sri Lanka. *International Journal of Mental Health Systems*. 7, 3, 3 (2013).

[25] P. R. Smith, Resilience: resistance factor for depressive symptom. *Journal of Psychiatric and Mental Health Nursing*. 16, 829 (2009).

[26] P. R. Smith, Resilience: resistance factor for depressive symptom. *Journal of Psychiatric and Mental Health Nursing*. 16, 831 (2009).

[27] P. R. Smith, Resilience: resistance factor for depressive symptom. *Journal of Psychiatric and Mental Health Nursing*. 16, 835 (2009).

[28] B. Montgomery and L. Morris, (n.d), Psychological Responses to Disasters – Facilitating Preparedness and Recovery. Retrieved from: http://csrp.hku.hk/files/1010_3818_941.pdf

[29] D. Somasundaram and S. Sivayokan, Rebuilding community resilience in a post-war context: developing insight and recommendations – a qualitative study in Northern Sri Lanka. *International Journal of Mental Health Systems*. 7, 3, 4 (2013).

[30] R. Gordon and P. Fleming, Red Cross. News Release: Red Cross Continues Its Support for the People of Christchurch. Retrieved from: https://www.redcross.org.nz/yk-files/836f6024aca36c04a2e6368e42534223/Feb%2022%20media%20release%20.pdf (20 February 2013).

[31] World Health Organization, *The Constitution of the WHO*. (Geneva: World Health Organization, 1948).

[32] F. H. Norris, M. J. Friedman, P. J. Watson, 60,000 disaster victims speak: part 1. An empirical review of the empirical literature, 1981–2001. *Psychiatry*. 65, 3, 216–217 (2002).

[33] S. M. Weine, Developing preventive mental health interventions for refugee families in resettlement. *Family Process*. 50, 3, 410–430 (2011).

[34] S. M. Weine, Developing preventive mental health interventions for refugee families in resettlement. *Family Process*. 50, 3, 400 (2011).

[35] S. M. Weine, Developing preventive mental health interventions for refugee families in resettlement. *Family Process*. 50, 3, 401 (2011).

[36] A. O. Hirschman, *Exit, Voice and Loyalty: Responses to Decline in Firms, Organizations and States*. (Cambridge, MA: Harvard University Press, 1970).

[37] R. Dynes, The dialogue between Voltaire and Rousseau on the Lisbon earthquake: the emergence of a social science view. *University of Delaware Disaster Research Center Preliminary Paper*. 293 (1999).

[38] Y-N. Lien, H-C. Jang and T-C. Tsai, A MANET based emergency communication and information system for catastrophic natural disasters. In *2009 29th IEEE International Conference on Distributed Computing Systems Workshops*. (2009). p. 412.

[39] J. Quintanilla, Disaster communications: covering the last mile. *Guardian Professional*. Retrieved from: http://www.theguardian.com/global-development-professionals-network/2013/apr/03/disaster-communications-ict-internews. (2013, April 3rd). Para. 2.

[40] Y-N. Lien, H-C. Jang and T-C. Tsai, A MANET based emergency communication and information system for catastrophic natural disasters. In *2009 29th IEEE International Conference on Distributed Computing Systems Workshops*. (2009). p. 414.

[41] J. Quintanilla, Disaster communications: covering the last mile. *Guardian Professional*. Retrieved from: http://www.theguardian.com/global-development-professionals-network/2013/apr/03/disaster-communications-ict-internews. (2013, April 3rd). Para. 5.

[42] M. K. Lindell, Disaster studies. *Current Sociological Review*. 61, 5–6, 806 (2013).

[43] D. P. Aldrich, Social, not physical, infrastructure: the critical role of civil society after the 1923 Tokyo earthquake. *Disasters*. 36, 3, 412 (2012).

[44] P. H. Longstaff and S-U. Yang, Communication management and trust: their role in building resilience to "surprises" such as natural disasters, pandemic flu and terrorism. *Ecology and Society*. 13, 1. Retrieved from: http://www.ecologyandsociety.org/vol13/iss1/art3/ (2008). p. 3.

[45] J. Quintanilla, Disaster communications: covering the last mile. *Guardian Professional.* Retrieved from: http://www.theguardian.com/global-development-professionals-network/2013/apr/03/disaster-communications-ict-internews. (2013, April 3rd). Para. 13

[46] P. F. Anthonissen, (Edit.). *Crisis Communication: practical strategies for reputation management and company survival.* (London and Philadelphia: Kogan Page, 2008). p. 13

[47] N. Leighton, S. Pellegrino and T. Shelton, There is no substitute for media training – 'No comment' just won't cut it any more (pp. 132–141). In P. F. Anthonissen, (Edit.). *Crisis Communication: practical strategies for reputation management and company survival.* (London and Philadelphia: Kogan Page, 2008). pp. 138–139.

[48] F. H. Norris, S. P. Stevens, B. Pfeffferbaum, K. F. Wyche and R. L. Pfefferbaum, Community resilience as a metaphor, theory, set of capacities and strategy for disaster readiness. *American Journal of Community Psychology.* 41, 127 (2008).

[49] P. H. Longstaff and S-U. Yang, Communication management and trust: their role in building resilience to "surprises" such as natural disasters, pandemic flu and terrorism. *Ecology and Society.* 13, 1. Retrieved from: http://www.ecologyandsociety.org/vol13/iss1/art3/1 (2008).

Section 4

Human Development/Institutional Strengthening

Chapter 7

A Study of the Relationship between Foreign Aid and Human Development in Africa

Gabriel Staicu and Razvan Barbulescu

Additional information is available at the end of the chapter

http://dx.doi.org/10.5772/67483

Abstract

Why are some countries more prosperous than others? Why are some countries still poor? What can be done by the West to help the rest to overcome the poverty trap? Finding better answers to these questions still represents the *research agenda* for development economists and *political agenda* for government and international institutions. Of course, the first two questions are age-old ones and have been asked since the beginning of our history. The economic literature has identified important factors that influence the wealth of nations and they include: openness to trade, natural resources, capital accumulation, and innovation. Recent studies have found that cultural aspects and institutional framework tend to play a major role in a nation's development process. The researchers' work also helps policy makers to find a better answer to the last question. The purpose of this chapter is to evaluate the effectiveness of aid in eradicating poverty and improving life conditions in African countries since 1980. Since we are at the beginning of a new UN development agenda, it is important for all stakeholders (recipient, donors, international agencies, etc.) to identify the conditions that enable aid to work.

Keywords: foreign aid, millennium development goals, economic development, economic freedom, Africa

1. Introduction

The theoretical foundations of economic development as a full discipline go back to the 1950s and 1960s, thanks to the work of outstanding economists such as Arthur Lewis, Ragnar Nurske, Paul Rosenstein-Rodan, and Kurt Mandelbaum, considered as the founding fathers of classical development economics. The emergence of this new body of economic literature was accompanied by important political changes in Africa and Asia. As the European colonial empires began to crumble, more than 35 African and Southeast Asian countries gained their independence. And to get these countries back on their feet, especially Africa, was challenging. Just like an OECD report mentions, some of these countries are actually "creations of the great European colonial carve-up rather than traditional nation states" [1].

What were the appropriate policies these new countries needed to adopt? Being influenced by the work of Harrod and Domar, the early development economists strongly supported aid as a key engine of growth and development. Emphasizing the essential role of saving and capital accumulation in promoting economic growth, Nurske and others have argued that poor nations remain poor because of the vicious circle of poverty. And, according to the Big Push Theory, foreign aid was needed to help poor countries escape from the poverty trap [2]. The years that followed could easily be described as "glory years" for the development policies and foreign aid. By the end of the 1960s, many of the East Asian countries had started to grow rapidly and suspended shortly receiving foreign aid. In the following years, the African experiment (in particular, Sub-Saharan countries) registered disappointing results of foreign aid. "The '1970s' and '1980s' were pretty dire. It got worse rather than better ... countries got very economically out of balance," concludes Richard Manning [3], a former chairman of the OECD's Development Assistance Committee, when referring to the African countries. It was not surprising to observe a decline of enthusiasm among development theorists and aid supporters. The classical theoretical justifications of the development assistance based on "saving gap" and "trade gap" have come to be challenged. Many researchers suggest in their academic studies that aid is necessary but not sufficient for growth.

The economic literature on aid started to take into consideration various new paradigms. Some studies such as Riddell's are based on direct experience of aid experts [4], others have been developed by various academic researchers like Tarp and Peter [5]. However, in the 1970s the idea of "aid for growth" became seriously questioned. The holistic focus on growth did not prove to be enough to improve living conditions of the poor. In that context, academia advice for policy makers was to include accountable conditionalities for aid recipients, to direct financial assistance rather than to satisfy basic needs such as safe water, proper nutrition, education, and healthcare programs to promote economic growth.

But the dark clouds continued to linger over foreign aid in the 1980s. It is worth to mention here the increasing (real) cost of borrowing in the early 1980s that affected the poor and developing countries capacity to repay the loans. For instance, in 1982, Mexico defaulted on its debt. Many African countries defaulted too or were increasingly struggling with debt. The international debt crisis radically influenced the approach of international institutions and donors regarding aid. Considered countries with "profound economic mismanagement," as Jeffrey Sachs said, the aid recipients were asked to make substantial changes in their macroeconomic policies [6]. "Two ideas came to dominate: stabilization and structural adjustment." The first required developing countries to "stabilize" their economies, for example, by reducing fiscal imbalances; the second called for fundamental structural reforms such as trade liberalization. Aid came attached with ever more "conditionalities" and policy advices, which today are often criticized [1].

In line with neo-liberal mainstream approach and ignoring endogenous factors such as culture or prevailing institutional framework, the ingredients for economic success in the 1990s were: privatization of state-owned enterprises, open-up the goods and financial markets, giving up to protectionism practices, cutting government expenditures, and including spending for education and health. This development recipe was common for all developing countries around the world, from Africa to Central and East Europe.

The relative lack of positive results, in terms of improving economic performance, forced both scholars and aid community to abandon to some extent for the framework of traditional development economics. By the end of 1990s, as Riddell emphasizes, there was a wide recognition that "development is an extremely complex process [...] difficult for outsiders to help in promoting without an in-depth understanding of the attributes and constraints of each poor country" [7].

The rethinking of the concept of development was also reflected in the creation of Human Development Index (HDI) in 1990 by the United Nations Development Programme (UNDP). Since then, UNDP has annually published Human Development Report, which takes the position that "people are the real wealth of a nation." Its approach to development is about enlarging people's choices, focusing broadly on the richness of human lives rather than narrowly on the richness of economies. In partial response to aid programs critics, the global development community has agreed on setting firm targets for results. This led to the creation of the eight millennium development goals (MDGs) in 2000, which set down a series of economic and social progress indicators that were expected to be achieved by the end of 2015.

Especially after 2000, exploring unconventional determinants of development process has become a new trend in the academic world. The institutional paradigm, for instance, has proved its relevance for analysis of foreign aid and aid effectiveness [8]. Convinced by the fact that the quality of institutions matters, Martens et al. analyzed particularly the incentives problem that drives the behavior of agents (donor governments, agencies' experts and bureaucrats, recipient governments, etc.) involved in foreign aid policy. In their very influential article in 2000, Burnside and Dollar found that aid has a positive impact on growth in developing countries with good fiscal, monetary, and trade policies, but has little effect in the presence of poor policies [9]. Although their article does not follow a specific institutional approach, the conclusion is quite clear: institutional environment in recipient countries strongly influences aid's effectiveness.

The fresh focus brought by institutional economics, a subfield that grew rapidly since the 1990s, is accompanied with more and more academia debates on aid effectiveness, and the general tendency was to highlight its negative effects rather than positive aspects. As The Economist has stated, the MDGs managed to shift the debate away from how much is being spent on development to how much is being achieved. However, theoretical and empirical criticisms seem to overcome the political optimism. William Easterly, a New York University professor, has published a great number of critical articles and books on aid, arguing that "aid cannot buy growth" [10]. Moreover, based on his personal experience during his past career at the World Bank, Easterly considers that present aid policies do more harm than good for poor countries [11]. More recently, this perspective which underscores the negative effects of foreign aid is shared by Angus Deaton, a well-known economist from Princeton University. Deaton argues that aid rarely reaches the poor. Moreover, there is no unquestionable empirical evidence that aid promotes growth [12].

The next section of this chapter analyzes the conceptual framework of foreign aid, who are the donors and international institutions that channel aid to the third world countries. Then, our focus is on testing the effectiveness of aid on improving life conditions of the African people, measured by the Human Development Index. We prefer Human Development Index instead of economic growth because it is a more comprehensive approach, and reflects both quantitative and qualitative improvements in human life conditions. According to the UN, development can be described as the process of enlarging people's choices, which means allowing them to "lead a long and healthy life, to be educated, to enjoy a decent standard of living," as well as "political freedom, other guaranteed human rights and various ingredients of selfrespect" [13]. Therefore, to increase the theoretical and practical relevance of our model, we have opted to integrate other two exogenous variables (economic freedom and political freedom), as important determinants of human development. Economic Freedom Index, published by the Fraser Institute, reflects the quality of economic environment, scoring a country between two extreme regimes: interventionist and free-market based. Polity score measures the quality of a political environment, the scale moving from authoritarian to a democratic regime. The outcomes of our research might prove helpful for aid agencies to adapt their policies in order to increase aid effectiveness. The lessons and policy recommendations are found in the final section.

2. Concept of foreign aid

Aid is generally considered as one of the biggest part of the world's development cooperation effort and represents a flow of money from governments in developed countries to developing ones. Also known as official development assistance (ODA), this type of aid is mainly discussed in this section. But, as we will see, this is not the only form of financial support the developed countries provide. Even though, much less important than ODA, there are some other forms of assistance, both from government and nongovernment institutions[1].

Since 1961, 23 developed countries (including the European Union) have decided to work under OECD's Development Assistance Committee (DAC) to provide the world's official development assistance. Presently, the DAC members have reached 29, and the number is expected to increase in the next years. At the same time, OECD has the role to monitor and collect data on all development flows from DAC and nonDAC donors, as well as multilateral aid agencies, and other private investment and philanthropy.

[1]The conceptual framework presented below is based on OECD [1].

http://dx.doi.org/10.5772/67483

Referring to ODA, three key elements can be identified:

- It is targeted at improving living conditions and welfare of poor countries.
- It is provided by governments or by their national agencies.
- It could take the form of a grant, or a loan at an interest rate less than the market rate[2].

According to OECD practice, about 90% of ODA is represented by grants, a financial support that receiving countries would not have to repay. Much of the rest consists of "soft" loans with low interest rate and often with a longer repayment period. Such credit instruments are used in order to bring more financial responsibility and accountability in the recipient countries. This financial support mentioned above is usually planned in advance, preceded by agreements and conditionalities between recipients and donors. Along planned assistance, OECD operates emergency financial assistance also. This type of aid is specifically directed to those developing countries confronted with cataclysms, such as the 2004 Asian tsunami and the 2010 Haiti earthquake.

The donor countries sometimes accept debt forgiveness of borrowers, meaning either deferring loan repayments or canceling them altogether. According to OECD methodology, cancellations are recorded as "grants" in ODA, even though, in effect, no new funding is being provided at the time when the loan is forgiven. Most of the loans forgiven were not aid in the first place; typically, for example, they may have originally been export credits. But loan forgiveness frees the resources for developing countries to use as they wish, and so is counted as ODA [1].

Considering the donors' perspective, only 30% of ODA is multilateral and 70% is bilateral. The money channeled through international aid agencies, according to their own development agenda, represents multilateral assistance. In practice, because the developed countries impose the aid agencies where and how to spend money, this is counted as bilateral aid and not multilateral assistance. **Figure 1** shows the total net official development assistance since 1960 from DAC members. Net ODA represents, in fact, disbursement flows (net of repayment of principal) of the DAC donors. Ignoring short periods of time, it reflects a continuous increase of the effort of developed countries to help the rest, reaching 2014 more than 137 billion USD. And, according to preliminary OECD data in 2015, net ODA rose by 6.9% in real terms from 2014, which is the highest level of ODA ever achieved.

Another indicator, commonly used in aid literature to illustrate the aid efforts made by the developed countries to help the third world, is the percent of net ODA in gross national income (GNI) of donors as it is shown in **Figure 2**. Basically, it reflects how much of the wealth created in developed countries is transferred (or redistributed) to developing ones. Even though more informal than mandatory for DAC countries, UN has set a target of 0.7% of GNI to be directed to aid.

Another form of foreign aid is technical cooperation. Developed countries might help the poor countries by paying for training of people from recipients, providing study scholarships, etc. A more widely used form involves supplying technical experts (consultants, advisors,

[2]In the case of a loan, this has to have a grant element of at least 25 percent.

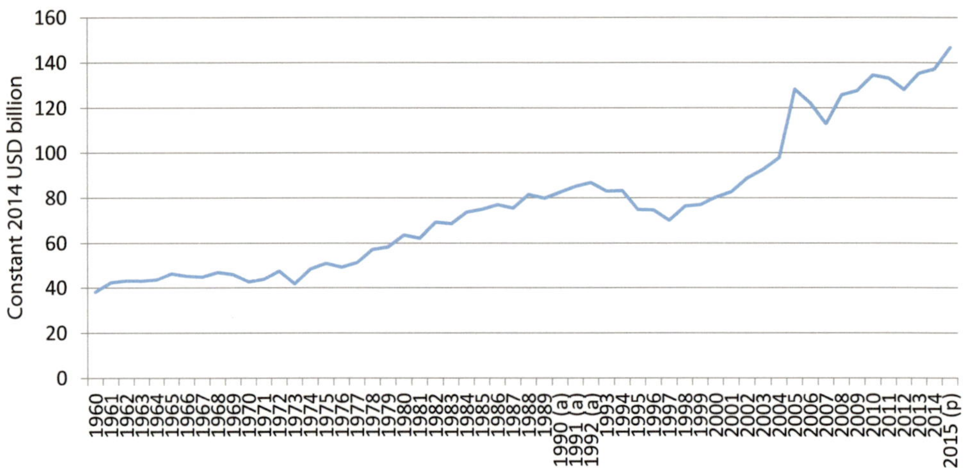

Figure 1. Net official development assistance, DAC members. (a) Total ODA excludes debt forgiveness of non-ODA claims in 1990, 1991, and 1992. (b) Preliminary data. Source: Authors' compilation based on 2016 OECD Report [14].

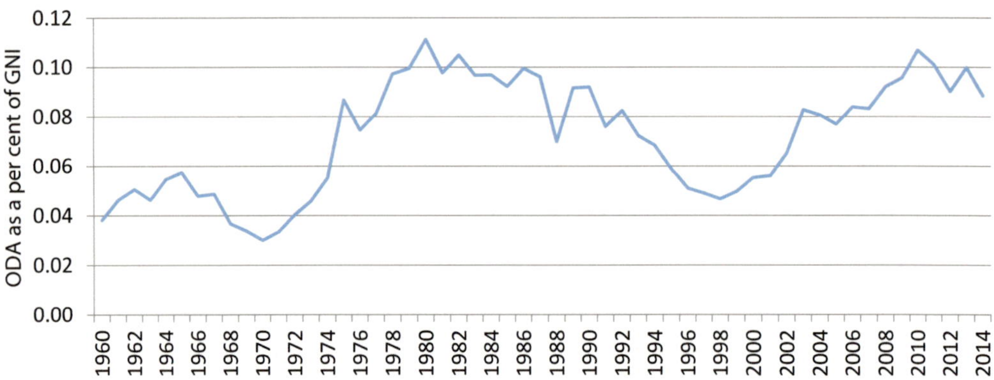

Figure 2. Net ODA/GNI, DAC members. Source: Authors' compilation based on 2016 OECD Report [14].

and administrators) to developing countries, but this method is widely criticized. The OECD admits in its official reports that technical cooperation is "perhaps the most controversial type of aid" [15]. And the critics add the attributes of "ineffective" are based on a multitude of negative cases. Some international experts have been accused of introducing technologies and procedures that are inappropriate to developing countries' needs. Also, technical cooperation has been criticized for failing to increase the local theoretical and practical skills. For instance, many students who were trained overseas have opted to stay there, thus fueling a brain drain of local human capital.

Who are the donors? As we mentioned above, a large part of aid is channeled through many multilateral agencies, such as the World Bank and United Nations. In one of the latest report, OECD [1] estimates around 200 multilateral donors and agencies involved in development assistance.

http://dx.doi.org/10.5772/67483

Considering administrative criteria, these agencies are: (a) national, being run by the governmental bodies; (b) regional, such as the European Union's agencies; and (c) international, such as UN.

More significant, from aid perspective, we can divide multilateral agencies into four categories:

- *Development banks*: World Bank, African Development Bank, and Asian Development Bank are focused mainly on lending funds to developing countries, as well as expertise and advice in different sectorial policies. Apparently confusing, the World Bank is organized into two separate bodies: the International Bank for Reconstruction and Development (IBRD), which focuses on middle-income countries and the stronger lower income countries, and the international development association (IDA), which focuses only on the world's poorest countries. The World Bank Group also includes a number of other agencies, such as the International Finance Corporation (IFC), which offers financial assistance, bank guarantees, and expertise to privately owned enterprises in developing countries.
- *United Nations*: UN efforts are directed at providing emergency and humanitarian assistance to poor countries (e.g. World Food Program) and to improve health and living conditions in those countries. MDGs, for instance, are longer term development goals aimed to eradicate poverty, to foster peaceful, just, and inclusive societies. According to the UN's General Secretary, the present 2030 Agenda goes beyond the eight MDGs that political leaders had agreed on in 2000. In order to meet sustainable development all over the world, UN has identified 17 sustainable development goals with 169 associated targets.
- *Europe:* The collective financial effort of EU members makes Europe the world's largest donor, even though much of the aid takes the form of bilateral assistance, considering priorities and interests of each country.
- *Global funds and institutions*: This refers to the emergence of a large number of special agencies that have been set up to pursue particular development goals. One of the best known example is the Global Fund to fight AIDS, tuberculosis, and malaria, which was created in 2002. The Global Fund is solely a financing agency, unlike UN agencies such as the World Health Organization.

3. The impact of foreign aid on human development in Africa: a multifactorial approach/model

Despite all efforts that have been made, the institutional framework of foreign aid still seems to function suboptimally. In September 2015, UN released a new Agenda for the next 15 years, suggestively entitled "Transforming our world: the 2030 Agenda for Sustainable Development." The purpose of the new agenda is to continue (and also to extend) the eight MDGs promoted since 2000. The main aim of this international project still remains the eradication of poverty and promotion of sustainable development in the third world.

Although UN has solved some pressing issues (better access to medicines and healthcare technologies, better school infrastructure, etc.), it becomes increasingly evident that aid has little effect on growth in a country with an institutional framework unfavorable to economic and political freedom. As mentioned in our introduction, we included potential explanatory factors for development as, in addition to ODA, two other independent variables. The first one is Economic Freedom Index (ILE) published by Fraser Institute, a famous Canadian think-tank. It is widely recognized in the economic literature that economic growth and development depend on (endogenous) economic, social, and political institutions. The second one is Polity score developed by Marshall in Polity IV Project [16]. This indicator reflects a spectrum of governing authority that spans from fully institutionalized autocracies through mixed, or incoherent, authority regimes (termed "anocracies") to fully institutionalized democracies.

Since foreign aid is expected to have better results in improving human life conditions (healthcare and education) rather than promoting economic growth, we have opted in our model to decompose Human Development Index and test the impact of ODA, ILE, and Polity on some HDI subindicators. The three-dimension index of HDI are: *Life Expectancy Index* measured by the indicator life expectancy at birth, *Education Index* based on indicators like mean years of studies and expected years of schooling, and *GNI Index* that is based on the indicator GNI per capita.

3.1. The data

African countries in the sample are Algeria, Angola, Benin, Burkina Faso, Botswana, Burundi, Cameroon, Cabo Verde, Central African Republic, Chad, Congo, Arab Rep Egypt, Ethiopia, Gabon, Gambia, Ghana, Guinea-Bissau, Guinea, Cote d'Ivoire, Kenya, Lesotho, Libya, Mauritania, Madagascar, Mauritius, Malawi, Mali, Morocco, Mozambique, Namibia, Nigeria, Niger, Rwanda, South Africa, Senegal, Sierra Leone, Swaziland, Tanzania, Togo, Trinidad and Tobago, Tunisia, Uganda, Zambia, and Zimbabwe.

The first data series we have worked with is the Human Development Index (HDI) for African countries shown in **Figure 3**. This is an indicator that emphasizes the importance of people development, in terms of health, knowledge, and standard of living.

The data available for this indicator consists of a panel of 41 time series between 1980 and 2014 with up to 11 cross section values for the 41 African countries that were included in this research. The main challenge regarding this data is that it consists of data for every fifth year between 1980 and 2010 and then yearly data between 2000 and 2014. This makes it impossible to test for root unit in first and second difference due to the very low number of remaining observations. The ADF unit root test for HDI allows us to reject the null hypothesis that the indicator follows a root unit process in level, with individual trend, and intercept for each of the African countries with a significance level of 5.2%, below the targeted 10% considering the issues with data.

The second series of data, presented in **Figure 4** is regarding ODA received by the African states to promote economic development and welfare. Only the official grants and loans that include at least 25% grant were taken into consideration. In order to make this information comparable between the states we have chosen to divide ODA by the mid-year population estimate and, thus, work with ODA per capita.

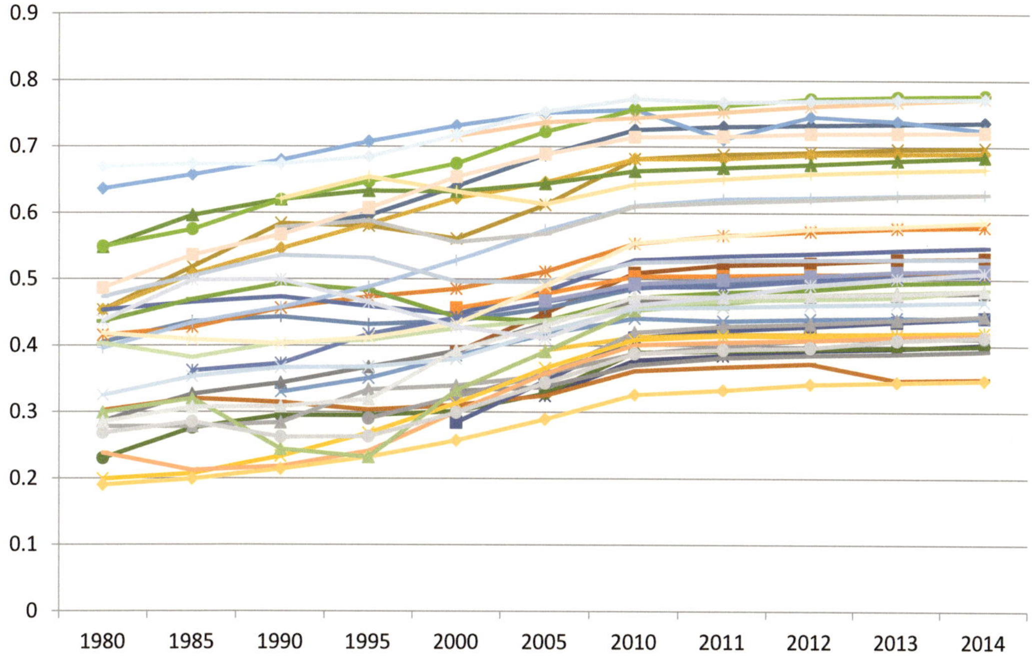

Figure 3. Evolution of HDI in African countries. Source: Authors' compilation based on UNDP Human Development Report 2015.

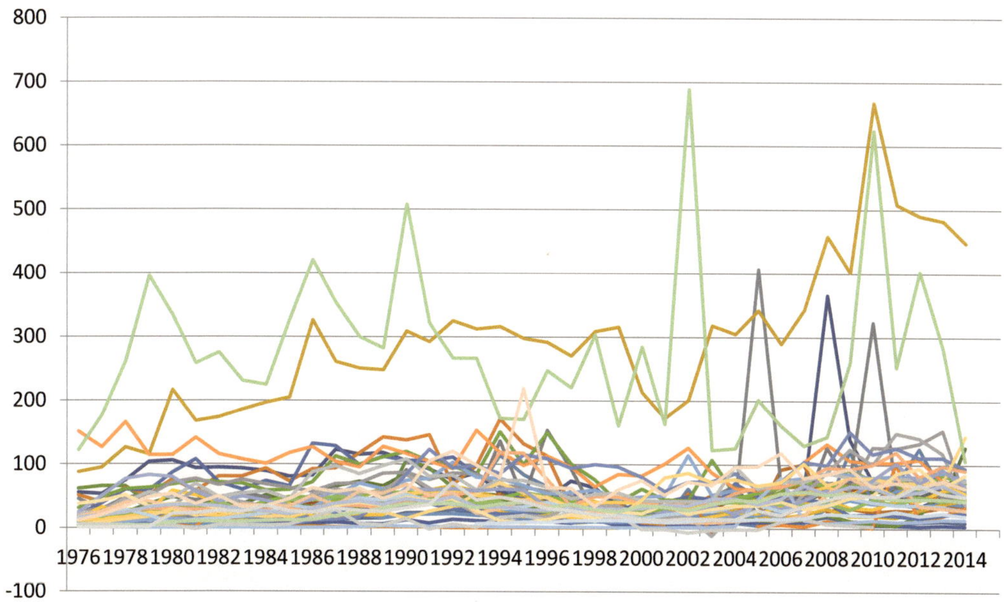

Figure 4. Net ODA for African countries. Source: Authors' compilation based on OECD and World Bank data.

ODA is a relevant indicator for the financial support received in order to develop the wellbeing of people in that country rather than poverty support. Also, ODA represents around 80% of the total development support that an African country receives. The other 20% is regularly coming from NGOs being focused on alienating poverty in specific areas.

For this indicator we will use a panel of data with 43 time series, one for each of the African countries and 40 cross sections for the period between 1976 and 2015. We have tested the series for unit root with multiple tests for both trend and difference, both for common root and for individual root unit, and the data proved to be stationary. We have rejected the null hypothesis of root unit with a significance level close to zero.

The third data series reflects the authority of the political regime in the country, measured by Polity score presented in **Figure 5**. The polity score captures this regime authority spectrum on a 21-point scale ranging from −10 (hereditary monarchy) to +10 (consolidated democracy). According to the authors, the Polity scores can also be converted into regime categories in a suggested three part categorization of "autocracies" (−10 to −6), "anocracies" (−5 to +5 and three special values: −66, −77, and −88), and "democracies" (+6 to +10).

When testing for unit root, the Polity2 series proved to be stationary both in trend and difference, taking into account both the individual effects and the individual linear trends, just like in all the other tests. Thus, the null hypothesis can be rejected and we can use the polity data in modeling.

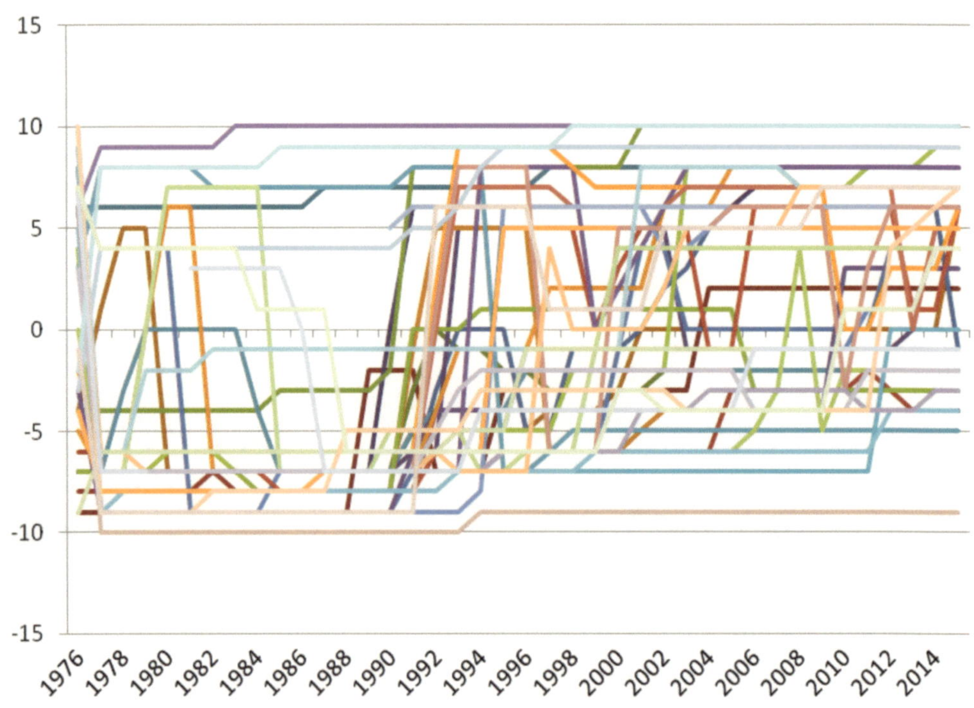

Figure 5. Polity scores in African countries. Source: Authors' compilation based on Polity IV Project data.

The last data series we work with is Economic Freedom Index (ILE), presented in **Figure 6**. In many ways, a country's economic freedom ranking is a measure of how closely its institutions and economic policies are compared with the idealized structure implied by the standard textbook analysis of economics. It uses 42 distinct variables to create an index, which is measured in 5 areas: size of government, legal structure and security of property rights, access to sound money, freedom to trade internationally, and regulation of credit, labor, and business [17]. The countries are ranked on a scale between 1 and 10, moving from the less free to the most free.

When testing for unit root, the series have shown that we cannot reject the null hypothesis for common unit root process according to Levin, Lin, and Chu test (548.454 statistical value) under first difference. Thus the series has been transformed to stationary by differentiation. ILE was tested for root unit with multiple tests and has proven to be nonstationary with an ADF-Fischer value of 81.7 (9.12% confidence level, higher than the targeted 5%). Thus, we have rejected the null hypothesis and transformed the data by first level differentiation. Thus, we will test the effects of Delta ILE over the endogenous variables. We found that the new series proved to be stationary.

GNI was tested for unit root with multiple tests and has proven to be nonstationary with an ADF-Fischer value of 84.3 (59.12% confidence level for the 44 cross sections, 1073 observations) for individual effects and individual trend. Thus, we have rejected the null hypothesis and transformed the data by first level differentiation. Thus, we will test the effects of the exogenous variables on Delta GNI. The new series proved stationary.

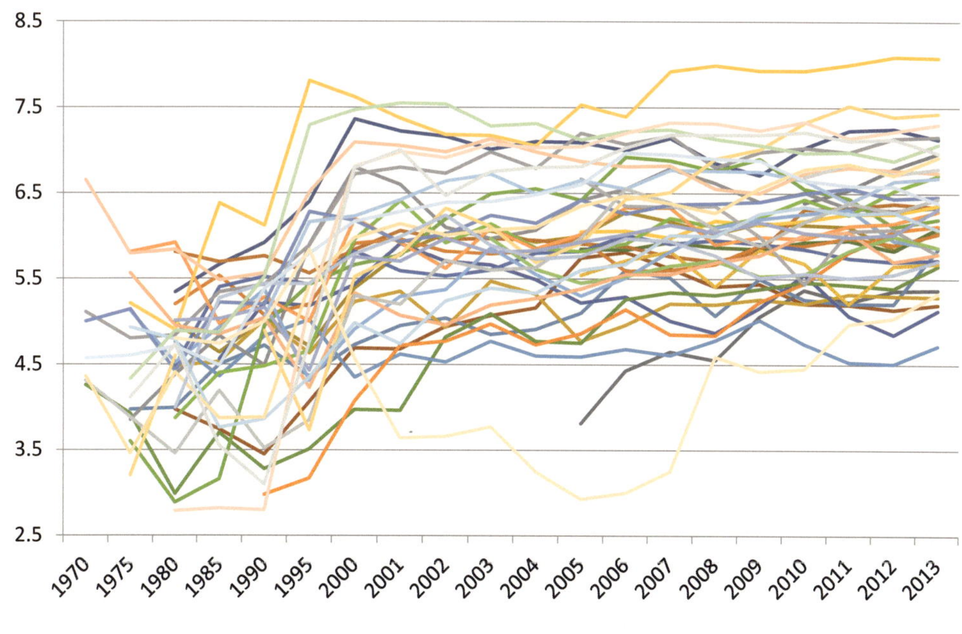

Figure 6. Economic Freedom Index for African countries. Source: Authors' compilation based on Economic Freedom Index of the World, 2015 Annual Report.

Life expectancy at birth data was tested for root unit with multiple tests and has proven to be nonstationary with an ADF-Fischer value of 102.5 (13.7% confidence level for 44 cross sections, 1010 observations). Thus, we have rejected the null hypothesis and transformed the data into percentage change of life expectancy at birth (DPLE). The new series proved stationary.

3.2. The methodology and findings

In the first model, life school expectancy was regressed versus the exogenous factors ODA, DILE, and Polity.

Equation	1	2	3	4
Dependent variable	SCH	SCH	SCH	SCH
Lags	None	ILE(−1)	ODA(−1)	ODA(−2)
Method	Panel least squares (unbalanced)			
	(fixed cross-section effects, white adjustment)			
Constant	5.944561	5.726093	5.449028	5.530522
	(0.463922)	(0.596327)	(0.573915)	(0.479372)
ODA	−0.013381	−0.01159	−0.002397	−0.004658
	(0.007355)	(0.007965)	(0.009202)	(0.007812)
DILE	−1.011094	0.469779	−1.027069	−0.996587
	(0.852597)	(0.988261)	(0.883243)	(0.865338)
Polity2	−0.093381	−0.179178	−0.122334	−0.114812
	(0.118211)	(0.149517)	(0.122132)	(0.121545)
Adjusted period	2001 2014	2001 2014	2001 2014	2001 2014
Observations	472/40	472/40	472/40	472/40
Adjusted R^2	0.426965	0.356552	0.422928	0.423342
Sum squared reside	6802.978	7640.24	6850.896	6845.982
S.E. of regression	3.98218	4.22012	3.99618	3.994747
F-statistic	9.355682	7.214153	9.218801	9.232748
Prob(F-statistic)	0	0	0	0

Depending on the lags used for ODA and ILE, the model explains between 35% (DILE lagged one period) and 42.6% (no lags) of the life school expectancy. Although the model partially explains life school expectancy, the parameters associated with the three variables used can be accepted as relevant with low probabilities. ODA is the most relevant variable in all models with 93% relevance in the model with no lags, 85% in the model with lagged DILE, and 30.5% or 45% in the two models with lagged ODA. In all models, the relation between ODA and life school expectancy proves to be negative showing that the main problems regarding the education in Africa are not improved with the development aid received by the countries.

Improvements in economic freedom appear to have a negative and weak short term effect with around 75% relevance in the models where the indicator is not lagged. With 1year lagged DILE, the impact of economic freedom becomes positive the next year but the impact is even less relevant (46% t stat relevance). This result may be commented that in the years when economic freedom improves, there is a slight incentive to give up schooling for other benefits. Political regime authority changes also prove to have a very limited effect on the life school expectancy.

In the second model we have looked for the impact of ODA, ILE, and Polity over the growth of GNI. Since, after the transformation, the domestic gross national income (DGNI) has a distribution that is different than the normal one, the residuals of all the GNI models have a skewness close to zero but a high kurtosis. Since the GNI data needed to be converted to stationary leading to negative values, the log transformation cannot be applied. We have chosen to accept the nonnormal distribution of the errors instead of performing other box-cox transformation of the data, based on the fact that when the sample size is large enough (472 observations in our case), the violation of the normality assumption does not cause major problems [18].

A sensitivity analysis was performed by modifying the lags of the data in order to see modifications past periods bring to the model.

Equation	**1**	**2**	**3**	**4**
Dependent variable	DGNI	DGNI	DGNI	DGNI
Lags	None	ILE(−1)	ODA(−1)	ODA(−2)
Method	Panel least squares (unbalanced)			
	(fixed cross-section effects, white adjustment)			
Constant	139.1449	85.22174	185.5918	115.8896
	(36.14561)	(62.09452)	(45.63961)	(30.34444)
DILE	43.63322	113.2846	41.62892	40.42955
	(51.55286)	(38.06388)	(51.07163)	(50.97066)
ODA	−0.016979	0.648237	−1.099133	0.568132
	(0.647223)	(1.010753)	(1.087195)	(0.375682)
Polity2	22.8524	21.5023	25.61406	21.14402
	(7.394513)	(10.3076)	(7.918873)	(7.068845)
Adjusted Period	2001 2014	2001 2014	2001 2014	2001 2014
Observations	472/40	472/40	472/40	472/40
Adjusted R^2	0.314585	0.242737	0.320044	0.316071
Sum squared reside	45495371	67643230	45133032	45396716
S.E. of regression	325.6529	397.085	324.3535	325.2996
F-statistic	6.147015	4.594694	6.278368	6.182571
Prob(F-statistic)	0	0	0	0

Delta GNI was regressed versus the exogenous variables Delta ILE, ODA, and Polity2. Comparing the coefficients for the three variables with their variance (under brackets), for each specification of the model we find out that in the model with no lags, explaining 31.4% of the DGNI variance, the Polity indicator is the most relevant exogenous variable with DILE less relevant and ODA almost not relevant at all. In this case, ODA is also negatively correlated with the changes in GNI. In the second model with lagged DILE, that explains 24.2% of the variance, this lagged indicator becomes the most relevant of all showing us that changes in economic freedom take time to produce improvements in GNI. ODA still has an extremely low relevance but becomes slightly positive while Polity2 becomes the number 2 indicator in relevance, very close to lagged DILE. The third and fourth models with lagged ODA, that explain 32% and 31%, respectively, are still showing a low relevance for ODA but an even lower relevance for the nonlagged DILE. Polity2 remains the only important exogenous variable in the model.

The third model is the regression for a double differentiated series of life expectancy depending on the same three indicators: ODA, DILE, and Polity2. Since the model has led to auto correlated residuals, we have preferred using the EGLS white consistent method of estimating the parameters instead of Cochrane-Orcutt. Since the volume of the database is high (472 observations), EGLS will maintain similar properties for the estimators as per the regular OLS [19].

Equation	**1**	**2**	**3**	**4**
Dependent variable	DDPLE	DDPLE	DDPLE	DDPLE
Lags	None	DILE(−1)	ODA(−1)	ODA(−2)
Method	Panel EGLS			
	(fixed cross-section effects, white adjustment)			
Constant	115.8896	0.001487	0.001832	0.001528
	(30.34444)	(0.000171)	(0.000146)	(0.000114)
ODA	40.42955	−0.0000228	−0.0000289	−0.0000243
	(50.97066)	(0.00000318)	(0.000003)	(0.00000246)
DILE	0.568132	−0.00015	−0.00007	0.0000458
	(0.375682)	(0.00016)	(0.000128)	(0.000099)
Polity2	21.14402	−0.000049	−0.0000429	−0.000035
	(7.068845)	(0.0000173)	(0.000012)	(0.0000124)
Adjusted period	2001 2014	2001 2014	2001 2014	2001 2014
Observations	472/40	472/40	472/40	472/40
Adjusted R^2	0.316071	0.480624	0.546168	0.530581
Sum squared reside	45396716	0.001696	0.00189	0.001972
S.E. of regression	325.2996	0.002051	0.002099	0.002144
F-statistic	6.182571	10.80471	14.49592	13.67543
Prob(F-statistic)	0	0	0	0

The most relevant parameter in all the regressions above is the one attached to ODA (99%) in all regressions, closely followed by Polity2 (approx. 95%) and then DILE (19–65%). Thus, between the three variables, ODA is the most important factor related to life expectancy as it is most often correlated with an inflow of know-how and pharmaceutical innovations.

4. Conclusions and policy recommendations

The HDI dimension, education index, has been tested only for life school expectancy. Due to lack of relevant official data available, our models have not included the indicator: mean years of schooling, and this can be a negative factor influencing the empirical relevance to the tested correlations here. As statistical data provided by international institutions will be improved, we are convinced that the quality of the following research will become more relevant. However, our findings show some important facts. Surprisingly, life school expectancy is not improved in recipient countries by getting development assistance. Therefore, it might be possible that better education is rather home-grown process, depending in a large extent by better domestic policies which take into account other cultural aspects in that particular region. The other two variables, ILE and Polity have also proved to have a very limited positive effect on life school expectancy indicator. We observed also that economic freedom tends to be positively correlated in time with this indicator.

Related to the changes in gross national income, our findings in the model without lags reveal that Polity and ILE are the most relevant, while ODA is negatively correlated. In the model with lagged ILE, economic freedom becomes the most relevant factor that contributes to growth. Thus, after doing this sensitivity analysis, we can emphasize that a less authoritative regime and improved economic liberties in the previous years are the most important factors of the three in terms of the impact over the GNI growth. This confirms some other recent findings in the development literature that quality of economic and political institutions matter for growth in a strong manner. Since aid is still channeled in most cases to governments and public agencies in the developing countries there is a little chance to stimulate growth, but corruption and social inequalities. As economic theory suggests, markets represent a better way to allocate resources and increase the living standards of people.

Analyzing the impact of these three variables on life expectancy at birth, our findings are favorable to ODA, as the most relevant factor, followed by Polity and ILE. Thanks to the work of UN World Health Organization, global funds, and other NGOs, healthcare problems in Africa have been reversed in trends.

Our findings and conclusions might be helpful to aid policy makers. However, it is not the goal itself of the international institutions and Western governments to eradicate poverty that is being questioned here, but the means by which they intend to achieve their objective. For instance, by analyzing separately HDI components instead of focusing on the aggregate HDI, we have identified some areas in which aid helps the poor, and areas in which aid seems to be wasted.

In the first place, if the developed countries want to promote economic growth, as main engine for sustainable development or to eradicate poverty in Africa, they should help the poor to have markets not bureaucracy and interventionism. A good example comes from the British Development Agency and it is worthy to be mentioned here. In southern Ethiopia, coffee farmer Feleke Dukamo is getting a better price for his beans. "My coffee sells for nine times more than it used to," he tells the British development agency DFID. The farmer is benefiting from the Ethiopia Commodity Exchange, established in 2008 with support from the United Kingdom. Before the exchange was created, Ethiopia's 15 million smallholders had no way of knowing the market price for their coffee, so middlemen were able to buy their beans cheaply and then sell them for a big margin. The new exchange has changed that: it sends farmer's regular updates on coffee prices by text messages via a dedicated phone line, which receives 44,000 calls a day. The result is a fairer price. "Now I can aspire to a better life," says Feleke. "I've been able to buy some cattle and, as my farm grows, I can employ people to help bring in the harvest" [1].

This challenge takes time and cannot be done overnight. But the first step in the right direction is to generally admit that aid cannot buy growth, as Easterly emphasized [20]. Development agencies should be more specialized, focusing more on small number of tasks in specific fields. The holistic approach of collective responsibility of hundreds of agencies should be replaced by a more accountable approach of individual responsibility, such as transferring knowledge on banking systems, developing stock markets, promoting sound macroeconomic management, or stimulating business environment by simplifying business and trade regulations. Basically, the main goal for aid agencies is to identify proper actions to promote institutional reforms favorable to free markets and fair competition in recipient countries. Simply giving money to a large number of national government bureaucracies helps public administration and the ruling parties, not the people. Additionally, a more focus on the alternative aid channel involving NGOs, global funds or other social entrepreneurs could increase aid effectiveness.

Second, for the UN and development agencies, there is an important task to be focused on in the future. Many healthcare and nutrition problems in poor countries have been solved, even if partially, with the help of the West. According to Easterly, by giving the poorest people vaccines, antibiotics, food supplements, fertilizers, or roads does not mean we make the poor dependent on foreign aid. On the contrary, better health, better nutrition, and better education represent more opportunities for the poorest to escape poverty and get better living conditions.

Author details

Gabriel Staicu* and Razvan Barbulescu

*Address all correspondence to: gabriel.staicu@economie.ase.ro

Bucharest University of Economic Studies, Bucharest, Romania

References

[1] Keeley, B. From Aid to Development: The Global Fight against Poverty. Insights, OECD Publishing, 2012.

[2] Temple, J. R. W. "Aid and Conditionality." In Handbook of Development Economics. Vol. 5. Edited by Dani Rodrik and Mark Rosenzweig, 4415–4523. Amsterdam: Elsevier, 2010.

[3] OECD. Development Co-operation Report 2011 50th Anniversary Edition, OECD Publishing, 2011.

[4] Riddell, R. C. Foreign Aid Reconsidered. Baltimore, MD: Johns Hopkins University Press, 1987.

[5] Tarp, F., and Peter H. eds. Foreign Aid and Development: Lessons Learnt and Directions for the Future. London: Routledge, 2000.

[6] Sachs, J. The End of Poverty: Economic Possibilities for Our Times. Penguin Publishing, 2006.

[7] Riddell, R. C. Does Foreign Aid Really Works? Oxford University Press, 2007.

[8] Martens, B., Uwe M., Peter M., and Paul S. The Institutional Economics of Foreign Aid. Cambridge, UK: Cambridge University Press, 2002.

[9] Burnside, C., and David, D. "Aid, Policies, and Growth." American Economic Review, 90(4): 847–868, 2000.

[10] Easterly, W. "Can the West Save Africa?" Journal of Economic Literature 47(2): 373–447, 2009.

[11] Easterly, W. The White Man's Burden: Why the West's Efforts to Aid the Rest Have Done So Much Ill and So Little Good. Oxford: Oxford University Press, 2006.

[12] Deaton, A. "Aid and Politics." In The Great Escape: Health, Wealth and the Origins of Inequality. Princeton, NJ: Princeton University Press, 2013.

[13] United Nations Development Programme. Human Development Report 1997. Human Development Report, 15, 1997. ISBN 978-0-19-511996-1.

[14] http://www.oecd-ilibrary.org/development/development-co-operation-report-2016_dcr-2016-en#statlinks

[15] OECD. Development Aid at a Glance, OECD Publishing, 2008.

[16] Marshall, G. M. Polity IV: Political Regime Characteristics and Transition, 1800–2013. http://www.systemicpeace.org/polity/polity4x.htm

[17] James G., Robert L., and Joshua H. Economic Freedom of the World: 2015 Annual Report, Fraser Institute, 2015. https://www.fraserinstitute.org/studies/economic-freedom-of-the-world-2015-annual-report.

[18] Pallant, J. SPSS Survival Manual, A Step by Step Guide to Data Analysis using SPSS for Windows. 3rd Ed., 179–200. Sydney: McGraw Hill, 2007.

[19] Pindyck, R. S., and Rubinfeld, D. L. Econometric Models and Economic Forecasts. New York: McGraw-Hill, 1991.

[20] Easterly, W. "Can Foreign Aid Buy Growth?" The Journal of Economic Perspectives, 17(3), 2003.

Chapter 8

Developing Competencies for Rural Development Project Management through Local Action Groups: The Punta Indio (Argentina) Experience

Ricardo Stratta Fernández,
Ignacio de los Ríos Carmenado and
Miriam López González

Additional information is available at the end of the chapter

http://dx.doi.org/10.5772/67046

Abstract

This chapter provides the foundations for a new approach in competence development for rural development project management, involving the role of higher education in the solution of real-life problems. This experience took place in senior courses at La Plata University and included the participation of students from this university. The research was carried out in Punta Indio, which is affected by rural depopulation, as are the rest of the territories inside the Buenos Aires Province. The process is developed through project-based learning (PBL) and the basis of the working with people (WWP) model, involving project management competencies according to the International Project Management Association (IPMA) standards. In the formation of local action groups (LAGs,) elements from the LEADER (Liaisons Entre Activités de Developement de l'Economie Rural) rural development model—applied in the rural territories inside the EU—were taken into account.

Keywords: project-based learning, rural development, professional competencies, project management, working with people, higher education

1. Introduction

The University represents new training paradigms, which establish the need for greater involvement with society and the environment; not only transferring, training and communicating, but also listening, learning and reflecting on the content of the messages sent by the community [1]. This vision regarding the role and remit of the University's activities within the community allows them to be integrated in a natural and permanent manner with teaching and research activities [2]. The UNESCO [3] report on higher education highlights the ability to adapt to changes imposed and demanded by today's society as one of the challenges faced by the university system. In this regard, not only the knowledge, personal attributes, skills and experience are important, but so-called professional competencies are also the key. There are many definitions surrounding the concept of competencies and although there is no agreement on a single definition, there are multiple different conceptual approaches. Among all of these, the International Project Management Association (IPMA) proposes a definition focused on project management and defines competence as a demonstrated ability to apply knowledge, personal attributes, skills and relevant experience in order to achieve success in a specific function [4]. As a result, competencies can be defined simply as the result of a process of integrating skills and knowledge: know, know-how, know-why, know-who [5]. However, this definition omits the fundamental role that context has with regard to competence development. According to the project management institute (PMI) [6], in terms of developing competencies for managing projects, knowledge must be adapted to the whole social and cultural system, which requires it to be used appropriately. The adaptation of this knowledge to different contexts can require a manager who is focused on solving problems. In the case of rural development projects, these managers have a fundamental role in channeling endogenous development. These criteria were used in the development of the doctoral thesis research titled "Rural development in Argentina: evolution and proposal of an intervention model for displaced rural communities in The Pampas." The research was carried out in an area called Punta Indio, in the province of Buenos Aires. A small group of part-time teachers participated in the research, as well as a group of interns formed of students in the upper years of their agricultural and forestry engineering degrees from the National University of La Plata, Argentina.

The research was aimed at identifying people who were interested in innovative proposals which would enable them to carry out new initiatives in order to implement them. As a result, training was carried out on project-based learning (PBL) [7–9] and a social activation experience from the Punta Indio region, with the objective of creating the necessary conditions to implement a development strategy. Furthermore, the research involved the creation of a local action group (LAG) (and the development of its competencies according to IPMA standards) [4], for managing rural development projects based on the specifications of the leader approach applied in the region.

2. Managing rural development in Argentina

The changes created by the technological modernization process in the Argentinian farming sector in recent decades have had a significant impact on the different social actors involved. Although agriculture is modern and thriving, some externalities have arisen, such as the advances in agricultural transformation in areas outside of the Pampas and vast movements of labor to urban environments [10–12]. It is evident that the loss of rural population is a phenomenon which is seen across the world, as societies develop and as a result of the changes and crises in economies which affect traditional farming societies [13]. Therefore, certain authors [14, 15] believe that the agricultural transformation in Argentina has accelerated the social and population changes seen in the sector. The rural towns that make up the social framework in each region are a reflection of this situation. In many cases, the lack of new nonfarming employment opportunities combined with a series of changes that affect employment levels (family and business) in the area's farmland is the most visible problem facing the smallest of villages. These have experienced a crisis due to the lack of economic activity, which leads to a population decrease, not only as a result of an aging population but also as a result of losing young people who want to live in a better location in cities. As a result, many villages have the same kinds of problems, in a type of vicious circle: economic structure strongly linked to traditional farming activity and with a lack of appeal for new projects and diversification of production, lack of employment opportunities and withdrawal or decline in local human resources (progressive deskilling of labor, technological alienation among production agents, aging population, etc.) [12]. According to Gorenstein [16], this situation causes diseconomies (external factor that affects the normal functioning of the economy) of agglomeration and cooperation, among other effects. Argentina's current agricultural development model (especially in the Pampas where it is dominant), which is based on the production of export goods, intensive technology for supplies and capital, favors larger economies with economic concentration and deeply harms the basis for food sovereignty among the rural, periurban and urban population [17]. The changes that have been seen in the Pampas' agricultural system and their social effects have led to a series of debates relating to the focus which has guided its development over these years. The shrinking agricultural structure due to the loss of producers and reduced population levels in rural villages forms an area of research and analysis of these transformations and the ways of addressing these. At a glance, it is clear that the economic and social imbalances, which have historically defined its evolution, far from disappearing or diminishing, have become more prominent in recent years. In a way, the rural development policies that have been implemented in Argentina in the last two decades have not achieved their proposed objectives, or it may be that these problems were not considered as such for the Pampas region [12, 18]. According to some authors [19, 20], rural development in Argentina has always been linked to policies aimed at poor rural sectors in marginal areas or regions outside of the Pampas. For Schejtman and Barsky [21], rural development in Argentina is a process, a way of working toward productive progress; improving the quality of life for the rural population; strengthening civil society and democracy; territorial development; conservation of natural resources and; respect for cultural diversity. Coinciding with this focus, Sili [14] relates rural development to a process of rural transformations which arises from the organization and revitalization of the territory with the following objectives: achieve a high level of innovation and economic diversification; drastically reduce the levels of poverty and marginalization; improve infrastructure; equipment and services for economic development; and improve the quality of life for the rural population [22].

These circumstances make it necessary to find other development alternatives, where the presence and commitment of the state and public polices can be guaranteed among the most unprotected sectors [23]. More recently, based on the information provided in the National

Farming Census [24], Obschatko [25, 26] created a new segment of producers, which considers "small producers" as those who directly carry out production tasks in farming operations without using salaried employees. As a result, family farming began to gather strength as a way of describing those producers in the country who are grouped in a different way to those from traditional farming and who promote other values such as: resource conservation, organization of producers, family production as a way of life and as a cultural matter. Finally, the definition indicates that the concept of family farming includes farming, livestock or cattle, fishing, forestry, agribusiness and traditional production, as well as the traditions of harvesting and rural tourism [27–29]. Toward the end of 2004, the National Federation of Family Farming (FoNAF) was created by the family farming commission, as part of the Ministry's remit and supported by the Argentine Agrarian Federation (FAA) and as a result of the proposals that emerged from the "National and Latin American Congress on Land Usage and Ownership", in which delegates from over 150 family farming organizations and indigenous communities participated. In March 2006, the Secretary of Agriculture, Livestock Farming & Fishing in Argentina officially formalized the FoNAF's remit as an area for debate and agreement of public policies for family farming. In May 2006, the FoNAF's 1st National Plenary Session took place in the city of Mendoza. This led to the creation of the FoNAF's 1st Document, known as "Mendoza Document" or "agreed diagnosis for the family farming sector." In December 2015, all of these innovative actions in the field of rural development culminated in the approval by the Argentine Congress of the family farming law known as the "Historical repair of family farming to build new rural life in Argentina."

3. Case study and shortcomings or levels of competence

The participation of the National University of La Plata, Argentina, in the research involved a small group of part-time teachers, as well as a group of students in the upper years, who were studying courses that are part of the rural development department of the Faculty of Agricultural and Forestry Sciences, including: rural extension, introduction to management, introduction to agricultural and forestry sciences, socioeconomics and curriculum integration workshops I and II.

Through an open call addressed to all students who were part of these courses, they were offered the opportunity to participate in a research experience that would allow contact with rural stakeholders, as well as the opportunity to establish this research as a basis for their future final degree dissertation. Of the 190 students who took part in these courses, a total of 23 students voluntarily registered to participate in this research experience.

The process of selecting students was conducted based on the activities developed in the framework of the applied research project: "A development strategy in rural villages: application in the Town of Punta del Indio," which was approved and funded by the National University of La Plata, Argentina.

The departmental board made the final selection of students to be enrolled, based on academic merit, knowledge of certain tools to work in the rural-social sector and interest in the

http://dx.doi.org/10.5772/67046

Figure 1. Location map. Punta Indio. Source: Google maps and http://heraldicaargentina.com.ar/1-BA-PuntaIndiomapa.jpg.

topics addressed. Of the 23 students enrolled, four principal members and four substitutes were selected.

The research project was carried out in the region of Punta Indio (administrative area) in a small town of the same name and with a population of 600 people. This region is located to the northeast of Buenos Aires province on the banks of River Plate in Samborombón Bay (**Figure 1**). The main town is Verónica, which along with Pipinas, Punta del Indio, Álvarez Jonte, Las Tahonas, Luján del Río, La Viruta, Monte Veloz and Punta Piedras are the main populated areas. The total area of land in the Department (Partido) of Punta Indio is 1550 km^2 and the total population is 10,660 people.

This area can be described as a vast plain which forms part of the Salado River Basin (the main water basin in the Province of Buenos Aires). Its characteristics primarily stem from the conditions which characterize this basin: generally flat topography; mild humid climate; limited water network; land with limited drainage and hydromorphic features, with limitations due to high sodium levels; the presence of floodplains which have historically been subject to regular flooding; and seasonal drought cycles [30]. The ground in this area is fairly level and whilst it is not suitable for farming use, it is mainly suitable for livestock farming [31]. As a result, the economic activity in the area is primarily focused on livestock farming, with other sectors still providing a small contribution to overall GDP. This situation has contributed to a stall in population growth and, moreover, an exodus in rural areas, especially among youth and families of producers who move to urban centers in the search of a better future. This, without a doubt, creates a complex social and economic backdrop as well as an uncertain future, as there are no policies or actions aimed at reverting this process of permanent decline.

A general review of the literature regarding development from a territorial perspective shows us that there are many concepts of territory applied in order to facilitate social, economic, cultural, political and institutional analysis within a given geographical area, which also help to form the basis of public policies aimed at resolving the problems identified across these dimensions. Therefore, Cazorla [32] indicates that with territorial analysis, development should not be considered as simply combining a group of resources and methods, but rather as improving the quality of life. As a result, it makes sense to get close to the local population, to learn about their history and customs as well as to plan the development with them, in a bottom-up approach in which a territory's complex history and culture require them to identify those factors that have the greatest impact on development planning.

Within this framework, the rural development management models have provided important changes over time; the emergence of territorialism in the current rural development debates is no coincidence. It is a response to economic and social changes, where the debate promotes a different vision in terms of the territorial problems and directly involves rural populations in the design of new development perspectives [33].

In the EU, the *Leader* program has been able to stimulate the development of local actors' abilities through social capital [34]. Through these programs, innovative horizontal integration has been established with the objective of allowing local agents to develop an organic group of actions thanks to the creation of nonprofit organizations called *local action groups* (LAG) [35]. The importance of these groups lies in the fact that they are public-private associations that promote connections between governments, civil society and economic sectors to train mixed groups. This requires the involvement of local actors in the development process and facilitates improvements in the skills of administrative employees and the population in general [34, 36]. In the long term, the general objective of this local development is to transform the local economic and social system. In turn, this overall objective translates into two objectives in the short term in order to achieve its goal: the promotion of business activity and the coordination of all activities and programs which have a local impact. The promotion of business activity relates to the local business owners in their dynamic role as well as economic and social growth [37]. When setting out the need for change, local development plays a role that includes the promotion of endogenous growth and internal investment which facilitates the creation of new SMEs, cooperatives, community businesses, innovative companies and in particular social economy entities.

In this context, it makes sense to carry out activities aimed at strengthening the development group leaders' abilities and to become the focal point for management processes and project implementations in the rural area [5]. The project management institute (PMI), in line with other authors [38], describes project management as "The application of knowledge, skills, tools and techniques to meet the project requirements" [6]. According to Meghnagi [39], each person builds their own competencies and knowledge at the heart of a process that is not just limited to straightforward contact with the actual or symbolic situation, but equally takes place through social intervention, favored by the most competent individuals or their peers.

In contrast, Morris [40] criticizes these definitions for being too focused on the execution tools and processes and advocates a wider definition of project management with an emphasis on the importance of a wider business and strategic context as well as a focus on people leadership. Blackburn [41] reinforces the first concept, supporting the idea that, in order to work in the rural development field, individuals require competencies and abilities in order to manage projects in a more efficient and sustainable way. Other authors [42–44] also agree that the project management is a complex process with multiple results in terms of focusing on competencies and which requires a variety of skills and knowledge to be acquired. One of the most interesting aspects of competency-based project management is the significant change in the focus that is placed on people's work. Rather than simply concentrating on determining what people do, or what people should be doing at a given time in their professional duties, the key is to create an intermediate step that determines the support that is expected from people in order to achieve the strategic objectives expected by the organization [5]. All of the organizational actors are important in the identification of competency-based management processes. Each one should contribute their experience and creativity to the project management process [45]. In order to develop competencies in rural development project management, it is necessary to incorporate a number of factors aimed at achieving development objectives. Therefore, the competencies of the groups or people themselves should be included in the analysis and should be positioned on three main axes which together form the focus for any activity: (1) what it wants to be, (2) what it is and what it knows to do and (3) what it is capable of doing. This creates a strategy which includes wishes, goals, resources and capabilities which facilitate development, with some authors defining this as sustainable competitive advantage [5].

4. Methodology

The methodology used in this study was based on the criteria established in the "working with people" (WWP) [46–48], a planning model that is based on planning guidelines as social learning and competencies development through project-based learning (PBL) [7–9] addressed to local communities. This model forms part of a new understanding of planning, aiming to transform society, connecting thoughts with actions through gradual changes in accordance with the local population's idea of live [46, 49]. The process of social learning involves the use of theoretical-practical training methodologies and strategies that are focused on action research with the aim of diagnosing, intervening in and resolving development problems in the territory. Therefore, social learning is a methodological process in which the knowledge of reality and practical experience are equally influential and is known as mutual learning [50].

The methodology consists of five main sections:

1. Diagnosis of the characteristics of the productive elements in the Department of Punta Indio.

2. Identification of potential elements that could be of importance when it comes to designing a rural development strategy for the department.

3. Initial contact with the region's rural communities to involve them in the design and evaluation of these options.

4. Organization, ranking and articulation for practical application.

5. Financial evaluation and securing sources of finance.

In order to progress to the design, development and implementation of these elements, it was necessary to carry out an initial study of the territory in question, from both an anthropological and cultural perspective, as well as a natural environment perspective. The aim was to get a detailed understanding of which elements might be attractive when evaluating them as mechanisms for driving development. Similarly, the region's unique environmental aspects were taken into consideration.

In order to implement this methodology, the participation of the population is required. Furthermore, in order to guarantee flexible planning, it is essential for there to be a knowledge-action-competence link so that a fruitful backdrop can be formed, against which science creates a frame of reference which comes to life and transforms as the population starts to set out its interests and incorporates knowledge in order to impact reality [50]. Discussing about social learning it is also synonymous with "working with people" (WWP) [46–48], a model developed by the GESPLAN research group at the Technical University of Madrid (UPM), which is based on planning guidelines for development, devised by Friedmann [49] and Cazorla [46]. Accepting this focus on competencies means rethinking our experience of acting in the territory, the ways in which we organize and implement activities within the community. Therefore, the WWP model aims to transform society through social learning, by connecting thinking with action through gradual changes, in accordance with the local population's view of life. It involves mutual learning between the technical team and the community which implements the capabilities, by both parties, in order to develop competencies through: continuous practice in challenging contexts; a high level of interaction and communication; ongoing investigation and critical reflection; and proposing challenges which stimulate curiosity and interest, increase commitment and the extent to which people are happy with the actions in response to the challenge and stimulate and enable imagination and innovation.

5. The integration of competencies in the development strategy in Punta Indio

Punta Indio's strategy is the outcome of applying a development model that arises from reflecting on rural depopulation problems in "La Pampa" region, Argentina [51]. The action planning process was participative, in which the population (through its representatives from public and private entities) addressed the problems facing their communities.

This development model incorporates the working with people (WWP) approach [46–48] as a scientific basis, the principles of planning as social learning and elements of the leader initiative as an experimental approach for rural development based on a territorial approach, the creation of new participatory local government structures and decentralized management. The model is applied in the territory of Punta Indio (Argentina) [51], by highlighting several of the relevant aspects to address the problem of rural depopulation: the active participation of beneficiaries in the design of their own development, territorial approach, bottom-up approach, the creation of a local action group (LAG), innovation, integrated and multisectoral approach.

While development activities were taking place, a learning process was applied with members of the LAG of Punta Indio, which integrated capacity building for the application of project management competencies. This process was based on project-based learning (PBL) [7–9] and it was structured taking into account the application of technical, behavioral and contextual competencies in the territory, according to IPMA standards [4] and its most suitable combination within the framework of three specifications of the leader rural development model: (1) Bottom-up focus, (2) creation of local action groups and; 3) innovation.

As a result, the learning process was heavily geared toward a sustainable development strategy based on competencies, improving the community's work in search of greater efficiencies. Thus, certain competence elements were taken into consideration from the following fields: technical, behavioral and contextual. These competencies were evaluated throughout the implementation of the development strategy in order to improve the benefits for all of the agents involved.

The following *technical competencies* were explored:

1. Project management success: project management achieves success and avoids failures in its projects. An understanding of which criteria would be considered is required in order to determine the success or failure of a project and how it will be evaluated.

2. Parties involved: this refers to the people or groups who are either interested in the development or success of a project, or who are part of the project.

3. Project requirements and objectives: this consists of identifying, defining and agreeing the requirements in order to meet the needs and expectations of the parties involved in the project.

4. Quality: is the extent to which a group of inherent characteristics meet the project's requirements.

5. Project structure: this element includes the design and management of the project, organizational structure, the most appropriate responsibilities and skills for a project.

6. Teamwork: this is a fundamental element as one person's strengths make up for another person's weaknesses. The team is not a group of people, rather a group in which everyone rows in the same direction, sharing the same values and enthusiasm for the project.

7. Problem solving: the ability to solve problems is the efficiency and agility in providing solutions to problems that have been identified, taking the necessary corrective actions using common sense, focus on cost and initiative.

Communication: the effective exchanges between parties and summarizing information. In projects of a social nature, it is crucial to correctly communicate information to the population.

The following *behavioral competencies* were explored:

1. Leadership: involves directing and motivating others in their roles or tasks in order to achieve a project's objectives. It is particularly important when a project is facing difficulties.

2. Behavior and motivation: is the support of those involved in a project. Commitment means that people believe in the project and want to be part of it.

3. Self-confidence: is the ability to express points of view in a clear manner, but without being authoritarian. It is the effective way of communicating within the team without creating differences.

4. Creativity: the ability to think and act in an original and imaginative manner. It is necessary to explore the group's collective creativity in the face of the difficulties and challenges posed by the project.

5. Efficiency: is the ability to use resources and time in an effective manner, in accordance with the stated objectives, to meet the expectations of the parties involved.

6. Negotiation: is the ability to resolve disagreements or problems. It is the means by which parties can resolve their disagreements with the project or program in order to reach a satisfactory solution.

7. Conflicts and crises: this competence element covers the ways of managing conflicts and crises which may arise between different people and the parties involved in a project or program.

8. Appreciation of values: is the ability to notice other people's intrinsic qualities and understand their points of view. It also includes the ability to communicate with people and be receptive to their opinions, value judgments and ethical standards.

The following *contextual competencies* were considered:

9. Implementation of projects and programs: the involvement of an organization in this instance results in establishing better processes, methods, techniques and tools, changing attitudes and applying organizational changes in a process of continuous improvement.

10. Permanent organizations: have a long-term purpose. It is crucial to secure support and overcome any internal resistance within a project's permanent organization. Therefore, it is important to choose the right methodology and undertake adequate planning in order to establish good initial conditions and achieve satisfactory results.

11. Systems, products and technologies: this competence element covers the link between the projects and the program. The systems are an organized group of elements that are connected in order to form a complete unit with specific objectives. At the same time, the various components that form a system can be grouped into three subsystems: natural,

technological and socioeconomic subsystems. The interaction between these components represents a system with a specific aim.

12. Management of personnel: personal development is a key concern in every organization. From the organization's point of view, it is important to have suitable human resources, thus it is also important to provide individuals with opportunities to learn new skills to support the stated objectives.

13. Security, hygiene and environment: this element covers all of the activities aimed at ensuring that the organization behaves in an appropriate manner in the context of security, hygiene and environment during the planning and implementation phases of the project.

Table 1 shows the process that was implemented for the methodology in order to develop competencies in the community of Punta Indio and the competence elements that were chosen in relation to each leader specification applied within the territory. The competencies have a score of between 1 and 5. 1 is the lowest score, which could indicate negative aspects or conflicts within the project; 2 is an average score, indicating a desire to improve; 3 is a good or acceptable score which adds to the project; 4 is very good, very positive attitude and; 5 is excellent.

The scoring criteria were defined by a panel of experts in which the following five entities participated: (1) representative of the National Institute for Agricultural Technology (INTA). Regional centre of 'Cuenca del Salado' based in Chascomús, Buenos Aires Province; (2) representative of the Ministry of Agricultural Affairs of Buenos Aires Province- Rural Development Directorate-; (3) representative of the Department of Rural Development at the Faculty of Agricultural and Forestry Sciences UNLP; (4) representative of the Development Directorate of Punta Indio Municipality; and 5) municipal delegate of Punta Indio Municipality based in the town of the same name (Punta Indio).

5.1. Bottom-up focus

Within the bottom-up focus, it is the population affected by specific problems and/or needs, who participate in researching possible solutions and designing strategies that can be applied and implemented during the observation of the results. This focus means that the population provides active, creative and highly committed contributions, when it becomes involved through work teams. The advantage of this focus is that participants are encouraged to think in a more creative way. This enables them to feel involved in the development of the project as they feel that their initiatives are valued. The bottom-up focus shown in **Table 2** has been a key element in this research, encouraging participation among the community through themed workshops and surveys, organized with the aim of obtaining different information in response to the problems facing each sector: (1) farming; (2) environment; (3) commerce; (4) tourism; (5) creation of associations; (6) handicrafts; and (7) cultural heritage. As a result, the main problems facing each sector were identified, so that the work could focus on designing the development strategy, establishing the priority axes, development guidelines and actions for the community of Punta Indio. The integration of these aspects of the bottom-up focus with the competence elements suggests an assessment geared towards the success of projects, defining the criteria required to achieve the objectives within the agreed limits.

Competence elements	Leader specifications		
	Bottom-up approach	Creation of LAG	Innovation
Technical competences			
Success in project management	3	4	3
Parties involved	4	4	2
Pro ject requirements and objectives	4	4	3
Quality	4	4	2
Project structure	3	4	3
Teamwork	4	4	3
Problem solving	3	4	3
Communication	3	3	3
Totals	28	31	22
Behavioral competences			
Leadership	4	4	3
Behavior and motivation	3	4	3
Self-confidence	3	3	2
Creativity	3	4	3
Efficiency	2	3	3
Negotiation	4	4	3
Conflicts and crises	4	4	3
Appreciation of values	3	4	3
Totals	26	30	23
Contextual competences			
Implementing projects and programs	3	4	3
Permanent organizations	3	3	3
Systems, products and technology	3	4	3
Management of personnel	3	3	3
Security, hygiene and environment	3	4	4
Totals	15	18	16

Source: Compiled by authors.

Table 1. Development of competences in Punta Indio.

The competencies demonstrated within this focus correspond to these elements: technical, behavioral and contextual. In the technical area, the following competencies were taken into account: project management success; parties involved; project requirements and objectives; teamwork; problem solving; and communication. In terms of behavioral competencies:

Decisions	Participative elements	
Diagnosis	• Semi-structured questionnaire • Questionnaires for key people • General workshops • Themed workshops • Use of participative tools • Integration of project management competences Group dynamics	Objectives: • Identify key development factors • Reach agreement in terms of development priorities for actions plans and projects • Development of competences in the local community with regards to managing rural development projects, based on the Leader specifications for the region of Punta Indio
Definition of priorities	Themed workshops • Development of tourism and handicrafts • Diversification of production • Use and preservation of natural resources • Stimulating commercial activity • Promoting cultural heritage • Training & Development	Objectives: • Strengthen the results of the data collected in the questionnaires, with supporting information
Priorities	SWOT analysis (strengths, weaknesses, opportunities, threats)	Objective: Definitive diagnosis
Definition	Definition of the competence development strategy in order to carry out rural development projects	
Source: Compiled by authors.		

Table 2. Participative competence elements from the experience with the community of Punta Indio.

leadership; creativity; negotiation; conflicts and crises; appreciation of values. With regards to contextual competencies: project implementation and permanent organization.

5.2. Creation of local action groups (partnership)

The creation and strengthening of the institution was one of the most important factors in promoting local development in the region of Punta Indio. Therefore, it was found appropriate to create a new institution—local action group—or partnership in the community of Punta Indio, as one of the distinguishing and fundamental aspects of this study. The LAG is a form of horizontal cooperation, in which agents and institutions which represent the local society become members, with the purpose of identifying a common development strategy and managing its implementation [52]. In the case of Punta Indio, the creation of the LAG involved bringing together agents and institutions which represent the local society, with the aim of implementing the development strategy in Punta Indio. As a result, a LAG was established in Punta Indio called "Amigos del Parque Costero" (Friends of Parque Costero). The inclusion of competencies in this Development Strategy also provides the possibility of carrying out tasks integrated within the community. In this context, it is important to highlight the LAG's role as an excellent tool for teamwork and as a means of ongoing education [53, 54]. Making decisions that are both in the public interest and for the benefit of third parties lies at the organization's core.

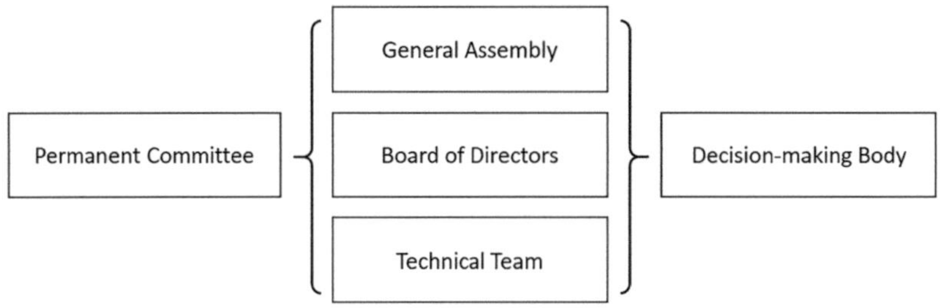

Figure 2. General organization chart of the LAG.

Figure 2 shows a typical organization chart for a local action group.

The decisions taken by the group based on its technical competencies are supported by a professional support team and, occasionally, by consultancy from local experts. As a result, the LAG takes on all of the competencies for developing the region, establishing a constant relationship with the population, not only to strengthen the development of competencies to implement projects, but also to ensure the sustainability of these projects.

The technical elements that were considered include: project management success; parties involved; project requirements and objectives; quality; project structure; teamwork; problem solving; and communication.

In terms of behavioral competencies: leadership; behavior and motivation; self-confidence; creativity; efficiency; negotiation; conflicts and crises; and appreciation of values. With regards to contextual competencies: project implementation; permanent organization; and personnel management.

5.3. Innovation

Rural development's integrative outlook requires innovative responses, so that it does not remain at the sidelines of new economic and social ties [34]. In this case, innovative actions were sought in order to promote the development of the region. The LAGs carried out various actions and projects, a total of 18 (**Table 3**), which were hugely innovative for the region, given that new solutions for the community's problems were sought, promoting economic diversification as well as multisector and multifunctional links.

Here, the work on competencies for researching the innovative nature of project management implied the evaluation of eight elements, of which four were from the technical field: project management success, project requirements and objectives, quality and; project structure. One from the behavioral field: creativity. Three from the contextual field: project implementation; systems, products and technologies; security, hygiene and environment.

Themed areas	Development axes	Measures	Actions
Use and preservation of natural resources	Natural resources	Protection and preservation of the environment	Design and construction of an Interpretation Center and themed museum in the 'Parque Costero Sur'
			Creation of a native plant nursery, in order to repopulate deteriorated areas in the 'Parque Costero Sur'
Development of tourism and handicrafts	Tourism	Promoting tourism heritage	Design and installation of signage
			Creation of maps for historical sites which are important for tourism
			Creation of tourist routes
			Organization of a calendar of local festivities
			Creation of a tourist information center
Change in economic activity	Diversification	Improve the perceived value of other local products	Production of aromatic plants
			Production of edible mushrooms
			Strengthen the development of arts & handicrafts, linked to the area's history
			Strengthen the development and transformation of organic products in the area
			Improve honey production
			Development of the farming innovation center
Training & development	Improved human resources	Develop and strengthen knowledge, competences and skills among people in the community	Tree nursery program for youngsters (32 youngsters aged between 12 and 17)
			Arts & crafts workshops (12 people)
			Design workshops for clothing and learning traditional weaving (16 people)
			Creation of a training center for alternative activities in Punta Indio (24 people)
			Development of an innovation center (14 people)

Source: Compiled by authors.

Table 3. Projects implemented by the LAG in Punta del Indio.

6. Conclusion

The research on rural development carried out by the UNLP was a result of the university's increased involvement with society and its surroundings. As a result, the university's contribution facilitated work which benefited the community and also reinforced academic training among degree students, through the work experience they took part in across different communities. This work has facilitated the creation of cooperative processes between the university and the community in Punta Indio, with a dual objective: (a) the creation of a development strategy to strengthen the socioeconomic base and; (b) the development of a competence process with the local action group for managing projects according to IPMA standards, based on three leader specifications applied across the region. The purpose of developing competencies in the community is deeply linked to the idea of strengthening the capabilities of the developed group leaders and being at the very heart of project management and development in rural areas. In order to develop these competencies, it was necessary to incorporate a series of factors aimed at achieving the objectives of the development across three areas of competence: technical, behavioral and contextual. From the competence process that took place, it was clear that the leader specification used by the most elements from the three areas is "local action group or partnership." As would be expected, the skills of those who have to decide which projects should be chosen and the reasons why, relate to: the project's requirements and objectives, quality, project structure, teamwork, problem solving, etc., among others elements. All the elements that commit and motivate people's activity and confidence to make their work more reliable ultimately guarantee the sustainability of the activities carried out. The experience achieved the following results: (1) creation of the LAG in Punta Indio: "Amigos del Parque Costero Sur"; (2) creation of a development strategy with 10 main priorities, 17 measures and 154 specific development actions to achieve. The LAG's activities have so far produced 18 projects, focused on the following areas: assessment of local production, training, promoting tourism heritage; protecting and preserving the environment and treating places of interest for Punta del Indio.

The local action groups have great potential in countries such as Argentina, when it comes to carrying out rural development. The creation of these local governance structures is a key element of a new concept of planning for rural development, based on a territorial focus and decentralized management.

Acknowledgements

First, the authors would like to thank Doctor Adolfo Cazorla, Director of the GESPLAN Group at the Technical University of Madrid for being a fervent advocate and ongoing supporter in the application of ideas and models developed by this research group, which are happily shared across different parts of Latin America. Second, they would like to thank the UNLP for its support and development of innovative ideas for the rural environment in The Pampas. Third, they would like to thank the community of Punta Indio, for being welcoming and supporting new ideas for their community.

Author details

Ricardo Stratta Fernández[1], Ignacio de los Ríos Carmenado[2]* and Miriam López González[2]

*Address all correspondence to: ricardo.stratta@agro.unlp.edu.ar; ignacio.delosrios@upm.es and miriam.lopez@upm.es

1 National University of La Plata, La Plata, Argentina

2 Technical University of Madrid, Madrid, Spain

References

[1] Coraggio JL. Universidad y desarrollo local. In: Consejo Nacional de Educación Superior (CONESUP), UNESCO y el CIESPAL, editors. La educación superior y las nuevas tendencias; 23–24 July 2002; Quito, Ecuador.

[2] Sousa Santos B. La universidad en el siglo XXI. Para una reforma democrática emancipadora de la universidad. 1st ed. Buenos Aires, Argentina: Miño y Dávila, Laboratorio de Políticas Públicas; 2005. 88 p.

[3] United Nations Educational, Scientific and Cultural Organization UNESCO. Global Monitoring Report 2015: Education for all 2000–2015: Achievements and challenges. Paris: UNESCO.

[4] ICB – IPMA Competence Baseline, Version 3.0. Nijkerk: International Project Management Association (IPMA); 2009.

[5] Herrera Ortega H. Perfil de competencias del Agente de Desarrollo Local. Definido mediante el método. Empleo tipo estudiado en su dinámica, ETED. Tesis para optar al título de psicólogo y al grado de licenciado en psicología [dissertation]. Universidad de la Serena. Chile:2009. 173 p.

[6] A Guide to the Project Management Body of Knowledge (PMBOK® Guide). 5th ed. Newtown Square, Pennsylvania: Project Management Institute (PMI), Inc; 2013. 596 p.

[7] Chinnowsky P, Brown H, Szajnman A, Realph A. Developing knowledge landscapes through project-based learning. Journal of Professional Issues in Engineering Education and Practice. 2006;**132**(2):118–125.

[8] De los Ríos I, Cazorla A, Díaz-Puente JM, Yagüe JL. Project-based learning in engineering higher education: two decades of teaching competences in real environments. Procedia-Social and Behavioural Sciences. 2010;**2**(2):1368–1378.

[9] De Los Ríos I, Rodríguez F, Pérez C. Promoting professional project management skills in engineering higher education: Project-based learning (PBL) strategy. International Journal of Engineering Education. 2015;**31**(1-B):1–15.

[10] Barsky O, Gelman J. Historia del Agro argentino, desde la conquista hasta el siglo XXI. Buenos Aires: Grijalbo-Mondadori; 2001. 460 p.

[11] Rabinovitch JE, Torres F. Caracterización de los síndromes de sostenibilidad del desarrollo: El caso de Argentina. In: CEPAL (Naciones Unidas/Comisión Económica para América Latina y el Caribe), editor. Taller Síndromes de sostenibilidad del desarrollo en América Latina; 16–17 September 2002; Santiago de Chile. Serie Seminarios y Conferencias-CEPAL No. 38; 2004.

[12] Stratta Fernández R, De los Ríos Carmenado I. Agricultural transformations and depopulation in rural communities of the Pampas Argentina. Estudios Geográficos. 2010;**71**(268):235–265.

[13] García Pascual F. Políticas públicas y sustentabilidad en las zonas desfavorecidas y de montaña de España. Boletín de la Asociación de Geógrafos Españoles. 2003;**41**:151–182.

[14] Sili M. La Argentina rural: de la crisis de la modernización agraria a la construcción de un nuevo paradigma de desarrollo de los territorios rurales. Buenos Aires: INTA; 2005. 108 p.

[15] Manuel-Navarrete D. Análisis sistémico de la agriculturización en la pampa húmeda argentina y sus consecuencias en regiones extrapampeanas: sostenibilidad, brechas de conocimiento e integración de políticas. Santiago de Chile:CEPAL, United Nations Publications; 2006.

[16] Gorenstein S. Agricultura familiar pampeana: tramas, territorios y políticas. Revista interdisciplinaria de Estudios Agrarios. 2008;**29**:1–21.

[17] CIPAF, editor. Manual de aplicaciones CIPAF y sus IPAF. Buenos Aires: INTA; 2006.

[18] Carballo González C. Desarrollo Rural. Nuevos enfoques y temas claves a considerar. In: VI Jornadas interdisciplinarias de estudios agrarios y agroindustriales. Eje temático: Instituciones y políticas públicas sectoriales; 11–13 November; Buenos Aires. 2009.

[19] Piñeiro M, Villareal F. Modernización agrícola y nuevos actores sociales. Ciencia Hoy. 2005;**15**(97):32–36.

[20] Manzanal M. Regiones, Territorios e Institucionalidad del Desarrollo Rural. In: Manzanal M, Neiman G, Lattuada M, editors. Desarrollo Rural: Organizaciones, Instituciones y Territorio. Buenos Aires: CICCUS; 2006. pp. 21–50.

[21] Manzanal M, Nardi MA. Modelos de intervención de los proyectos de desarrollo rural en la Argentina a partir de 1995. In: Schejtman A, Barsky O, editors. El desarrollo rural en la Argentina, un enfoque territorial. Buenos Aires, Argentina: Siglo XXI; 2008. p. 429–525.

[22] Enfoque de desarrollo territorial. Programa Nacional de apoyo al Desarrollo Territorial. Buenos Aires: INTA; 2007.

[23] Barsky O, Dávila M. La rebelión del campo: Historia del conflicto agrario argentino. 1st ed. Buenos Aires: Sudamericana; 2012.

[24] INDEC 2002 y 2008. Censos Nacional Agropecuario 2002 Y 2008. INDEC. Buenos Aires, Argentina.

[25] Obschatko E, Foti MP, Román M, editors. Los pequeños productores en la República Argentina. Importancia en la producción agropecuaria y en el empleo en base al Censo Nacional Agropecuario 2002. Buenos Aires: SAGPyA-IICA; 2006.

[26] Obschatko E, Ganduglia F, Román F. El sector agroalimentario argentino, 2000–2005. 1st ed. Buenos Aires: Bib. Orton IICA / CATIE; 2007.

[27] Feito MC. Agricultura familiar para el desarrollo rural argentino. In: Misiones, Argentina, editors. Avá 23. Editorial Universidad Naciones de Misiones; 2013. pp. 139–159.

[28] Lattuada M, Nogueira M, Urcola M. Tres décadas de desarrollo rural en Argentina. 1st ed. Buenos Aires: Universidad Abierta Interamericana. Teseo; 2015.

[29] Tsakoumagkos P. El trabajo agrario en la agricultura familiar de la Argentina, aproximaciones conceptuales. In: RED Sociales; 2014. pp. 1, 2–18.

[30] Gabellone N, Sarandon R, Claps C. Caracterización y zonificación ecológica de la Cuenca del Río Salado. In: Maiola O, Gabellone N, Hernández M, editors. Inundaciones en la región pampeana. La Plata: Editorial de la Universidad Nacional de la Plata; 2003. pp. 87–122.

[31] Panigatti JL. Argentina 200 años, 200 suelos. Buenos Aires: INTA; 2010. 345 p.

[32] Cazorla A. La nueva planificación: hacia una estrategia de desarrollo basada en el Aprendizaje Social. In: Experiencias de desarrollo rural en una iniciativa LEADER. Madrid: Dirección General de Agricultura y Alimentación; 1997. pp. 289–332.

[33] De los Rios-Carmenado I, Díaz-Puente JM, Cadena-Iñigue J. The initiative LEADER as a model for rural development: implementation to some territories of México. Agrociencia 2011;**45**(5):609–624.

[34] Cazorla-Montero A, de los Ríos-Carmenado I, Díaz-Puente JM. The LEADER community initiative as rural development model: application in the capital region of Spain. Agrociencia. 2005;**39**:697–708.

[35] De los Ríos I. Innovación para el Desarrollo Rural: la Iniciativa LEADER como Laboratorio de Aprendizaje. Madrid: Comunidad de Madrid; 2002.

[36] De Los Ríos I, Ortuño M, Rivera M. Private–public partnership as a tool to promote entrepreneurship for sustainable development: WWP Torrearte Experience. Sustainability. 2016;**8**(3):199.

[37] Sanchis Palacio JR. Local development and business creation. The role of local development workers in project management. The International Entrepreneurship and Management Journal. 2006;**2**(1):57–78.

[38] Kerzner HR. Project management: a systems approach to planning, scheduling and controlling. 11th ed. New York: John Wiley & Sons; 2013. 1296 p.

[39] Meghnagi S. Il sapere professionale: competenza, diritti, democrazia. 1st ed. Milano: Feltrinelli; 2005.

[40] Morris PWG. The validity of knowledge in project management and the challenge of learning and competency development. In: Morris PWG, Pinto JK, editors. The Wiley Guide to project organization and project management competencies. New Jersey: John Wiley and Sons, Inc; 2010. pp. 193–205.

[41] Blackburn S. The project manager and the project-network. International Journal of Project Management. 2002;**20**(3):199–204.

[42] Cleland DI. Leadership and the project-management body of knowledge. International Journal of Project Management. 1995;**13**(2):83–88.

[43] Greer M. ID project management: Tools and techniques for instructional designers and developers. New Jersey: Educational Technology; 1992. 227 p.

[44] Tinnirello PC. New directions in project management. Florida: CRC Press; 2001.

[45] Pereda S, Berrocal F. Gestión de Recursos Humanos por Competencias. Madrid: Centro de Estudios Ramón Areces; 1999.

[46] Cazorla A, De los Ríos I, Salvo M. Working With People (WWP) in rural development projects: A proposal from social learning. Cuadernos de Desarrollo Rural. 2013;**10**(SPE70):131–157.

[47] Cazorla A, De los Ríos I. Rural development as "Working with People": A proposal for policy management in public domain. UPM: Madrid, Spain. 2012; pp. 29–35.

[48] Sastre-Merino S, Negrillo X, Hernández-Castellano, D. Sustainability of rural development projects within the working with people model: Application to Aymara Women Communities in the Puno Region, Peru. Cuadernos de Desarrollo Rural. 2013;**10**:219–243.

[49] Friedmann J. Planning in the public domain: From knowledge to action. New Jersey: Princeton University Press; 1987. 501 p.

[50] Herrán Gómez J. Modelo de integración del conocimiento-acción a través del Proyecto de Comunicación para el Desarrollo: 25 años de experiencia en comunidades indígenas andinas en Ecuador [Doctoral thesis]. Universidad Politécnica Salesiana; 2015. Available from: http://dspace.ups.edu.ec/handle/123456789/11234

[51] Stratta Fernández R. El desarrollo rural en Argentina: evolución y propuesta de un modelo de intervención para las comunidades rurales despobladas de la región pampeana [Doctoral thesis]. Technical University of Madrid; 2011.

[52] Cazorla A, editor. Planning experiences in Latin America and Europe. México: Colegio de Postgraduados de México. Montecillo; 2015.

[53] De los Ríos- Carmenado I, Rahoveanu AT, Gallegos AA. Project management competencies for regional development in Romania: analysis from "Working with People" model. Procedia Economics and Finance. 2014;**8**:614–621.

[54] De los Ríos-Carmenado I, Cadena-Iñiguez J, Díaz-Puente JM. Creating local action groups for rural development in México: methodological approach and lessons learned. Agrociencia (Montecillo). 2011;**45**(7):815–829.